THE MAKING OF AN UN-AMERICAN

THE MAKING OF AN UN-AMERICAN

A DIALOGUE
WITH EXPERIENCE
PAUL COWAN

A DELTA BOOK

A DELTA BOOK

Published by Dell Publishing Co., Inc.
750 Third Avenue, New York, N.Y. 10017

Copyright © 1967, 1968, 1970 by Paul Cowan
All Rights Reserved

First published in 1970 by The Viking Press, Inc.
625 Madison Avenue, New York, N.Y. 10022

Published simultaneously in Canada by
The Macmillan Company of Canada Limited

SBN 670-45166-5

ACKNOWLEDGMENTS
Harcourt, Brace & World, Inc., and Faber and Faber Ltd.:
From "Ash Wednesday" by T. S. Eliot from *Collected Poems
1909–1962*. Reprinted by permission. Sanga Music Inc.:
From "Letter to Eve" by Pete Seeger. © Copyright 1967
Sanga Music Inc. All rights reserved. From "Gotta Travel On"
by Paul Clayton, Larry Ehrlich, Dave Lazar and Tom Six.
© Copyright 1958, 1966 Sanga Music Inc. All rights reserved.
Used by permission.

Delta ® TM 755118, Dell Publishing Co., Inc.
This edition published by arrangement with
The Viking Press, Inc.

Printed in the United States of America
First Delta printing—September 1970

THE day we left the Peace Corps we discovered that Rachel was pregnant with our first child, Lisa Pilar. The day the manuscript of this book went into production we discovered that Rachel was pregnant with our second child.

I intend this book as a letter to them, mailed through time.

After all the tragedies and frustrations of this past decade, I still believe that someday we will create an America which realizes, with the great Cuban revolutionary José Martí, that *"los niños son la esperanza del futuro del mundo"* and create a society based on that homily.

That is my prayer for my children.

APPRECIATIONS

I WANT to thank the Institute for Policy Studies in Washington, D.C., for a fellowship which enabled me to get a good start on this book at the same time as I was readjusting to life in the United States;

Aaron Asher for invaluable editorial advice which helped me to add breadth and texture to my book, Ann Hancock, who read the manuscript at a later stage, asked some very useful questions, and helped me to tighten scenes that still seemed flabby, and Faith Sale for performing the job of copy editor, one of the most thankless in the literary world, with as much care as if she were the book's editor, or even its author;

Lynn Nesbit, my agent and very good friend, who gave me wonderfully helpful literary and personal advice, especially during times when I couldn't believe this book would ever be born;

And I especially want to thank my parents for showing me, by their constant, loving example, the importance of remaining open to the world, sensitive to its people, responsive to their hopes and ideas.

PREFACE

WHEN I finished serving in the Peace Corps in Ecuador, nearly eighteen months ago, I wanted to write a book about some of the State Department, AID, and Peace Corps officials I had known abroad, a sort of updated, radical's version of *The Ugly American*. That spring I published six such sketches in the *Village Voice*, but I was dissatisfied with them. Alone, they seemed one dimensional, a misleading representation of a very complicated experience. So I decided to make the behavior of the United States officials, and its effect on me, part of a broader, more personal book, *The Making of an Un-American*.

My experience had helped me to gain confidence in my own discontent, learn to trust nonconformist instincts which I had sought to suppress while I was at the Choate School and at Harvard. But they also forced me to confront the side of myself that was part of the problem that I had hoped to help solve. In Mississippi in 1964 and in South America in 1966–1967, I saw that even the liberals I had wanted to emulate, men who seemed to be devoting their lives to fighting injustice, were unable to accept people from alien cultures on any terms but their own.

That reaction, I realized, was characteristic of most Americans, whether they supported Ronald Reagan, Eugene McCarthy, or their own particular brand of revolution. Instinctively, we insist on our moral and intellectual superiority: with Abraham Lincoln, we continue to believe that America is "the last, best hope for man" despite the awful events of this decade. I learned that the only way I can fight that instinct in myself is to persist in redefining my loyalties through actions: to call myself an un-American (citizen of the world), to be willing to fight against my own government whenever that is necessary.

Throughout this book I have concentrated on my own evolution, not on the evolution of the institutions and places through which I have passed. Thus, for example, I have failed to mention the fact that the Choate School, which was lily-white when I graduated in 1958, included twelve blacks in its student body of 577 in 1969. Rachel and I spent an afternoon there during alumni weekend 1969, and we were impressed with the hip anger that some of the black and white students we met felt toward the school, which remains conservative and elitist despite the few symbols of change it so proudly displays.

Similarly, I ended the book with my departure from the Peace Corps, instead of trying to evaluate the changes the organization has undergone in the past eighteen months.

Some staff members contend that select host-country nationals are now included in the decision-making process, that few training programs are as rigid as ours was, that the agency is trying to recruit people with special skills and giving everyone it sends abroad more freedom. But others claim that morale inside the Peace Corps, which declined sharply in the years after Jack Hood Vaughn replaced Sargent Shriver as director, is still lower now that Nixon has appointed Joseph Blatchford to the position. Volunteers who have returned to the United States within the past six months tell stories which indicate that relations with the staff are generally worse than when we were abroad, and that they had at least as much trouble as the people in our group in finding rewarding work. In any case, it seems to me that the contradictions which beset the Peace Corps are so deep that whatever changes have been made must be virtually meaningless.

An article that appeared in the *Washington Post*, June 22, 1969, shows how unlikely it is that the Peace Corps will adapt itself to the needs of the countries in the Third World. Shortly after President Nixon appointed Joseph Blatchford as the agency's director, the story begins, Blatchford hired a "lady political boss" named Betty Williams. She serves as a "political screener," in the words of one veteran staff member, with a mandate from Blatchford to hire Republicans for staff jobs. The Peace Corps seems to have become a nesting ground for the most ambitious citizens of Nixonia: ". . . Republicans across the land, realizing that only so many ambassadorial plums are available, now are lowering their sights a bit and angling for becoming a Peace Corps representative abroad, a job which can pay up to thirty thousand dollars," the reporter observes.

Soon the period of time in which *The Making of an Un-American* is set may begin to seem like the Peace Corps' golden age.

The hardest decision I had to make while writing this book was when to identify the people I describe, when to disguise them. How could I tell the truth without hurting anonymous people because they happened to know me? No solution is entirely satisfactory.

The problem is not so acute in the early sections, when most of the Americans I mention by name are semipublic figures. But when I make unfriendly statements about people who are still unknown I give them disguises. Thus, Wade Eastbrook is not the real name of the boy who caused me such trouble at Choate. I have chosen to call the black project director about whom I felt so ambivalent during the Freedom Summer by the rather barbarous nickname I invented for him, Papa Doc. In his case, I would rather expose myself than my subject.

In the sections on Israel, Mexico, and Ecuador, I have preserved the names of local people except in a very few cases (like that of the Ecuadorian I call Hector Montoya) when I present information that might cause someone needless difficulties. I have not disguised any public officials or any private citizens with appreciable power.

Of course I am proud to include the names of my family and friends in this book. In a way it grew out of a sustained dialogue with my wife, Rachel, my brother, Geoff, my sisters, Holly and Liza; Rachel's mother, Margaret Brown, and her sisters and brother, Connie, Peggy, and Richard; and with Peace Corps friends like Nick Zydycrn, Margot Jones, Ed Fagerlund, Ralph Craft, Bill and Joyce Dodge; such friends from the movement as Tom Hayden, Richie Rothstein, Todd Gitlin, John McAuliffe, Adam Hochschild, Fred Gardner; friends from New York like Harold Ickes, Paul Gorman, Jack Newfield, Dan Wolf, Susan Thomases, Jane Eisenberg.

But the decision about names becomes difficult when I attack people in the Peace Corps, AID, and the State Department. Most readers would never have heard of them if I hadn't happened to be a volunteer in Ecuador. When does muckraking become invasion of privacy?

I have drawn an imaginary line for myself. In some cases, when a character is incidental to the rest of the book (like the man who taught Latin-American studies during training) I suppress his name and cite his position instead. The names of the volunteers I criticize are all inventions. There is no Hank Dawson, no Libby White, no Gerald Erlham, no Sammy Bernstein. I knew the people on whom they are based at a time in their lives when they were particularly vulnerable, and I hope that their experiences abroad will twine with the shock that so many volunteers receive when they return to the United States to provide them greater self-knowledge and compassion. My intention is to show the effect that a stint in the Peace Corps had on a variety of middle-class Americans who joined it, not to expose individual volunteers and thus, perhaps, compromise them in the future.

I have also disguised the Peace Corps doctors, whose involvement with our work was only peripheral; the University of New Mexico psychiatrist I call Sandra Long who, unpleasant though she made our training session, was still connected to the Peace

Corps only by the accident of a government contract with her university that was never renewed; and the AID technician I call Rudolfo Benitez, whom I met only in training, after his two-year contract with the agency had expired.

But I have used the real names of the Peace Corps, AID, and State Department officials whose actions affected our Ecuadorian friends and us directly. Many of them are careerists. If they don't remain in the foreign service or in foreign-assistance work, they will take equivalent jobs elsewhere—as employees of corporations with considerable international interests, for example, or as poverty bureaucrats inside the United States. They will move from community to community, country to country, drawing high salaries (often tax-free), living in considerable luxury, while they boast of their idealism and generosity and make decisions which affect the lives of millions of people whose cultures they barely understand.

Their anonymity is often a shield for incompetence and brutality. But there are few mass publications in America whose editors have the will or the wit to investigate such people or the institutions they represent.

During the Nixon years those faceless civil servants will be acquiring unprecedented amounts of power. That is why I feel obliged not only to show those I knew in action but also to call them by their correct names.

Finally, the fact that I have been so critical of other people has made me feel a special responsibility to be as honest as possible about myself. For I believe that the crisis through which we are living has been created largely out of our habitual dishonesty: our inability to look past myths and metaphors, past the emotions we think we should feel, to our genuine reactions and the reactions of the people around us.

I am committed to discovering and describing the truth of my own experience even if it means embarrassing myself and enraging people who believe that loyalty and decency are synonymous with discretion and silence.

—Concord, Massachusetts, July 16, 1969

THE MAKING OF AN UN-AMERICAN

PART ONE

I

An Image to Last a Lifetime:

I am a Fifth Former at the exclusive Choate School—a gawky Jew from New York City with a face so thickly covered by acne that one classmate has called me "the traveling muzzy."

My parents decided to send me there because I did so badly in grade school at the progressive Dalton School in New York City. Though I read a great deal at Dalton and spent a lot of my time discussing books with my primary-school friends, I could never concentrate on the studies that were assigned. I was too busy practicing basketball and baseball, flirting with the girls in our class, playing poker. "Paul will have to make a Herculean step to get ready for high-school English," my parents had been warned when I finished eighth grade. Most of my teachers were agreed that I would never get into a decent college unless I was enrolled in a school that forced me to acquire self-discipline. When Exeter rejected my application, I insisted that I be allowed to accompany a classmate to Choate. But the transition had disoriented me completely. My grades were even worse than they had been at Dalton. Most of my friends still lived in New York. From the day I entered Choate I felt, and acted, like a clumsy alien: the kind of vague, dreamy boy whom most undergraduates called a "weanie."

Now I am sitting in a math class in front of Wade Eastbrook, one of the many boys in my form who preserve their self-respect by tormenting people like me. He clamps his feet on the back flap of my jacket, as he has done every day for the past month: if I lean forward too impulsively the jacket will rip. But today Wade has discovered a new kind of entertainment. He swipes my math book and puts it on his desk. I make no effort to retrieve it. The thought of a fist fight paralyzes me. Finally the bell rings and Wade gives the book back.

That night I am in my math teacher's apartment reviewing a complicated geometry problem. He sees a note scrawled on the top right-hand corner of my book and asks me about it.

FUCK YOU, YOU KIKE, Wade has written.

I had not noticed the message before then. Now it takes nearly fifteen minutes to persuade the teacher that I didn't write it myself.

"Anyone who uses the word 'nigger' must be evil," I wrote in an English paper later that year. It was the furthest I dared go toward defending myself.

At Choate, during the Eisenhower years, racist remarks were as much a part of our daily lives as the chapel services which we were required to attend each night. In fact, at the first Sunday service I attended there, Seymour St. John, the school's headmaster and also its chaplain, began his sermon with a joke about "Old Darky Joe" and his friend "Moe." The humor that the sons of America's (mostly Republican) elite shared with one another was considerably blunter. A boy who left damp marks at the tip of his cigarette had "nigger lips"; a generous act was "mighty white" or, more ironically, something "I'd do for a white man"; a common piece of repartee when two boys shook hands was "left hand for niggers"; at breakfast the tough Southern boys often ordered their coffee "strong and black, like my women"; if someone gave you the finger you automatically asked, "Is that your I.Q. or the number of white parents you have?"

There wasn't a single black person at the school then (one pronounced the word with a capital S), and I was one of the few Jews. One week we staged a small revolt by refusing to bow our heads for evening prayer. But the Reverend St. John threatened to make serious trouble for anyone who persisted in mocking that most cherished of all the school's traditions. "When in Rome do as the Romans do," he enjoined us in a sermon. We hadn't the wit or the knowledge to ask how his Anglican ancestors would have felt about such advice. Our rebellion collapsed immediately.

My four years at Choate left me permanently convinced that there is a class of people in America who consciously regard themselves as members of the master race. But I was scared to fight them while I was there and transformed my private hatred for them into an effort to prove that I was their moral superior.

I also accepted Choate's moral terms for material reasons: if I went "the extra mile," as Dr. St. John was always exhorting in chapel, I might persuade the school's faculty to help me get into Harvard. No one in my family had ever gone there before. (My father was an executive at CBS television; his father had sold used cement bags in Chicago.) When I was a senior I used to force myself awake at five o'clock each morning to memorize French verbs and the genus and species of the plants we studied in biology while my classmates still slept. I suppose that was the sort of self-discipline my teachers at Dalton had wanted me to acquire.

By then I had a small group of friends, and we controlled the school's newspaper. But I am embarrassed to recall how intimidated we all were. Once, for example, we published a front-page picture of some boys bowing before a brightly painted pole near the chapel. Our faculty adviser (a man whose breath always smelled of liverwurst) forbade us to send the issue through the mails for fear that some alumnus might regard the spring rite as a phallic symbol and be so offended that he would never donate money to Choate again. It didn't occur to us to protest that decision. Or to write editorials asking why the headmaster and his faculty were the school's sole legislators, the Student Council their rubber stamp. Or to criticize Choate's segregated admissions policy, though President Eisenhower had used Federal troops to integrate the Little Rock school system during the fall of our senior year. We ignored the newspaper's content and devoted all our attention to its form. Our favorite book was called *Functional Newspaper Design*, and throughout the entire year we debated the subtle points it raised about make-up and graphics with the same intensity that high-school students a decade later would display toward Fanon's ideas about colonialism, Che Guevara's theories of revolution.

It symbolized our sole means of escape. Once or twice a week a few of us were allowed to spend several hours at Van Dyck's, a small print shop in near-by New Haven where we put the paper to bed. Van Dyck's was our mecca. There, older workmen taught us how to read slugs almost as quickly as we could read the printed page, to set headlines, to put the finished form onto the press. Technical terms like "font," "pica," "widow," "em dash," "em rule" took on a significance that was almost cabalistic. When we invoked them during those leaden months at Choate they allowed us to imagine that we were worldly reporters and editors. They allowed us to imagine that we were free.

But we were all good citizens of the police state in which we lived. I must have been one of the most naïvely obedient members of my class. The thought of expulsion terrified me. I never broke the rules against smoking or drinking, never "cut out" downtown to date local girls. Once, in my Fourth Form year, I broke the school's honor code and cheated on a Latin examination, but the guilt I felt as a consequence plagued me for months. Finally, I flunked the course—to punish myself, I now think.

When I was a senior, though, I felt relatively confident of my ability to survive at Choate. Our clique was quite stable, and we were always inventing fantasies and diversions to amuse ourselves. But these were within the framework of the school's laws and traditions. For example, that year we tried to use our imaginations to make the dance weekend more enjoyable. For several months I waged a private campaign, as priggish as it was ironic, to persuade my classmates never to litter the school's lovely lawns.

In my last term I wrote a short story which showed how bullies like Wade Eastbrook made life miserable for the boys they considered "weanies" and I read it as a chapel sermon. My tone was moral, my manner grave. I made it clear that the fable was fiction, named no one, never mentioned the anti-Semitism and race prejudice that had made me so unhappy. The speech won a favorable response. The faculty, particularly, praised it as an outstanding example of the humane attitude which the school instills in most of the young people who pass through it.

II

ALTHOUGH my grades improved considerably during my last year and a half at Choate, my over-all record was still poor enough that Harvard nearly rejected me. But then some influential faculty members intervened in my behalf. When I discovered that my name was toward the top of the waiting list I wrote a long letter to the admissions office telling its deans how much I wanted to become part of the tradition they represented. I had just been reading *Look Homeward, Angel*, and I was heavily influenced by Thomas Wolfe in the eager, hungry style I used to describe some of the deepest emotions I had ever felt. For Harvard, to me, was a treasured idea: hardly a place, not a social force. There I would be liberated from the fears that afflicted me constantly at Choate.

Finally, I was accepted into the class of 1962, but the debt I felt I owed to the university haunted me most of the time I was there. I constantly worried that I was unworthy of the tradition which its elders had permitted me to share.

I decided to major in American history and literature. Writers like Dos Passos and John Steinbeck and James Agee, folk singers like Pete Seeger and Woody Guthrie had carried my imagination far beyond the prejudices and silly rules that surrounded one at Choate into a nation that seemed to be filled with energy and decency. I was convinced that it still could be found if one looked beneath the dull, conformist façade of the Eisenhower years. Whenever I attended one of Seeger's concerts I felt a belief, nearly religious, that there was a generation of people like myself preparing to help America break free. That year Seeger became my spiritual President.

But I could never find the same excitement in my courses at Harvard, and I blamed myself for that failure, not my professors. They were some of the most brilliant men in the country—Perry Miller with his baroque lectures on Jonathan Edwards, Cotton Mather, and the rest of the New England divines whose theology was so difficult to fathom; Oscar Handlin, confident that he could summarize the immigrant's experience in a few optimistic phrases; Arthur Schlesinger, Jr., master synthesizer, intent on proving that men like Theodore Parker, William James, Thorstein Veblen, Oliver Wendell Holmes had provided a durable theoretical foundation for the wise pragmatism that always guided the men who inhabited America's "vital center"; Louis Hartz, short and stentorian, rolling off the names of obscure European thinkers whose complex theories were supposed to have provided the basis for America's elastic liberal tradition. Their lectures rarely included the sort of material that I wanted to learn about. None of them paid much attention to the great labor struggles, or to the human details of slavery, the Civil War, and Reconstruction, or to the violent battles between immigrant groups like the Molly Maguires and the rigid society they wanted to enter.

I am convinced now that those aspects of American history were omitted because they contradicted the ideology that the liberal professors had created for themselves: the belief that the nation's genius lay in its unfailing ability to harmonize conflicting interests, to channel its citizens' energy into social and technological innovation. But at the time I thought that it must be my ignorance which made me feel so bored by their lectures, confused by their abstractions and their theories.

At the *Crimson*, where I spent even more time than I had at the *Choate News*, I found some of the excitement that was lacking in my classes. I was elected to the newspaper's staff during my freshman year, and its office was my real home. I loved the sensation of walking through the Yard during Cambridge's soft, sweet spring, down narrow, shady Plympton Street, and into the *Crimson* building with its sharp smell of newsprint, so alien to the academic world. Often I would stay there, talking with anyone who happened to be around, until the paper went to press at two or three in the morning.

But when we discussed politics at the *Crimson*'s editorial board meetings I often felt as inadequate as I did when I tried to understand what Schlesinger and Handlin were trying to tell me about American history. In 1959 and 1960 pacifist groups in New England were launching direct action campaigns designed to prevent the launching of nuclear submarines, and students all over the country were protesting segregation at Woolworth stores in the South. Their activities stirred me in the way Pete Seeger's concerts had, but when I tried to translate those emotions into arguments about editorial policies the older members of the board would embarrass me, silence me, with sophisticated arguments, rich with data and impressive references, which proved that pacifism was naïve, that rapid integration was unfeasible. I began to worry that my opinions were more sentimental than rational. I was reluctant to commit them to print except in news stories, where I could attribute controversial views to other people.

In 1961, after John Kennedy's Inauguration, progressive ideas became a little more popular in Cambridge. I had a special, private reason for believing that Kennedy was more sensitive to problems like segregation than the Harvard professors he had named as his advisers. He was a member of a minority group and he had graduated from Choate. My fantasy was that his apparent concern for the poor had grown out of the same bitter dislike of the Protestant elite that I had developed during my years at boarding school. When he urged people to "ask not what your country can do for you—ask what you can do for your country," I wanted to believe that he was talking about an America that included poor people, sensitive young people, liberal adults, but excluded the self-fish bigots he and I had both known at Choate.

Soon his Presidency would inspire thousands of young people like me to leave their middle-class environments and work in the Peace Corps or the civil-rights movement. But not quite yet. At Harvard that year hundreds of students, suddenly awakened to political awareness, joined a campus organization called Tocsin that was working for nuclear disarmament. It took us into libraries and lecture halls, not to the ghettos and barrios where some of us would be forced to redefine our political identities a few years hence. We sought to master all the relevant scientific information so that we could devise practical suggestions for arms reduction and pass them along to men like McGeorge Bundy. The most gentlemanly form of protest imaginable, it was based on the assumption that a rational dialogue between Harvard faculty and Harvard students would save the world from destruction. Still, many undergraduates considered Tocsin extremely radical that year, especially when we staged public demonstrations. So we spent a great deal of time arguing with the conservatives on campus about issues like underground testing and phased inspections systems.

But those technical subjects seemed dull and irrelevant to me, though I was ashamed to admit it. It was the same conflict I had felt on the *Crimson* and in my courses, a conflict that seemed to be afflicting dozens of my friends, too. The fact that our educations seemed pointless, unrelated to any future we could imagine, made us feel especially guilty, for it meant that we were unable to make use of the magnificent opportunities that Harvard was supposed to offer all of its undergraduates. The guilt produced an alarming kind of paralysis. Ever since my freshman year many of the people I knew rarely went to class, never studied, spent a great deal of time worrying about the nervous breakdown that always seemed to be one frustration away. As a result our conversations were often elliptical forms of self-mockery. We discussed ourselves and our doubts in brittle phrases and carefully contrived accents—to disguise our true identities, I often felt. One *Crimson* editor wrote an article which described the entire syndrome as "academic suicide."

Now Kennedy's administration had begun to harness those swirling emotions to a new kind of politics. The disarmament movement had released emotions in many of its adherents that were far stronger than anything Tocsin's technologically precise proposals could suggest. Ghoulish fantasies of imminent destruction had become almost fashionable within our small group of liberals. Sometimes we even seemed to be indulging ourselves in subtle competitions to see who was the most obsessed. Fishermen in the troubled sea of our psyches, we often exchanged yarns about our nightmares of buildings exploding, of charred victims of nuclear attacks gagging from the radiation poisoning they had suffered. But when we shared those fearful images with our elders they hinted that the pressures of academic life must be addling our brains. They would remind us that the buildings we dreamed about were always standing the next day. Our apocalyptic premonitions made no sense, they would argue. The country we were living in was the most stable on earth. Its new President promised to be one of the greatest in its history.

Those arguments sounded so reasonable that most of us continued to blame ourselves for our discontent. We believed that we were experiencing "identity crises"—the term was quite popular that year—not a first, faint realization that there were forces loose in America which would change the nation (and Harvard College) beyond recognition in just a very few years.

That spring, 1961, I flunked the examination that would have allowed me to write an honors thesis. I had studied for weeks— memorized texts as I'd done during my senior year at Choate—but I was literally unable to understand the terms of the questions we were asked. The failure confirmed my fears about my own inadequacy. So I decided to drop out of college, leave America, explore the world and myself until I was fit to graduate from Harvard.

For twelve months I wandered. I tried to study at the London School of Economics and found myself more depressed than ever.

I was reading T. S. Eliot during that autumn and soon the sterile rhythms of "Ash Wednesday" made me their slave.

> Teach us to care and not to care
> Teach us to sit still

Those lines, Eliot's plea for grace, seemed to me a terrible threat. I did care, I cared about something, and I could do nothing but sit still. Finally, my fear of total emotional paralysis forced me to move on: I forfeited my tuition at the LSE, left my flat, my few friends, all my books and papers, and one weary morning in December 1961 dragged myself to the Paddington station, where I embarked, desperate voyager, on a slow journey to Israel.

A week before I had been sexually impotent for the first time in my life, and the memory of that abysmal night and the hungry woman I had failed haunted me across a continent. I was in pieces, fragments held together by the arbitrary fact that I possessed a body. For the moment that, too, seemed useless.

A single small incident still signals for me the degree of my collapse. Though I had plenty of money—my parents were subsidizing my adventure—I had, for some reason, failed to buy myself socks. My feet were naked except for some shoes whose soles were in decay. They got grubbier as I crossed the continent: what had been a patina of dust in Paris was a film of dirt in Naples and a layer of grime in Athens. Finally, when the ship I boarded in Peiraeus docked in Cyprus I bathed my feet in the Mediterranean, and my first act when we landed in Haifa was to buy myself a pair of shoes. Shoes, mark you, not socks, so on that first night I journeyed to Jerusalem, my extremities almost bare. Of course my clothes were ragged and smelly as well, and my face was stained with a few days' growth of stubble.

At the Hebrew University, where I found a room, I made a friend who invited me to spend the weekend with his family in Tel Aviv. His younger sister was so shocked by my appearance that she asked her mother about the meaning of my visit. No kibbutznik had ever been so filthy: what sort of tramp was her brother bringing home? "Don't be so narrow-minded," her mother an-

swered. "Maybe people in his country always look that way. Customs differ all over the world. Why don't you teach him how we
dress here?"

Soon I went to a kibbutz, and the work I did there helped me
to rid my mind of the morbid impressions I had collected in Cambridge, Massachusetts, and in London. Planting tomatoes in driving rain, hauling forty-five-kilo stalks of bananas until my back
throbbed, I found it hard to take T. S. Eliot's desiccated pleas
quite so seriously. On one side the kibbutz was bounded by the
Mediterranean Sea; if you walked just five miles down the beach
you arrived at the town of Caesarea, where Pontius Pilate had
presided. Mount Carmel was across the highway that formed the
other boundary of the kibbutz. It was not hard to ascend to the famous cave that contained the bones of a being who had lived there
ten thousand years before. Sometimes, as I explored those ruins, I
was accompanied by some of the Jews who had lived on the kibbutz for years. Our conversations covered millennia. Standing on
the jetty at Caesarea, where the first of the Crusaders landed their
vessels, we would talk about the guns that had been smuggled in
along the Mediterranean Coast during World War II.

Such Israelis showed me something that was lacking in myself.
They possessed a past they could see, a present they had created, a
future they were building. None of those things belonged to me.

One day, shortly after I had left the kibbutz, I hitchhiked to Ti-
berias. The man who picked me up had spent all of World War II
working with the Haganah to smuggle immigrants into Palestine.
For hours he told me stories of his adventures, and as I compared
them with my own tiny repertoire of exploits I became quite en-
vious. Then, after nightfall, we entered the Galilee and began to
drive past its rich green fields. At about nine o'clock we drew close
to Mount Hermon. My new friend stopped his car. He took his
young daughter by the hand and, with a flashlight to show the way
beneath the Galilean sky, began to wander through the large
meadow. "I have studied the flowers of Israel for years," he explained to me. "Now I know every plant that grows in my country. I feel them as part of my life. Near here is the first kibbutz I

worked at. I came here from Poland, a young boy who knew nothing of crops and cultivation. Now I want to share with my child what I have learned, what my country has done."

A young man with no real home, I longed to feel that emotion, too. Israelis thought I was crazy not to accept their solution to my problem. I had only to return from the Diaspora. "This is the only place in the world where a Jew can walk down the streets of any city without worrying that someone will make an anti-Semitic remark to him." That was the first thing an Israeli ever said to me: a gnarled, tough, old Russian I met the day my ship landed in Haifa. He had encouraged me to tell him about my life in America, and I had told him about my experiences at Choate. I guess he began to see me as a potential immigrant to the homeland. He sent me to the kibbutz near Mount Carmel and kept track of me from then on. Months afterward, when I told him that I still felt my work was in the United States, he seemed hurt and angry. "You must feel the way I do, even though you're an American and nearly a *goy*. When will you learn that there's no place for us Jews out there?"

By then I had drifted to the immigrant town of Beersheba, where I was earning my keep by teaching English to the children of North Africans who had just arrived in the country. It was work I enjoyed, for it allowed me to enter a world I had never imagined. I loved to watch the old bearded patriarchs, dressed in long robes, their heads wrapped in turbans, as they grazed their goats along the shallow valley that set their poor dry community off from the rest of Beersheba. Near there, it was said, Abraham's tribesmen had dug their first underground homes and had lived in the caves for decades. Now, after centuries, their children were home from the Diaspora. Israelis called them the desert generation, and the meaning of that biblical term was clear. Their bodies had reached the promised land, but in their minds they were forever sealed off from the modern world. While they grazed their sheep, their sons, my students, yearned to possess motorcycles, television sets, Minox cameras. They would conserve their earnings by practicing a form of birth control that seemed barbaric to their fathers.

The more deeply I entered their lives, the more remote Harvard became. The abstract questions that had haunted me there seemed, in the midst of all the poverty, the energy, the concentrated intelligence that surrounded me now, sheer self-indulgence. If a Harvard student read two magazine articles, I thought, one about a college senior who had cracked up under pressure of work, the other about an African child who had died of malnutrition, he would be haunted by the first and forget the second. But the real problem in the world was poverty, not middle-class neurosis, and a decent man would turn his attention from the problems that luxury bred to the more substantial problems of deprivation. Perhaps my notion indicated the best way of overcoming the fears and confusions that had paralyzed me: the more luxurious one's life, I decided, the more intent one becomes on the throbbings of one's own psychic pulse. Certainly, the work I was doing in Israel allowed me to achieve a new kind of self-control.

But the freer I felt of the depression that had chased me to Israel, the more eager I was to return home, though I couldn't explain that feeling to my Russian mentor in Haifa. I remember reading William Styron's *Set This House on Fire* and deciding not to travel to Alexandria with a girl friend because the novel aroused my interest in the Florida Keys. I had read Durrell, too, and loved the *Quartet* as much as the girl did, but now I wanted to be near the Virginia Tidewater. I conceived a crazy desire to spend a year in Delaware because it was such an anonymous little state that I thought some American writer should do it justice. There was a bar in Beersheba, The Last Chance, and I went there every night to hear Odetta's latest album. The owner came from Newark but he hadn't been back in the States since World War II. He always cried when it came time for her to sing "The Battle Hymn of the Republic." I did, too. Somehow her rich, passionate Negro voice was the perfect expression of the America I now knew I could discover when I returned home.

A friend at Harvard had been sending me copies of the *Crimson*. I received one late in April, on a morning when I didn't have to teach and was still a bit hung over. The night before, to my great surprise, I had outfaced a man named Itzhak, the town's leading stud. He had been a gigolo on the French Riviera, had run drugs from Israel to Syria, and now owned the Barsheba, a bar where you could often find the sort of brawl that seemed so exciting in Westerns. At least once a week Itzhak would receive a communication from someone who threatened to kill him: he was always stealing women. He had taken my girl from me, made her a hostess in his bar, and, I had heard, put her on a daisy chain—each night she had to service five or six of his friends.

But I had never summoned the nerve to challenge him until that night at The Last Chance. After the Barsheba closed he had come there with Cynthia, a Hungarian prostitute. She had fled after the revolution of 1956, arrived in Israel with no money, and had been screwing for a living ever since. Now she was said to be madly in love with Itzhak.

As soon as they walked through the door Itzhak ordered her to strip. She refused. "But everyone here wants to see your big tits," he said. There were twenty people at The Last Chance that night, most of them regulars. No one said a word. Then I heard myself talking: "I don't want her to strip." And I felt it deeply: I'd be damned if I'd let the arrogant brutality behind that demand triumph. I was terrified, but willing to fight if I had to.

"Who doesn't want her to strip?" he demanded. "I don't, Itzhak." My voice cracked as I uttered those three short words.

He seemed to decide that a fight with me wasn't worth the trouble—he could have taken me quickly, I'm sure—for he simply said, "All right," took Cynthia by the hand, and left. Afterward, everyone who had witnessed the episode congratulated me. It was the first time in my life that I had ever been praised for risking physical danger to say what I believed. I liked the feeling very much.

So I was still a little exultant, if a little nauseated from drinking too much cognac, when next morning I read in the *Crimson* a short article about a group of Negroes called the Student Nonviolent Coordinating Committee which was working for civil rights in the South. The writer described how they had been harassed for trying to help black Mississippians register to vote. I read the article as I walked down Rehov Negba, past a row of comfortable stucco houses. Many of my good friends lived there, Europeans who had fled to Israel. Now they were safe and happy, building their land. The community where I taught was behind Rehov Negba, across the shallow valley. At that hour of the morning my students' fathers, those ancient Oriental men who earned their keep by cleaning Beersheba's streets, were just returning home. Their sons and daughters would have decent jobs and live in better homes than millions of people in the United States. Of course there was some tension between the generations of North Africans, even more between the Europeans who settled the country and the Orientals who composed the majority of its population. But most of those conflicts would be healed. Israelis cared too much about each other to let their internal problems rip them apart. As long as I stayed in their country I would be a free man, too. (It never occurred to me at the time, though, that the Palestinian refugees were paying heavily for that freedom. When I thought of them in those days it was as enemies, not victims. Now the situation in the Middle East seems to me the most tragic in the world; the Arabs have joined the Jews as casualties of Western anti-Semitism.)

My Russian friend was right: on Rehov Negba none of the Americans I went to Choate with would call me a kike. But in their own country they still used the word "nigger" when they talked about the SNCCs who were working for integration in Mississippi. I had never been brave enough to confront them in school, not even after I delivered the chapel speech that won the faculty's approval. Just a few weeks later I had remained silent, frightened, while the captain of the hockey team, the boy I liked least in my entire class, spent an entire lunch mocking a Third

Former who reminded me of myself. He and I were the only Sixth Formers at the table. My silence made me his accomplice, the villain of my own fable.

By their example, my Israeli friends had helped me begin to acquire the sort of pride that allows one to fight back. I was learning that I liked to take risks to defend other people. Now, the civil-rights movement seemed the best place in the world to test my new manhood.

III

I COULDN'T find any civil-rights projects that wanted white volunteers to work through the winter of 1963. Besides, my parents kept arguing that I should graduate from college. So I followed the impulse that had brought me home from Rehov Negba only as far as a summertime commitment to tutor Negro kids on the eastern shore of Maryland. Then I realized that I wanted a Harvard degree as badly as my parents wanted one for me. I might have resented the college for the lifeless education it gave me, but I also needed its formal approval to consider myself a success. Without a diploma I would have trouble facing the adult world.

The work we did in Chestertown during those two months was much more enjoyable than frightening. I had plenty of time to learn about the Negro community and to explore the complexities of my personal relations with my black contemporaries on the project's staff. In those days the conflicts which would tear the civil-rights movement apart seemed manageable. Sometimes, indeed, the effort to cross cultural barriers presented a challenge that was even exhilarating. The more one expanded one's psychic plurality, the richer one's life became.

There were just four of us working in Chestertown that summer, two black men, a white girl, and myself. To raise money our project director had pledged not to organize any disruptive direct-action campaigns. Chestertown whites, who had attacked a bus-load of freedom riders the winter before, never harassed us. We didn't threaten them enough. A few people even seemed proud that the town could tolerate our small integrated group. One day when I was walking toward the small church that served as our headquarters I saw an elderly white woman turn to a friend, point at me, and boast, "There goes our outside agitator."

That summer I felt that I had found the American history I'd been looking for in my college courses. An older nation seemed to be preserved in the slow-paced Negro community, and it was a wonderful place. I took a delighted scholar's pleasure in learning how black society worked, sharing its pleasures, learning its language. It was far more real, for example, to hear Mrs. Alberta Deacy, who had spent thirty years of her life "working private" in Philadelphia, recount kitchen gossip about the rich people who sank with the *Titanic* than to take notes on Oscar Handlin's droning lectures about American millionaires. In college classrooms it had been difficult for me to understand the meaning of phrases like "the impact of technological innovation on poor societies," even after I had taken sociology courses devoted to that theme. Now, when I watched the sixty-five-year-old woman at whose house I was living struggle to understand the workings of the dial telephone that had just been installed, I understood that her look of confusion reflected the same sense of displacement as the lost expressions on the faces of old Oriental men in Israel, who listened to Doris Day songs on their transistor radios as they grazed their sheep near Abraham's caves.

It was clear that a distinct black culture had developed out of segregation. That was something my austere abolitionist's view of the South had blocked me from realizing before I went to Chestertown. I had thought that daily life for a black man was constant agony: that he was a "nigger" from morning till night with no real pleasures of his own. But the people I met that summer lived lives that were at least as rich and complicated as my friends' back at Harvard. They had remained entirely human. Their capacity to make spontaneous jokes about the system didn't even seem inhibited by my white presence. For example, one day I was sitting with some friends in Mrs. Sarah Bradford's front parlor waiting to go to a picnic that Campbell Soup, the town's leading employer, had organized for its workers. At the last minute Mrs. Bradford decided to stay home, and she told us to watch out for her son. Then she gave him instructions. "Take care, boy. Mind you don't eat watermelons, hear. You don't want a white man to catch you doing that. But bring one home for me, boy. Because, you know, they're right: niggers do like watermelons."

We all laughed, in what I thought was comfortable harmony.

Of course ugly things happened that summer, too, and each injustice we encountered exposed the tremendous psychological distance between the black staff members and myself. But I was so eager to understand the new world I had entered that I regarded their angry comments as lessons rather than rebukes. Learning a new culture, I told white friends of mine, is even more complicated than learning a new language.

One of our main jobs in Chestertown was to tutor the girl who would integrate the white high school the next fall. She was entering her senior year, and the gaps in her education astonished me. She was supposed to take a second-year French course, for example, but it was impossible to review the rudiments of the language with her because she had never learned English grammar, not even the difference between an adjective and an adverb. We were talking about books one day and she told me that her sophomore English class had spent nearly a month on a single text, "Oh Susanna." I was outraged. I told the two black men on the project that we should complain. I had amused them all summer, I amused them now. "Complain to whom?" the project director asked. "You're in the South now, not at Choate or Harvard. Do you think the white people who run the school here are going to worry about what happens to a bunch of little nigger kids? The worse they're taught the less trouble they make, that's the way the white folks see it." Besides, he explained, the principal of the Negro high school had deep vested interest in inferior segregated education. "Now he calls himself 'doctor' and uses fancy words, struts around and plays 'big nigger' in his own community while he Toms all the whites. Do you think that he wants to change a system that gives him such power?"

There was an integrated group of labor organizers in Chestertown trying to unionize the Campbell Soup plant. The town regarded them as its real enemies ("furriners," the weekly newspaper said), far more threatening than our tiny project. One day a white woman who was working with them felt ill and was rushed to the town's only hospital by a black friend. For hours the doctors ignored her. And when they finally decided that she had suffered a heart attack they refused to put her in an oxygen tent, until a union executive from Baltimore telephoned an angry protest.

That kind of callousness horrified me, and I described it at a church meeting the next night. But the audience didn't seem to respond at all. "You really don't understand us, do you?" the project director said afterward. "You know, there's not a day when one of our people doesn't experience segregation at that same hospital. When they're admitted they're sent to the damp Negro ward in the basement. What makes you think that they're going to get angry now because some white lady suffers the same treatment as they do?"

One day I was playing outside our church headquarters with some children from town, trying to teach them to make a loud, clicking sound I had adapted from a Miriam Makeba record. I knew them all by name, and I felt flattered by the fact that they all seemed to know me. I was sure that they liked me, too. Whenever I walked through the streets of the community kids would holler out friendly greetings from houses and apartments everywhere.

But that afternoon Bill, the black organizer with whom I worked most closely, began to denounce me, enraged, insisting that my easy relations with the kids were built on hypocrisy: "What kind of game did you come down here to play, anyway? Who do you think you are, some modern Jesus who is going to lead all the poor little darky urchins away from the hovels where they live and into the promised land? Don't you realize that they flock to you because your skin is white, not because of anything you do? I wish you'd learn what's happening. I don't want our black children to model themselves after you."

I wasn't very surprised by Bill's tirade, for he was frequently moody and provocative. The first day we met he showed me some Swiftian essays he had written in college that year, Modest Proposals, which argued in coldly ironic tones that genocide was the only means by which white people could deal with the race problem in America. I turned on the manners I had learned at Choate and, as graciously as a prep-school fund raiser, tried to shift the conversation to a more neutral theme.

But most of the time we worked together quite effectively. For example, in church meetings we were able to use the fact that the project director was dark black, Bill café-au-lait, and I white, as a wedge into discussions of the sort of integrated future we sought to create for our country. Whenever we sang freedom songs in church we would lift our three arms high in the air and hold them up, side by side.

And in our personal relations Bill's contempt for my naïveté about black people was tempered by a desire—which in retrospect seems almost desperate—to show me what America was like for him. We would talk for hours about the gradations of prejudice inside the black community; about the anger he felt at his parents because they didn't want him to date any girl whose skin was darker than his own. Or he would tell me about the conflicts he experienced when he attended integrated schools. He always felt a temptation to be whiter than the white man, he said: to talk a more precise English, to dress more tastefully, to rise to the top of the professions we dominated. Sometimes he imposed disciplines on himself so severe that they nearly drove him mad. He used to smoke three packs a day but now had given up cigarettes altogether. He would study in his room for days at a time, never sleeping, cooking all his meals on a one-burner hot plate. As a teen-ager he had weighed almost three hundred pounds; during his senior year at college he had fasted down to one-eighty. Now he did exercises every day, to keep himself in shape for the violent future he feared and desired.

Such confessions seemed to provide a perspective into which I could fit Bill's angry outbursts. By the summer's end I was convinced that I understood him quite well, that I could transform myself and win his trust. And I was sure that I could communicate his reality to my contemporaries at college; encourage them to transform themselves, too.

It was a faith that seems embarrassingly dewy as I write now, in 1969. But during that summer just seven years in the past it was possible to believe that by changing ourselves we could change, and redeem, our America.

IV

My spring in Israel, my summer in the movement, gave me a self-confidence I had never before possessed. Some articles I had written about Chestertown for the *Crimson* seemed to me very good. I felt as if I had found a subject that would hold my interest long enough to let me learn my craft. And the woman I had failed in London was now visiting America. On weekends that summer we had stayed together in Washington. Now I was able to imagine myself as a talented artist taking dangerous risks each week to change the world while in his nation's capital, its fairest, sweetest city, a mysterious foreign woman waited. It was a kind of manhood.

That fall at Harvard I realized that hundreds of students were now committed to progressive ideas, as I was. Civil rights had replaced disarmament as the reigning issue on campus, and it allowed one to express one's hopes and anxieties through practical activities like tutorial programs instead of scientific abstractions about the arms race. I spent almost no time with the cynics whose paralyzed complaints had twined with my own mood during my first three years of college. Now my friends were people like Fred Gardner, Adam Hochschild, Todd Gitlin, Richie Rothstein, people who realized that politics were not just material for unhappy midnight bull sessions, a way of expressing one's private discomfort, but the substance of ideas and analyses that would dictate the direction of one's own life. Though I was still somewhat less radical than many of the left-wingers at Harvard, I was grateful to be part of a community in which issues like integration and pacifism were discussed seriously. Its existence gave me confidence in the ideas I had been embarrassed to present to the *Crimson* editorial board two years earlier.

I also was confident that I could argue intelligently with the liberals whose courses had confused me at Harvard, many of whom were now scholar-activists in the Kennedy Administration. My discoveries in Beersheba and Chestertown helped me to find words to express my objections to their style. It seemed to me that Arthur Schlesinger and McGeorge Bundy debased the government's policies when they sought to serve as spokesmen for people they scarcely knew. In the privacy of the White House or their Georgetown homes they debated the Negro problem, the Middle East, or Cuba, and based the decisions they made on ideas and theories they had developed in libraries at Harvard or at meetings of the Americans for Democratic Action, not on anything they had ever experienced.

But my criticisms were more technical than moral. I didn't question their right to administer, but rather the way they did the job. So, at the age of twenty-two, I resolved to give myself a better preparation than my elders had. I decided to continue viewing America from its slums and its ghettos, to spend as much time as possible living with its least privileged people so that, when my time came, I could govern them sensibly. Part of my reason for remaining in the movement, then, was a modern version of *noblesse oblige* tied to a radical definition of the interests of my class.

It was a wisp of a notion when I was in the South, for in the heart of the movement a member of the establishment is the same as a spy, and I cared too much about the people I was working with to let them consider me a traitor. But when I returned north, to New York or Cambridge, the problems that were so immediate and compelling in Maryland suddenly became abstractions. And when the poor black man who lived next door to me in Chestertown became the subject of classroom speculation at Harvard, the wisp of a notion began to billow. It was not hard to view the movement as a springboard to a successful, satisfying career.

There were times when immediate ambition dominated my long-range plans. To my surprise, I had become something of a celebrity at Harvard. The Southern civil-rights movement is the only popular war Americans have fought during the last twenty-five years, and people were eager to learn about its heroes. Even summer soldiers like me, who had never been in any danger. The pieces I published in the *Crimson* won the Dana Reed prize for undergraduate writings, and swiftly brought offers from book-publishing houses and magazines. The *Crimson* seemed an ideal place for my articles, though, since it was said to be one of the newspapers that President Kennedy read daily. There were times when I consciously wrote to him, to combat the bad advice that Schlesinger and Bundy must be giving. I remember insisting that an essay about the movement be held until the Yale-Harvard game because the President was expected to attend. I must have expected that my mind-blowing prose would distract his attention from the action on the football field.

I thought I could influence the President because of the attention that people at Harvard seemed to be paying to my work. White, twenty-two, with just a few months' experience in the South, I was supposed to be one of the university's resident experts on Negroes. A professor of mine, whom I knew to be a conservative, told me one day that I should stick with the civil-rights movement. "Oh, I don't believe in all the morality you people talk about," he said, "but sometime soon those colored people are going to have enough money to be substantial consumers. Then businesses will need people like you who are experts on their habits."

One afternoon I received a telephone call from a dean of the college who wanted to talk with me as soon as possible. He was worried that the black students were dissatisfied with Harvard. I was known to have some militant friends. Perhaps I could talk to them, then write a report describing the things that bothered them. I refused and asked the dean why he hadn't selected a black student to do his research. But though his request seemed crazy to me, it was also very flattering. It was the first time in my life that professors and administrators had taken me seriously.

The day before my graduation with the class of 1963, Medgar Evers was murdered by Byron de La Beckwith. I heard about it as I was driving to meet my parents at Logan Airport. I was ashamed that I'd spend the next day in sunny Harvard Yard, hearing speaker after speaker praise the university and the nation. They should mourn. They should put themselves on trial; they were accomplices in the crime of segregation.

For a moment I considered asking my parents to return to New York while I flew down to bloody Mississippi. I would confront the state, hands on hips, chin sticking out (sweat dripping from my reddened face, horn-rimmed glasses skidding from my nose); I would praise free speech in full voice, bellow its glory throughout the land. What an appropriate commencement that would be! The best possible way to begin my life in the adult world.

But my parents had been waiting a long time for me to graduate. They wanted to see me receive my diploma, and I had to admit that the part of me that had been battling Harvard wanted to participate in the ceremonial triumph. Besides, I didn't know anyone in Mississippi. What would I do once I got there?

So I rewrote an editorial I had published in the *Crimson* three months before, when William Moore was assassinated during his lonely hike to Alabama. I told the Americans who happened to be gathered in Cambridge that festive week that their moral nerve would decay unless they responded at once to the atrocities that were occurring with increasing regularity in the Southern states;

and those who knew me praised my prose style (they didn't realize that I had cribbed the metaphor from Norman Mailer) and my courage for publishing such bold opinions.

I was a Harvard pundit that year. People regarded me as an authority, and I was proud to act as one. It was a fleeting experience, but it did me enormous harm. A dissenter gained respect too easily at Harvard College during John Kennedy's short administration. He became confident of his opinions much too early. It was a sure way to acquire very bad habits.

V

I HAD decided to go to graduate school at the University of Chicago's Committee on Social Thought in the fall of 1963. I had enrolled there to stay free of the draft, and attended only the classes that interested me most. I spent most of my time working on a novel about a graduate of a New England prep school who had fallen in love during a tense civil-rights conflict like the one that had occurred in Cambridge, Maryland, where I had spent several weeks after I graduated from college.

It might have been a pretty good book, too.

But for months after President Kennedy was murdered I couldn't write anything at all. Instead, I spent most of that year trying to help some black people on my block build a playground for their kids. I was more interested in negotiating with the university over a fenced-in patch of land it owned on the rim of the ghetto than in attending the lectures its professors offered.

Each night the image of a crouched gunman invaded my brain; for months I was possessed of a fantasy which put me alongside John Kennedy in that car in Dallas, protecting him. But I couldn't avenge him, I hadn't guarded him.

The Mississippi Summer Project seemed the best place to commemorate him. There, by sheer main force, one might help realize the promise one had sensed in the President's words. I told myself that I was going south in the summer of 1964 to help Negroes win the right to vote. Now I'm sure that at some level of my mind I wanted to work there because I still believed that I could stop a man in Dallas from murdering my President.

But now that I was really going to Mississippi I was scared. In the spring I persuaded my fiancée, Rachel—the heroine of my unfinished novel, whom I had met in Cambridge, Maryland—to take judo lessons so that we would know how to respond when the rabid white Mississippians attacked us. But after three lessons we quit, battered, our apprehensions intensified by our obvious physical incompetence. Through one May morning we sat over bagels and lox at the Unique 47 Mt. Zion Delicatessen in Chicago's Hyde Park listing the places we really wanted to visit that summer. I liked the idea of Alaska. I considered myself a great poker player, and a friend of mine had won five thousand dollars there gambling with the money he had earned fishing for salmon. Rachel had always wanted to go to France. But the exact place didn't matter so much as the time we would have together. We were deeply in love, we wanted enough privacy to explore each other. So we wrote down all the places that interested us, then lanced a pen on the piece of paper; where it struck we would wander.

Of course the game was a lark, a morning's relief. We were both political puritans: the more frightening the prospect of a summer in Mississippi, the more obliged we felt to be there. Besides, the action was there, nowhere else. Part of my brain echoed that passage in *This Side of Paradise* where Amory Blaine proudly lists the great prep-school football stars who would be his classmates at Princeton. On demand I could produce a list twice as long as Amory's of the great civil-rights workers who would work out of the movement's headquarters in Jackson.

But that game ended the night that Andy Goodman, Mickey Schwerner, and James Chaney disappeared in Neshoba County,

Mississippi. Rachel and I were then still in training at Western College for Women in Oxford, Ohio.

A few hours after we had learned that they were missing, I heard a girl yell at her mother, who had phoned her in a sudden panic, "If someone in Nazi Germany had done what we're doing then your brother would still be alive." Later hundreds of us marched solemnly to the farthest boundary of the campus behind a car that was carrying five SNCC members toward Neshoba County, where they would search for the missing men. We sang, "We have hung our heads and cried, cried for those like Lee who died." The song, written after another civil-rights murder, was a dirge: "Died for you and he died for me; died for the cause of equality"; and an oath: "But we'll never turn back, no we'll never turn back"; and, finally, a vision: "Until we've all been free, and we have equality."

The car shot off, through America's twilight.

Many of us had confronted death only once before—but now it was not a remote figure like the President who had been assassinated. That night news broadcasts showed films of Andy Goodman sitting, just a week before, in Western's auditorium, where we now spent most of our days. Though his body would not be found until August, we were all certain that he and James and Mickey had been murdered.

"Mississippi is hell, that's what you people have to understand. You won't change it until you know how bad it is." It was an hour after the carful of SNCC workers had left for Neshoba County. A slender black man had interrupted a dull technical lecture a white lawyer was delivering, a survey of the legislation which the state had passed to contain our invasion. "These academic things won't help you at all down there. Mississippi is hell. Listen to me! H-E-L-L! Mississippi is hell. You can get killed in Mississippi." His passion made the statement extremely moving, and we all applauded him. He walked out of the auditorium, insulted. A black girl who had been working in Mississippi stood up. All week she had been one of the few staff members at the camp with whom we felt completely at home. She loved to do imitations of Southern society women; it was funny and relaxing to listen to her. "You white people better get over that damn ignorance very quick," she said. "Don't you know enough not to applaud like that? See, we've all been hurt so much that your applause is an insult. Do you know about that man who just talked? His name is Jimmy Travis. A year ago three machine-gun bullets went through his neck. It's a miracle that he's still alive. That's right, three machine-gun bullets. So he doesn't give a shit for your approval. He was trying to tell you something, and you wouldn't listen."

The night after the murders Bob Moses, the black man who had initiated the Mississippi movement nearly four years earlier and was now director of the Summer Project, gave a speech urging us to go back north if we had any doubts about the work we were going to do. But how could we turn back? Were we such cowards that we would retreat now that the dangers to which people like Bob had grown accustomed were finally apparent to us?

Bob seemed as anxious to forgive himself for the tragedies his planning had caused as he was to persuade the uncommitted to return home. His tone that night was almost confessional. "At least we've never asked anyone else to take risks that we weren't willing to take." The thought seemed to provide him little solace. "Anyway, we can't give up. White people in Mississippi have always killed Negroes who tried to gain their rights. And we want to change that, not succumb to it." He paused for a moment. "But the problem is that when you fight evil for so long you become part of evil yourself, and terribly, terribly tired."

Then for a second he snapped back from that mood. "Now I want to say a few things to the Freedom School teachers"—he had been a teacher at the Horace Mann School in New York before he gave up his comfortable life in the North to work in Mississippi— "Please be patient with your students. You must remember that there is a difference between being slow and being stupid. The people you'll be working with aren't stupid. But they're slow. So slow."

He finished his speech, stood still for a minute, then walked out the door. Far in the back of the auditorium a woman started to sing. "They say that freedom is a constant struggle." A sweet, solo voice in the quiet, crowded room. Each of us put his arm around the person standing next to him. We began to sway gently, back and forth, and to join her. "We've struggled so long, O Lord; We must be free, we must be free." Black and white together, their voices reverent, turning the emotions Bob Moses' words had aroused into a passionate prayer.

That week Bob became, for me, the embodiment of the America for which I had been searching.

His quiet modest personality was so compelling that many of us who hardly knew him strove to get close to him by imitating his manner. For example, his habit of sitting toward the back of the auditorium during important meetings: it was his way of forcing others to be leaders. Or his careful silences. When one asked Bob a question there was always a long pause before he answered, sometimes a pause of several minutes. He had been a math major at Hamilton College, a philosophy student in graduate school at Harvard. I had never met anyone who chose his words with such care, whose sentences were accordingly so lucid and precise. He told us once that he had decided, that most people talk too much and that he would use words only when they were absolutely required. So he shared what he knew by example and not, like most of us, by making long speeches or issuing orders.

His actions showed me my own hypocrisy. Someone who had known Moses while he was still a schoolteacher in New York told me that the year before Bob went to Mississippi he had spent a great deal of time listening to old Odetta records. He would play them over and over, night after night. Well, Odetta had created the same stirrings in me in Beersheba—something similar must have been reaching thousands of Americans in those years after John Kennedy's election—but Bob had acted while most of the rest of us talked. And he took terrible risks. The three machine-gun bullets which had lodged in Jimmy Travis's neck were aimed at him. An unmarked car had pulled up alongside the automobile he was driving, a white Mississippian had thrust his machine gun out the window, then fired seventeen bullets. Since Medgar Evers' assassination, Bob's name had been at the top of the list of those the Ku Klux Klan wanted to kill.

I compared my admiration for Bob with my attitude toward John Kennedy. Kennedy might have inspired a generation by talking about courage; Bob was trying to transform a state by living courageously. Kennedy had won great power for himself through the skillful use of wealth and influence; Bob's example, his endurance, had helped Mississippi Negroes gain a little power for themselves. John Kennedy talked about the value of democracy. Bob Moses tried to be a democrat. He could have belonged to any elite —for years he had been one of the "first Negroes" wherever he went—but instead he fought elitism. While Theodore Sorensen and Burke Marshall conferred in Washington about the "Negro problem," Bob stayed in Mississippi through four cold, lonely winters organizing black people to demand things for themselves.

The Kennedys boasted that they had learned about poverty during a brief campaign tour through West Virginia. Bob spent years of his life in the midst of terrible poverty. In that way he learned about America.

VI

THERE is a kind of Jesus Christ complex that many middle-class whites bring to their relations with people whom they consider oppressed. I used to see it in myself all the time, revealed in the crudest ways. I'd be walking down a street in Chicago, for example, notice a black child who looked broke and unhappy, and reach out my arm to touch his head. I felt that the mere fact of my attention would change the poor lad's life—my generosity would flow through my arm and convert to good fortune once it entered his brain—what a spreading, luxurious sense of power that thought afforded!

In a sense the Summer Project synthesized the deepest desire that possessed many of the volunteers: the desire to be used. A white girl I met in Mississippi confessed to me one night that whenever she walked through Harlem she burned to be raped; but now her work in a rural community center was satisfying the same longing. An extreme example, perhaps, but not an inaccurate metaphor. She despised the self she had inherited from middle-class America, wanted to obliterate it and move on to something more humane.

Most of us, eagerly assuming that we could heal whomever we sought to serve, shared a reverent belief in the Summer Project's vast political potential. We felt that our actions during those few months would not only bring limited kinds of progress to Negroes in Mississippi but would also insure the collapse of segregation everywhere in the country. The project seemed to be a turning point in America's history. We were an army of love, and if we integrated Mississippi we would conquer hate's capital. But if we were repulsed that summer then racism would triumph everywhere. My brother, Geoff, summarized our mood in a sentence. "I'm going," he told our parents, "because I won't know how to tell my grandchildren why I stayed home."

If you talk with Mississippi Negroes, rather than the black militants who comprised the SNCC staff, you will probably hear favorable comments about the Summer Project: "Thank God for those civil-rights workers who came down here and opened up our eyes."

And our efforts did benefit many local people, no matter what the SNCC organizers began to claim the next year. Or at least our presence did, for there was, in many cases, a sharp distinction to be made between the consequences of a white Northerner's decision to go to Mississippi and the work he did while he was actually there. If our goal was to focus national attention on the most severe of the state's problems, then our success was indisputable. Of course there was a great deal of silly talk, foolishly flattering to the white volunteers—just as there would be about our descendants who worked for Eugene McCarthy four years later—but the press and the public also paid enough attention to the worst aspects of segregation in Mississippi to force some changes. A few schools were integrated, public accommodations were opened, tens of thousands of black people registered to vote. By the spring of 1969 there were numerous black candidates for political office in Mississippi, and Charles Evers was elected Mayor of Fayette.

It was an effective public-relations campaign, then. But the changes I have just listed would probably have occurred if we had sat indoors from the day the television cameras recorded our arrival until the day they recorded our departure. The project itself was nothing like the project we'd imagined when we volunteered.

Most of us had come south with a set of romantic illusions. (Mine had been fortified by my memories of that pleasant summer in Chestertown.) We had expected to work in the black ghettos and rural slums with people just like ourselves, only poorer, darker, more saintly. That idea was the legacy of the leveling liberalism that we had inherited from a generation reared on the nationalistic idealism of Roosevelt's New Deal. But as we saw ourselves through the looking glass of the local culture we slowly began to realize that we were different people than we had believed, so were the Mississippi Negroes, so were the black SNCC staff members. (The looking glass had already created some grotesque impressions on my block in Chicago: during those summer months my neighbors, their playground only half-built, were telling each other that I had run off with the funds we had raised from the community and was now living lavishly in Mississippi. It was the only way they could understand my abrupt intrusion into their lives, my abrupt departure.)

Throughout the summer there was as much conflict as cooperation between the volunteers and local Negroes, and our relations with most of the movement staff members were a constant struggle. Schlesinger's "vital center" was not ample enough even to contain blacks and whites who had come together voluntarily to help Mississippi Negroes gain benefits more modest than those Roosevelt's Administration had conferred on most of white America during the 1930s.

The conflicts were produced by misunderstandings so profound that they could not possibly have been healed by patience or good will. American history, our own private histories, had made integration impossible.

At a meeting late in the summer one white girl on our project cried out in despair, "I wish Negroes spoke their own language. At least that would force white people like us to realize how badly equipped we are to come down here and work with you. Then if we wanted to talk with you we would have to learn your vocabulary and accept your definitions."

During the next years hundreds of us would try to incorporate such new, painful perceptions into our lives, to change our personalities accordingly. But for most of us that process did not begin until after we had left Mississippi.

The job I was given that summer in Vicksburg made me especially conscious of the tensions which provided the real emotional foundation of our project.

I was a communications officer: but more like a nursemaid than a journalist. (And separated from Rachel, who was working on a medical project in Jackson.) Someone on each project had to make sure that all the civil-rights workers in his area were back at headquarters within half an hour of the deadlines they had set for themselves. How else could we know whether Harold Ickes or Shel Stromquist, our two most skillful, energetic Freedom Democratic Party organizers, were still signifying with a local leader, sharing his fried chicken, or whether they were lying in a local gully with local bullets in them. Now places that had always seemed to me wonderfully American—supermarkets, miniature-golf courses, drive-in movies—were symbols of flaring danger. If a girl who had taken a load of wash down to the laundromat didn't return on schedule, I had to make a badgering phone call to the FBI. In that assignment lay a large part of my contribution to the cause of freedom in Mississippi.

When you spend your time inside an office you learn about everybody's problems. It is hard, even now, to sort the kind of gossip that occurs in organizations everywhere from the specific issues that divided volunteers from local people and the movement staff. Indeed, it was precisely the most ordinary difficulties that produced some of the summer's deepest tensions.

In mid-July a romance between a white girl on our project and a local black teen-ager collapsed. It had never really gotten very far anyway: the first tentative sparrings of puppy love, a few dates, maybe a night or two of passion. But the week after it ended the black man robbed a gas station, the first crime he had ever committed. What could any of us say? The girl had made great sacrifices to come to Mississippi and now she was one of the best Freedom School teachers in Vicksburg. But one could see why a black Mississippian would think she was hungry for sex, no more: the tight blue jeans she often wore when she taught, those open shirts that hung out at the waist must have made every gesture seem like an invitation. But so far as she was concerned there was nothing even remotely unnatural about those clothes. What could she do if a black man to whom she felt no attraction accepted an invitation which she didn't know she had offered? To reject an advance was to exhibit racism, or so it would certainly seem. But to begin a loveless affair in the name of racial harmony was to insure disaster.

It was one of the most complicated problems in the movement, but one rarely discussed it for fear of sounding like a bigot or a prig.

The next winter the black teen-ager from Vicksburg was serving a five-year sentence in a Mississippi reform school. The girl who had felt obliged to spurn him was home free, back at school, eager to share her memories of that exciting summer in Mississippi.

We all showed our misunderstanding of the community we lived in. For example, the problem of clothes. We were aware that in Vicksburg, which had one of the largest middle-class Negro populations in the state, most black people had conservative, church-going values. Even the poorest people expected you to be as neat as you were financially able and were insulted if you seemed to be dressing down to them.

Nevertheless, almost all of us always dressed badly. Part of the problem was our living conditions, which did make it difficult to be clean. Eight of us shared a room in the Vicksburg Freedom House. There was just one double bed, and a rickety old fan; so six of us had to sleep sweating on the dirty floor.

But that was no real excuse. Most of us would have dressed sloppily even if we'd had our own private room and shower. It was part of our personal rebellion, tied to the fact that the Summer Project was as much an effort to work free from our own pasts as to help black people build a better future for themselves. The lie we told was that we wore shoddy clothes in order to identify with the poor. For the main effect of our appearance was to make the vicious rumors spread by local white people seem plausible to some of the Negroes in town. Why shouldn't they have wondered whether the outsiders who looked so grubby weren't escaping from their families in order to lead lives of love-making and drug-taking?

In Chestertown I had been very impressed with the importance the black organizers attached to the churches in town. Local people always socialized during the hours after the services, and an outsider seemed more legitimate if he was seen on the church steps. Afterward, one was usually invited to someone's house for lunch, and once in a while, during those drowsy afternoons, one could move past the formal relationships that organizers at first establish with their new acquaintances, toward genuine friendships. But in Vicksburg most of us usually spent our Sundays reading or writing letters. Of course we had a reason to explain why we rarely went to church—we rationalized nearly everything we did that summer. We claimed that the church, as an institution, was much too conservative for the movement we wanted to build. We mustn't sanction it with our presence.

To a certain extent that argument was a disguise for our fatigued laziness. But it also reflected our desire to turn the communities where we lived into the utopias we harbored in our book-stuffed imaginations. Children of the white upper middle class, we told each other that we wanted to overthrow the conventional, materialistic middle-class black people who exercised leadership in Vicksburg. The beauticians, barbers, doctors, and post-office workers who held power in the Negro community weren't genuinely interested in the welfare of their own people, we said. A local doctor could be an outspoken member of the NAACP, at great cost to himself and his family, but if he spent more time that summer developing his practice or remodeling his home than he did working with us, we tended to regard him as a class enemy. To help his people we had sacrificed a summer which affluence had provided. Now we expected him to dedicate himself to our version of the movement, on our terms.

Of course SNCC staff members shunned black professional people and celebrated the very poor, too. Our attitude had been deeply influenced by theirs. But in Vicksburg, particularly, with its large black middle class, it put us in a painfully ambiguous position. For there were no poor people who seemed willing to become local leaders. We had to work with the middle-class blacks whom we criticized so frequently.

A scene from that summer continues to nag my memory. An earnest Northerner, dripping sweat from the midday heat, is giving his politely compliant protégé advice about the intricacies of local politics, though the protégé is a barber who has lived in Vicksburg all his life and has a deep, detailed knowledge of the relations among most people in the black community. Then, satisfied that he has taught a good day's lesson, the Northerner returns to the Freedom House and complains to the other volunteers that the barber's greedy wife wants to install a washing machine and may buy a new car.

We were so intent on transforming Mississippi in a summer that we were unable to relate to its people as human beings.

VII

VERY few of the black SNCC staff members ever shared the volunteers' illusions about the Summer Project. Most of them had been in the movement for years and were even more cynical about their relations with white people than my partner Bill had been in Chestertown. During those months I realized that Bill's angry remarks, which had sounded somewhat paranoid just two years before, might seem rather moderate in the years ahead.

The Freedom Summer had been a source of conflict inside the movement from the day it was proposed. Although most of the people affiliated with the Council of Federated Organizations (COFO), the umbrella organization which supported it, agreed that the Project would certainly draw attention to segregation in Mississippi, many of the SNCC workers who would have to administer the white volunteers proposed that there be a fixed ratio according to race, ten blacks to every white, so that they could be certain their organization was not dominated by outsiders. They dropped the plan when Bob Moses called it "racist" at an extremely emotional meeting in Greenville, and when it became clear that a summer project with a built-in quota system could not attract much money or support. But the danger the proposal foretold materialized quickly. The project became oriented toward its Northern backers and dependent on the specialized skills of the white volunteers. Many of the black staff members felt insulted and soon developed a lasting bitterness toward the volunteers.

They were in charge of projects throughout the state, and sometimes they treated us as brusquely as sergeants treat buck privates during the first month of basic training. Often they seemed annoyed when we proposed new ways to register voters or to establish Freedom Schools. When we complained about their attitude, it became apparent that they could not imagine how deeply they had hurt us. To most of them it was still inconceivable that a white man would think he wasn't being treated as an equal (who did he imagine had all the power in America, anyway?); he must mean that he wanted to run the show. When a graduate student in political science claimed that his way of running a voter-registration project was perfect from an academic point of view, most staff members heard him saying, "Move over boys. We're going to do things my way from now on."

They mistook our arrogant assumption that we could show them how to transform Mississippi's institutions for a Machiavellian desire to control the movement. We, in turn, saw their quick, wounded assertion of authority as brutish rejections of the selves we so desperately wanted them to use.

No matter how much we tried to talk we could never really understand each other.

I nicknamed our project director Papa Doc, after Haiti's dictator. In retrospect, of course, it sounds like a barely disguised code: a liberal's way of saying Rastus or Burrhead. But at the time it was one of the few outlets I could find for my frustration with the project.

Vicksburg, a safe place that summer, did not provide us with the external threats that made real battlegrounds like Greenwood or McComb such exciting places to work. There was not enough danger to unify us. Nor were there any local movement heroes like Fannie Lou Hamer in Ruleville to provide us a link with the city's most oppressed people. During our first month in Mississippi the Freedom School lost students every week, the community center kept faltering, the voter-registration campaign seemed irrelevant to one of the few areas in Mississippi where black people never had much trouble registering. We were all thoroughly demoralized, and Papa Doc, twenty-two, a native Mississippian who had not yet graduated from one of the near-by Negro colleges, had no idea of how to guide us past our confusion.

We all admired him for his physical courage. There must have been some deep deposit of idealism in him, barely visible to us, which caused him to quit college for a year and go to work for SNCC long before the movement offered any rewards. The previous fall, when the Freedom Democratic Party organized the mock election in which Aaron Henry ran for Governor of Mississippi, Papa Doc had proved his bravery time and again by driving full ballot boxes from their hiding places deep in local black communities through police lines to the movement's central headquarters in Jackson, where they could be counted. In a car, he was a genius.

I saw him operate late one night, in the middle of the summer, after we had taken some Freedom School students back home. At the far end of a one-way street a white man drove his car out of a hiding place, tried to block Papa Doc's path, and confronted him with a gun. Papa Doc's reactions were perfect. Tail gate toward the main road, he shifted into reverse, steered off the dirt path into a gully, and backed down it until he was free of the white man's car. He made the getaway seem easy. As we drove back home I decided that I was already too clumsy, too bookish, too citified ever to make an adequate revolutionary.

But Papa Doc was not nearly so bold in his dealings with the volunteers. Now I realize that it must have been torment for him to enter the Vicksburg office and listen to us discussing local problems as if they were issues that had arisen in a college seminar. A fear as large as a cannonball must have filled his stomach whenever he was around us. How could he fail to despise us for putting it there?

But I was unable to muster such sympathy for him while we were still in Mississippi. During our first week in Vicksburg a small group of us had a private conversation with Bob Moses in which we promised him that we would never make an important decision without consulting Papa Doc. Since he was gone from

Vicksburg for days at a time, we used to delay plans to extend the Freedom Democratic Party's registration drive, or to negotiate for a new community center, until we could talk to him. But even when he was in the office he seemed unwilling to listen to our ideas or complaints. We organized meetings in which all the volunteers would describe their activities to Papa Doc and showed him the agenda days in advance. Sometimes he skipped the sessions without giving us any warning or any explanations. When he was present he usually remained silent, noncommittal.

We decided to ask the Jackson office to send us a new project director. Surely someone with more sensitivity and self-confidence than Papa Doc would find ways of converting the volunteers' frustrations to enthusiasm and thus release a torrent of ideas and programs that would benefit Vicksburg's Negroes. A staff member would hear us out, make us a promise, then, it seemed, forget us. Later I learned that Papa Doc was lobbying too, complaining about us. I suppose that Bob Moses and his associates felt that it was better for twenty white Northerners to spend an irritating few months in Mississippi than for a potential black leader like Papa Doc to lose all confidence in himself because he had failed under pressure.

Bob's emotional loyalty was to Papa Doc; because of my job, I think, or perhaps because of my background, my loyalty was to the volunteers who discussed their problems with me every day and to the project in which we were all involved.

So I moved to assume the leadership that Papa Doc seemed incapable of exercising. After we had been in Mississippi for a month, I began to criticize him openly, as harshly as I have ever criticized anyone in my life. I continually complained about his frequent absences and his evident inability to understand the kind of planning that had gone into sophisticated programs like Freedom Schools and community centers. When volunteers would tell me that they felt like failures in their work I usually suggested that Papa Doc was the real reason for their unhappiness. I tried to translate each sign of low morale into an argument against his capacity to direct the project. The situation was so discouraging that most of the other volunteers needed a scapegoat as badly as I did. We allowed each other to blame Papa Doc instead of examining our own immature reaction to a very complex situation.

It took very little time to get rid of Papa Doc. Soon he quit coming to the Freedom House altogether.

Now we had to solve the problem that had worried us since we arrived in Vicksburg. How could we realize the promise of the Summer Project? Didn't we have a responsibility both to local people and to ourselves to produce some specific accomplishments?

Some of us were influenced by a strategy we had learned from a white girl who had spent the past year working in the Jackson office. Before that she had lived in Africa, and her experience there had provided her with the sort of reference point that my six months in Israel had provided me. She thought that the Mississippi Freedom Democratic Party should look to socialist parties in countries like Tanzania for models. It would not gain much popular support simply by running candidates in local elections, she argued. There had to be a variety of institutions throughout the state that were connected to it. Educational institutions, welfare agencies, publications would attract thousands of new people to the FDP.

We thought that Northern science teachers should come to Vicksburg, to show teachers in the local high schools how they could teach physics and chemistry by film; we hoped to get a labor organizer into some factories that weren't yet unionized; there was a little surplus food from a supply that some Northern friends had sent earlier in the summer, and we thought we could use it to establish a rudimentary food-stamp program.

We founded a newspaper that month, the *Vicksburg Citizens' Appeal*. The first community civil-rights newspaper in Mississippi, we called it in our fund-raising speeches—and it probably was. In any case, our friends in the North were glad to believe that claim, and it took just a few days to persuade some of them to donate the thousand dollars we needed to put out the first issue. Four of us were experienced journalists. We planned all the articles, wrote some of them ourselves, assigned a few to local people, and drew up a dummy. A Wall Street lawyer who had devoted his summer vacation to the movement explained the complexities of incorporation and promised that his highly respectable firm would help us when we got back to New York. Then we formed a local board of directors and named a chairman and a vice-chairman.

The most enjoyable work I did that summer was at the scruffy little shop of a job printer in New Orleans, where I supervised the composition of the *Citizens' Appeal's* first issue. It was like being back at Van Dyck's in New Haven, nursing the *Choate News* until it went to bed.

Of course we started the newspaper and planned the other programs without ever consulting Papa Doc. He was staying away from Vicksburg for weeks at a time now, working on the Freedom Democratic Party's convention challenge. There had been two local black men present at our meetings, but they never really said much. We assumed that they agreed with our ideas. We were too proud of ourselves to imagine serious opposition.

Whenever visitors came through town we told them about our plans, and soon our reputation started to spread. We began to hear that ours was considered one of the best projects in the state, a fertile area for innovation.

I was having a great time. With Papa Doc gone for good, I was able to act freely. The office was now my province. I used to sit on top of the long, rectangular table where we did our work, my legs crossed Yoga-fashion, and delegate responsibility while I made hip little jokes and imitated Lyndon Johnson or Martin Luther King.

I no longer felt like a usurper; or rather, I had successfully usurped. The telephone was my greatest joy, my medium for wheeling and dealing. A long distance call from Mississippi was nearly tantamount to a summons in the summer of 1964, and I loved using my psychological advantage to scavenge resources for our programs.

I called myself a magician and used the telephone as my wand, bringing forth from its depths large quantities of money or verbal support.

One night late in the summer we asked Bob Moses to come to Vicksburg for a meeting. At last, our grand design was well enough developed that we could share it with him. He would have to be impressed. I was thrilled by the prospect of his praise.

Papa Doc must have heard about the meeting, too, for he was back in Vicksburg and openly angry at us. Local people didn't want our newspapers, he said in a quiet, bitter voice, or our science teachers or our labor organizers or our food programs. They wanted freedom. And that was the one thing we would never be able to give them.

When I argued that our scheme was the logical extension of the strategy behind the Summer Project (using just those words)—a sure way of sustaining the connection between Mississippi Negroes and Northern institutions that Bob had tried to develop—Papa Doc laughed briefly then lapsed back into his customary silence.

He was at the office early that night, to make sure that he could greet Bob the moment he arrived. The two local black men who had sat through most of our planning sessions were with him. As soon as Bob entered the Freedom House the four blacks went into a small room off a library we were building to talk alone.

I remember feeling pleased that Papa Doc had arranged that prelude. Bob would have to talk with him only a few minutes before he realized that the project director's arguments were very flimsy.

When the meeting began, nearly three hours later, we tried to describe our plan for the newspaper. It became clear immediately that our ideas annoyed Bob more than they impressed him. We had assumed that the *Citizens' Appeal* would be controlled by the volunteers in Vicksburg and by the middle-class Negroes we had named to the board of directors. Bob disagreed. There was no way, he said, that the directors or the white volunteers could be directly responsible to the very poor people whom the movement defined as its constituency. If the *Citizens' Appeal* wanted to retain formal relations with the movement, it would have to be controlled by SNCC's communications people.

To us that meant censorship, so, very reluctantly, we told him that we would have to transform the newspaper into a completely independent entity.

It was clear that Bob was choosing words, making decisions, that would appeal to Papa Doc and the other two blacks in the room. Now, but not then, not at all, I realize that our small meeting in Vicksburg must have been connected to a sustained, serious battle that was being waged among the black people in the movement. Perhaps Bob felt that he had to show the SNCC staff that he was more concerned about their interests than about the ideas of the white Northerners who had journeyed to Mississippi at his bidding.

So he became angry and, I thought, profoundly sad when I converted my disappointment in his attitude about the *Citizens' Appeal* into a question about some political decisions the SNCC staff had made which seemed to us distressingly hypocritical.

Though the movement talked proudly about its belief in "one man, one vote," we had discovered that the slate of local people who were supposed to represent the Freedom Democratic Party at the Democratic Convention in Atlantic City had been chosen by a group of SNCC workers, including Papa Doc, the night before the state convention in Jackson. The organization decided which local people should be rewarded for their loyalty and then rigged the convention accordingly. They were afraid that too many middle-class Negroes would be nominated in an open convention, for it was clear that many of the poor blacks with whom we worked still accepted most of the ideas of representation and respectability that they had learned from their segregated society. Traditionally, ministers had always represented them, dressing well, speaking their painfully precise English: that was the kind of thing the movement wanted to change. But we had always assumed that the change would come through persuasion, not manipulation.

At the state convention, some middle-class delegates had been silenced by the SNCC staff when they sought to disagree with the method by which the slate had been selected. In an organization whose motto was "let the people decide" such behavior was unsettling. Now local people had less power than staff members like Papa Doc. I had a clear imaginative picture of the SNCC workers' place in a state-wide black political machine. (With the same kind of corruption as any political machine. We had been told by friends in Jackson that Papa Doc had invested about three hundred dollars earmarked for the project back into his car. He boasted, even to us, about the new set of spinners he had bought recently.)

I had always believed that the white volunteers were working in Mississippi to help make America a more democratic country, and I resented anything that threatened that ideal. But now Bob's quiet answer to my harsh question forced me to recall that we were all outsiders in the state, there for a brief time only, and that we should be extremely cautious before we passed moral judgments on people whose backgrounds were so different from ours. "I think a lot of people here know more about democracy in the country that killed President Kennedy than most of you who have lived in the North. They haven't studied it in universities, like many of you, but they've seen how the American system works on them. All of their lives they've been made to suffer in the name of democracy. So many terrible things have been justified by that word. . . . The convention in Jackson would not be one of the first I would criticize."

So: if we had to judge black activists we must be very careful: to understand them within the context of their own culture and traditions, and not condemn them because they failed to be the ideal citizens of our imagined utopias. But why did we have to spend so much time judging them, why had we felt obliged to politic against Papa Doc in the name of the local people? The answer was dismaying. Because we craved the redeeming purity we thought we would find in the movement, many of us responded to every event that occurred that summer with a more concentrated passion than we had ever responded with to events in our own white America. Thus, we struggled harder against the weaknesses we thought we spotted in the movement than we had ever struggled against injustice in the communities where we were raised. We needed to rid ourselves of the double standards on which so many of our opinions were based. Our job was to transform the America that had provided us the wealth and freedom to roam the streets of the world seeking to do good—the America whose history most black people saw as the embodiment of violence and evil.

Though Bob must have recognized that conflict years earlier, he seemed to have remained confident that he could mediate between the two cultures in which he had lived—until the Summer Project began. Then, dozens of conflicts like mine with Papa Doc must have persuaded him that mediation was virtually impossible. There was no way he could build a bridge between our psychic terrains, so distant from each other. And as he became finally, firmly, convinced of that, his belief in human generosity, which had shimmered for so long, must have begun to dissolve.

I had heard that just a few years earlier he used to dance freely down the streets of New York, singing show tunes with his girl friend. Now, he smiled rarely, and his long silences no longer seemed so patient and wise as they did resigned and depressed.

But he communicated more than he may have realized. When he rejected our grandiose proposals (the newspaper collapsed in 1966, the other projects were never launched) he taught me one of the most important lessons of my life. For the more I thought of our meeting in Vicksburg (I would brood on it frequently over the next year), the more certain I became that Paul Cowan, Choate '58, Harvard '63, conduit to the white power structure in the North, would-be adviser to Kennedys past and future, member of an elite class that continued to believe it could control events with a few well-placed phone calls, was still unsuited to the world he had first entered when he left Cambridge, then London, in a nightmare of self-disgust and tried to transform himself by working with North Africans in Beersheba and blacks in the South. He was still bound to the culture he was trying to escape.

VIII

DURING the summer of 1964 the forces that my friends and I had glimpsed, then ignored, while we were still at Harvard began to materialize, in forms that were nearly as ugly as the apocalyptic nightmares that terrified so many of us.

The Gulf of Tonkin resolution was passed in August while most Northern volunteers were still in Mississippi, and the American history lectures that Freedom School teachers delivered that week were the most bitter of the summer. But the escalation of the war was quickly overshadowed, at least for us, by the savage fight that split the civil-rights movement during the Freedom Democratic Party's challenge to the lily-white Mississippi delegation at the Democratic Convention in Atlantic City several weeks later. The battle between white liberals like Allard Lowenstein and Joseph Rauh and the black SNCC members, enlarged, grotesque versions of our small quarrels in Mississippi, forced hundreds of volunteers to re-examine the political and moral assumptions they had grown up with and to redefine their political loyalties accordingly.

Most of us were spectators. We were still too young, too callow to play for stakes like state-wide delegations, Vice-Presidential nominations, or, later, million-dollar organizations. I might have regarded myself as a hip wheeler-dealer while I was still in Vicksburg, but as soon as I began to watch Al Lowenstein operate in the North I realized that I was a naïve kid.

As I heard about the dispute, mostly from Lowenstein, with

whom I spent a great deal of time whenever I was in New York, I realized that if I had been five years older, or even if I hadn't spent the summer in Mississippi, I would have been the liberals' loyal supporter. Their insistence that they represented reason and democracy would have corresponded to the slightly bloodless, elitist views that so many of my Harvard classmates who regarded themselves as progressives carried into the adult world.

As it was, I followed the debate between SNCC and the liberals for nearly a year before I decided whose side I supported, whose view of America would influence my future actions.

I was much more impressed by Lowenstein than by any of his liberal allies. Indeed, it is no exaggeration to say that he seemed to be the kind of person I had hoped to become when I temporarily dropped out of Harvard three years earlier.

I had felt a special admiration for Al ever since I learned that he was one of the first white people to join Bob Moses in Mississippi. Al had taken a great many risks to serve the movement as a lawyer and had gained the respect of many of the black organizers who knew him. In those early days it seemed that his political sophistication, already legendary, could combine with the movement's moral fervor to produce a force that would rapidly transform the South.

It was Al who first conceived the Freedom Democratic Party, both as a strategy to attract Northern students and as a means of showing their parents' generation that black people didn't even have the right to vote in Mississippi. Bob Moses had been impressed with the plan. He agreed with Lowenstein that a small, mostly black movement full of courage and charisma would never force the segregationists to make any fundamental changes. But even at the start there was a profound difference between the way the two men defined political strategy. To Al, the FDP represented a temporary device as much as a permanent organization: he was as eager for it to gain substantial support in white Washington as in black Mississippi, thought that it might even give integrationists like Ed King, Aaron Henry, and Charles Evers enough leverage to reform the regular Democratic Party. Of course, Bob viewed the FDP as an organization whose first responsibility was to black activists like Papa Doc, poor blacks like Fannie Lou Hamer.

But the disagreement was not noticeable in November 1963, when the FDP organized the mock election in which Aaron Henry ran for governor. Lowenstein had excellent connections at Stanford and Yale, and from those colleges alone hundreds of students came to Mississippi to spend two weeks working alongside local organizers. They were chased by sheriffs, jailed and beaten, just as the black activists were. Soon their stories had spread along the campus grapevine to colleges throughout the country. Hundreds more students were moved to join the Summer Project by their example.

Lowenstein and Moses, architects of the swelling achievement, seemed to complement each other perfectly. Al's visionary belief in the inherent decency of America's young people seemed as intense as Bob's love of the dispossessed Mississippi Negro. Allard, in his mid-thirties, was old enough to remember the Roosevelt years, and he now seemed the medium through which the generous idealism of that period had been carried through the decades. When the Summer Project began he seemed to be the white Bob Moses—or, as many of the white students Al had recruited saw it, Bob was the black Allard Lowenstein.

Al developed his political creed in the late 1930s, while he was still a boy. At the age of ten he was following the Spanish Civil War with the same rapt attention to detail that his contemporaries must have been devoting to major-league baseball. He was, of course, an ardent supporter of the Loyalists, but he hated the Communists in Spain as passionately as he hated Franco's forces. When Madrid fell, Al wept for hours. The vicarious experience left him with a love for liberal democracy and a hatred for anything totalitarian.

It was not difficult for a young American with Al's ideals to be patriotic during those years, when this country had recently created the New Deal and was now planning to dedicate its resources to the long fight against Fascism. And Al was no mere flag-waver.

He seemed to feel that he had a special responsibility—like the Just Man among the Jews—to be sure that America's ideals were realized. Accordingly, he made sacrifices that must have seemed insane to his contemporaries. When he graduated from Horace Mann (a decade before Bob began to teach there) he certainly could have gone on to an Ivy League college, but instead he chose to enroll at the University of North Carolina so that he could combat segregation directly. Later, after he graduated from Yale Law School, he contested his 4-F classification (for bad eyes and weak ankles) and entered the army as a private. That was his duty as a citizen, he thought.

Meanwhile, Al gained stature as a liberal leader. He was elected President of the National Student Association in 1951 (the year before the organization established its formal but secret relations with the CIA) and worked in the Stevenson campaign in 1952. Before his hitch in the army he served as a legislative assistant to Frank Graham; afterward, he worked for Hubert Humphrey. But offices bored him. He taught history at the University of North Carolina and Stanford, ran for Congress in New York, fought *apartheid* in South Africa, Francoism in Spain, segregation in Chapel Hill and Mississippi.

His greatest following was among students. He tried to appeal to the moderates, the freckle-faced descendants of Tom Sawyer, the cashmere coeds, members of student Christian associations, young Democrats and Republicans—people whose consciences, filled with the egalitarian rhetoric of high-school civics courses, forbade them to join segregated fraternities, insisting instead that they support liberal causes on their local campuses (but always in wholesome ways, never like the noisy radicals who do such damage to each cause they adopt). As teacher, lecturer, elder statesman of the NSA, Al was always able to persuade them to support his causes, accept his strategies. In the mid-1960s he understood more clearly than almost anyone else in America that the idealistic rhetoric of the New Frontier, then Kennedy's assassination, had filled young people with a new questioning restlessness. Now they wanted to confront injustice in the part of America where it was

most blatant. For them, as for me, Al was a sort of Johnny Apple-
seed of activism.

His style was perfectly suited to the people he sought to reach.
They were hungry for inside information, gossip, and adventure
stories, and he always seemed to be in direct contact with the distant world they read about in the newspapers. Even as late as 1963
the hopeless mood of the 1950s still pervaded most campuses; that
mood was what we were trying to escape. And Allard was a living,
vibrant alternative to the parents and professors who counseled
their young to be cautious today so that they might gain suburbia
tomorrow.

One felt far freer to talk to him than with most of the celebrities who toured college campuses. At thirty-six, he still had the
manner of a student leader. His appearance was as sloppy as that
of the most casual undergraduate, and he was always making small
quips about his socks which didn't match, his glasses which, he
claimed, were as thick as the bottom of a Coke bottle. When you
met him you felt quickly at ease. And flattered, too, for he seemed
more interested in sustaining a midnight bull session with undergraduates than in sharing midnight sherry with their faculty advisers.

He seemed to talk politics the way Pete Seeger sang folk songs:
simply, but with great skill and eloquence. And he appeared as
eager as Seeger to draw his audiences into the process. He seemed
to be one of the young, only older, with an entree into regions of
vast power.

Or so I thought when the Summer Project began. But in the
months after the Democratic Convention my opinion of him
began to change. He had become much more disillusioned with
the Mississippi civil-rights movement than I'd been during my
glummest moments in Vicksburg. After I had spent several
months trying to sort out his bitter criticisms of SNCC staff members, I became convinced that the ideas which Al made so attractive when he brought them to the campuses were not really very
different from the ideas that were proving to be failures when his

liberal contemporaries brought them into government during those early days of Lyndon Johnson's Great Society. Like his former boss, Hubert Humphrey, like so many Democrats who loved to evoke the glorious 1930s, Lowenstein regarded the progress that had occurred in America during the New Deal as a model for development that could be applied to deprived and segregated societies everywhere, from Jackson to Johannesburg. And if it was always possible to create substantial, radical changes by democratic means, without bloodshed, as Lowenstein's generation of liberals insisted, then it followed that revolutionaries presented as serious a threat to progress as did the reactionaries. That was precisely the argument that the liberal administrators of the Great Society were using to justify the war in Vietnam. It was also the basis of Lowenstein's deepening distrust of Bob Moses and the rest of the SNCC staff.

In a way, Al was the contemporary incarnation of the theory of American history which I had learned from my Harvard professors. He was far more energetic than the academics, but at least as committed as they were to the traditional liberal definition of reason, of consent and compromise.

As I watched Allard's admiring friendship with Moses dissolve into a bitter quarrel, I grew increasingly suspicious—not only of Lowenstein but of myself, too. For I was inching toward the belief that my fight with Papa Doc had not been the outgrowth of our peculiar situation in Vicksburg, or of my own personal hang-ups, or of Papa Doc's relative incompetence. It had been characteristic of my class and my country. Could none of us work in alien cultures without fighting the people we had set out to support? Perhaps the faith which fused the brand of liberalism that Al still embraced and I had not yet rejected—that America really was a special land, "the last, best hope for mankind," as Lincoln had said—was finally so inflexible that it made us incapable of dealing with aliens on any terms but our own.

But when I first heard Al criticize SNCC, a few days after the Democratic Convention, I listened to him as carefully as I could, with none of the deep mental reservations I would begin to formulate later on. I hoped that his conclusions might somehow afford me a perspective into which I could put my own confusing experiences. Al seemed so anxious to talk about his disagreements with the movement, so eager to discuss each detail of his disputes with Moses, that I felt he must be as interested as I was in finding a way to redefine one's own political identity. Presently though, I realized that he wasn't at all interested in examining himself in order to change or grow. He knew exactly who he was and what he was doing. In his opinion, people like me were potential witnesses for the prosecution. We might add circumstantial evidence to his assertion that the movement had been subverted by people who were less interested in helping Mississippi Negroes than in using the segregation and poverty that existed there to foment angry, violent conflicts throughout the country.

Like any good lawyer, Lowenstein built his case on suggestive incidents, often letting the general conclusions present themselves. Since he did not argue in court, but at restaurants and parties and in university lecture halls, the specific technical arguments that concerned him sometimes seemed to be out of proportion to the passion with which he discussed them. For example, throughout the autumn after the Summer Project he kept arguing that the National Lawyer's Guild, which was supposed to be a left-wing group, had less justification to represent the movement in Mississippi than the moderate Legal Committee to Defend the Constitution. In Mississippi the issue would have seemed irrelevant, since there wasn't much tension between the two organizations, both intent on fighting the corrupt, segregated legal system. But in the North, where political intrigue was a way of life, the argument seemed significant. Al could deliver a half-hour speech relating SNCC's support of the Lawyer's Guild to the influence that extreme left-wingers possessed throughout the movement. He was always convinced that some awful plot against the liberals had been hatched at a meeting he hadn't attended, and could usually support his contention with a batch of notes taken by a friend he had sent in his stead. He supplemented all of his impromptu speeches with names, dates, and organizational affiliations. He might, for instance, reveal that a field director of the Southern Conference Educational Fund who had once been a member of the Communist Party had been meeting with several directors of SNCC who in turn were trying to rid all local Friends of SNCC chapters of their moderate leaders. Then, in his most boyish manner, he would profess to be astonished by such duplicitous behavior. That style, together with his self-assurance, made one extremely hesitant to challenge him.

To the volunteers who had returned from Mississippi believing that they had contributed something to the fight for equality Lowenstein's performance was particularly disturbing. I remember an unhappy girl interrupting him in the midst of his argument one night to exclaim, "I wish you would quit telling us all about this, Al. I learned so much from the Summer Project. Now you're saying that the thing we believed in was a lie." Al reminded her that all his life he had made a practice of fighting injustice. He wished that more people had spoken out against the far left in the 1930s, before it was too late and Joseph McCarthy caught hold of the issue.

So far as I was concerned, the problems that concerned Al seemed more bureaucratic than human: he seemed to be more worried by the possibility that there might be a few Communists in the movement than by the undisputed facts of segregation and poverty in Mississippi. Though I had wanted very much to admire him—had expected him, in fact, to be my mentor—I soon began to think of him as a political firefly: all glow but no heat. There was a great deal of motion, but not very much person. It seemed as though he used his suspicions of bureaucratic manipulations, of conspiracies and betrayals, as a means of avoiding direct, human relationships. He always had to be at the center of a crowd, never one of a group of friends, and for that reason he was always transforming small social acts into nightmares of frantic confusion. For example, when Al went to a movie it was as the leader of a hastily assembled coalition. There would be twenty different people to be mobilized, all of them from different parts of the city, all eager to see different films. But Allard seemed to feel that his mission was to unite them behind a common objective—this strange array of Stanford graduate students, African revolutionary leaders, newspaper reporters from North Carolina, divinity students from New Haven. So you would wind up on a street corner waiting for a group of people you had never met (and wouldn't recognize, since Al was invariably half an hour late) and then, frozen and bored, you would learn that the movie that had been chosen in the final caucus was no longer playing in all of New York City. Finally, the group would redivide into its component parts, and each person would see the movie he had originally chosen.

In many ways, I kept thinking, Al *was* a great man. He acted out the fantasies of his repressed contemporaries—those law-school classmates of his who talked a liberal line in Great Neck or Lake Forest—and he devised practical ways for the more courageous generation that followed to express its beliefs. But his crippling weakness was his inability to realize that when people are restless, questioning everything, they have to follow their own private impulses. He could not understand that almost everyone he sent into action would be transformed by his new experiences, sometimes beyond recognition. He regarded that fact of human nature as a form of betrayal.

He was convinced that a well-planned conspiracy lay behind our increasingly angry criticisms of the government, our increasingly militant behavior, and he fought it in a way that made him resemble the McCarthyites he had learned to despise in the 1950s. The tragedy was that his frenzied attitude lost him the respect of students and black people, the two groups he sought to restore to his beloved America.

IX

BUT many older Northern white liberals who had used their money and influence to support the Summer Project (while spending their summers in Europe or on Cape Cod) were quickly persuaded by Al's arguments. When the Mississippi movement stepped past service work—past community centers, Freedom Schools, voter-registration projects—and became involved in active politics at the Democratic Convention, many of its earliest allies began to share Lowenstein's distrust for black leaders like Bob Moses and James Forman. The FDP delegates, encouraged by the SNCC staff members who accompanied them to Atlantic City, insisted on making political decisions on their own terms and angrily rejected the advice of many of the liberal politicians who had been working with them. It was an unforgivable act as far as many white people were concerned.

The issue on which the dispute focused was a compromise which had been reached after long, tedious negotiations over the right of the regular, lily-white delegation to represent the state. The segregationists would remain, but the FDP would be granted two at-large seats. Joseph Rauh, Bayard Rustin, Wayne Morse, and others were convinced that the compromise represented a symbolic triumph for integration. But most delegates and SNCC organizers felt that the compromise was unacceptable. It did nothing to punish the regular party for segregating the entire democratic process.

Instead of sitting in the seats the Democratic Party had reserved for them, the FDP people sat-in on the convention floor. Within a week, the movement was split.

The Northern liberals received the same shock that many of us who worked in Mississippi had been experiencing throughout the summer. Like many of us, they simply did not believe that Southern black people, and the young, militant staff members who advised them, could make wise decisions about tactics for defeating the system that had victimized them for so long. Imagine Hubert Humphrey, whom Lyndon Johnson had appointed to negotiate an agreement between the FDP and the regular state party, whose own hopes for the Vice-Presidency were said to rest on his ability to achieve a peaceful settlement, respecting the political views of a semiliterate sharecropper from the Mississippi Delta. Humphrey was used to dealing with *leaders*, with Roy Wilkins, Martin Luther King, or even Bob Moses, not with *people*. Confronted with Bob and a Mississippi field hand, Humphrey would respond like most of the volunteers who had gone south and regard Bob's opinion as the important one—even though Bob, with more passion than anyone else in the movement, insisted that no one could speak for the field hand, and that politicians had to hear him express his own views in his own way. (Beneath all the political arguments, that was probably the human reason that Bob supported the manipulation of the Jackson Convention—because it meant that field hands, not ministers, would represent the FDP in Atlantic City.)

Humphrey was much too tied to the traditional political process to understand Bob's argument, let alone comply with it. He could view someone like Fannie Lou Hamer as a compelling symbol but could never perceive her as a partner. He could intone her name —call her one of those brave black people to whom America owed so much (as if she had won the medal of honor in Vietnam)—but he did not respect her ideas. He could not admit that she was able to determine the terms of the debt that the nation owed her.

What was true of Humphrey, whose relation to the movement was more political than personal, was even truer of Joe Rauh, whose commitment to the Freedom Democratic Party was voluntary and intensely emotional. Deeply as he felt about the FDP, though, Rauh still regarded the convention challenge as just one small tactic in a long-range strategy. It would be more important, he judged, to have Humphrey close to the White House for four years than to see Mrs. Hamer in one of the delegates' seats for four days. When he learned that Mrs. Hamer saw things differently—that she cared more about winning her own battle at the convention than about getting the most liberal traditional politician elected Vice-President—he disregarded her opinion. After all, Rauh had been around Washington for a long time, and Mrs. Hamer had been a sharecropper all her life. Was there any question as to who had more political savvy?

But when the FDP delegates persisted in rejecting the compromise, Rauh and his associates became angry and hurt. From their point of view, the intransigence of the black Mississippians suggested that there had been something suspect about the Southern civil-rights movement from its inception. They couldn't accept the fact that if Mrs. Hamer took Bob Moses' advice more readily than theirs it was because Bob had earned his influence during four years of dangerous work and because his political ideas were probably a more accurate reflection than theirs of the aspirations of the field hands and sharecroppers who composed the majority of the FDP delegation and the majority of Mississippi's black population. They couldn't believe that the Mississippians had rationally decided to reject their advice. So the liberals began to argue that poor black people had been duped by SNCC staff members whose interests had nothing to do with their own: men with un-American ideas who had worked their way into the movement's leadership and craftily managed to win the confidence of the unsophisticated.

And that, after all, was the way the Communists operated. An entire generation of idealistic liberals and radicals had learned that painful lesson in the thirties, forties, and fifties. If they hadn't seen the Reds first hand—and most of them hadn't—they had learned a little about their activities from the anti-Communist intellectuals who published their voluminous confessions in magazines like the *Partisan Review*. In the month after the convention Lowenstein clearly expressed his generation's gut reaction to the Mississippi movement: "I felt as if I was in Spain and the Communists were holding their guns at my back," he said of his relations with

SNCC. He wasn't talking about the fight over the compromise, during which he had been neutral, but about an entire year of tensions and disagreements. It was a view shaped by a distorted impression of another generation's failed liberalism. Lowenstein was his own tragic hero—an Orwell, a Koestler, a Dos Passos. By some odd inversion, he was suggesting that such people as Bob Moses were the evil outside agitators, while he and Rauh and the relatively few blacks who supported them were the legitimate indigenous leaders.

Soon the suggestion which the liberals sometimes made, that SNCC workers and some of their student sympathizers were disloyal to the United States, became an assumption as it spread out into cocktail-party rumors and then turned into a matter of public record when overt allegations were printed by columnists like Evans and Novak and Drew Pearson. The term "SNCC-baiting" gained currency on the left. It was a contemporary equivalent to red-baiting.

And particularly difficult to fight because it involved so many *ad hominem* arguments, so much innuendo. Who would want to stand up in public and insist that "Bob Moses is not a Communist" as a response to the hints, the whispers, the half-truths? That would only make the rumors more credible.

X

AFTER a few months of listening to Lowenstein discuss SNCC, I began to argue with him fiercely whenever we were together; but in private I still found myself inclined to accept a great deal of what he said. I would argue just as fiercely with friends of mine who insisted on celebrating the Summer Project with no reservations; and sometimes, to be shocking, to be spiteful, to win a small point, I would echo Allard himself and reveal my secret knowledge of SNCC's hidden relationships with left-wing organizations like the Lawyer's Guild. The summer's work had been so confusing, the apparent collapse of the movement so depressing, that I half-believed everything I heard. Like Lowenstein and Rauh, I was hurt by the hatred that blacks were beginning to express toward people like me who had worked for years to achieve integration. I could accept the cultural explanations for their efforts to rid their organizations of whites, but no rational argument really healed the pain of the personal attacks.

When I used Al's arguments I felt that I was getting revenge.

There was, besides, something soothing about the suggestion that the black militants' hatred of white people was the result of alien influences, not the logical outgrowth of American history. If there had been a conscious conspiracy to make men like Papa Doc disloyal to their country, then I could forget my own harsh criticisms of my behavior in Vicksburg. I could tell myself that my reactions were those of a smart, muckraking journalist who is always alert to phoniness and betrayal.

So I half-thought, half-hoped that there might be some truth to the liberals' assertions—even about Bob Moses, who had become the villain of their plot. Not that Bob was a conspirator exactly, but that the bitterness that had collected inside him after so many frustrating, lonely years—the attitude we had seen during that meeting in Vicksburg—had pushed him toward ideas that would undermine the America I still believed in; or at least the America I was again living in, for a few comfortable months in the North had erased my most vivid memories of Mississippi. Bob used to say that when you're outside Mississippi it never seems quite real, and when you're in the state the rest of America seems unreal. Though I quoted him often, I had forgotten the reality behind his remark.

There were rumors that year that money had come to the movement from Russia, China, Cuba, Algeria—that was the sort of thing the liberals in the North were talking about during the months that Lyndon Johnson was deciding to bomb North Vietnam and Dean Rusk was instructing the Marines to invade Santo Domingo—and while I felt contempt for people who gloried in such gossip, I still accepted the premise behind their accusations. I was as prejudiced against Communists, I discovered, as most Southern whites are against Negroes: that was the miserable inheritance of my childhood during the Cold War. If SNCC had received even a dollar of Moscow gold, then the organization must be polluted—that was my instinctive reaction to the rumor I heard. (I didn't know then that the civil-rights movement had received quite a bit more than a dollar of CIA gold during those years.)

It was a bout of hysterical fever, and it broke rather soon. As I compared reports from the real Mississippi with the stories that originated in the North, I was shocked into realizing just how little the liberals understood about the people they were criticizing. Bob Moses helped me recover. I saw him a few times, talked frequently with friends who had just come back from the South, and began to recall that Bob was simply not the demon the liberals portrayed. He was not basing his actions on the cold, cruel logic of revolutionary initiative. His decisions were not designed to further some distant cause.

In fact, if there was one thing for which people inside the movement criticized Bob, it was that he had become even less of a leader than he was during the Summer Project, more committed to his own idea of pure participatory democracy. He apparently couldn't stand the prospect of becoming an important national figure, or of reshaping his personality to the demands of constant, harsh factional fights. That people saw him as the head of the movement, the source of guidance or ruthless villainy, violated his deepest belief: that common men were better equipped to decide for themselves than any leader was. He referred almost everyone who sought his advice to the sharecroppers and field hands among whom he had been working for so long. "All our strength comes from the local people," he would remind the volunteers and staff members who stayed in the South throughout the next year. The homily became his theme.

"If the people of Mississippi want to organize sewing clubs, we'll help them organize sewing clubs," he told a reporter that year. "If they want to organize cooking classes, we'll help them organize cooking classes. It's their decision, not ours."

Had liberals like Lowenstein focused their attack on anyone else in the movement, their angry proclamations that they'd been betrayed might have continued to seem credible. But it was clear that their political prejudices had prevented them from understanding what Bob was trying to communicate by his actions, and occasionally his words.

They suggested that he might be disguising his real intentions beneath his libertarian rhetoric. He might be trying to dissemble for his detractors in the North, or craftily asserting his belief in the total decentralization of SNCC in order to create a vacuum which would allow his people to seize control of the entire movement. (Communists know how to take advantage of chaos, said Dean Rusk, in the spring when he explained the decision to send the Marines to the Dominican Republic.) To his enemies Bob Moses was Stalin—programed to resemble Jesus Christ. So deep was their suspicion of him that they could no longer imagine him performing a single act out of genuinely decent emotions.

One weekend late in the spring of 1965 Bob removed himself forever as a leader. At a SNCC conference in Atlanta he told the people who had worked with him the longest that he no longer wanted to be known as Bob Moses, and that he was determined to leave Mississippi, where he had struggled so long to build a movement. A cult of personality had developed around him, he said, and now it must vanish. People could be free only if they had no leaders, no idols.

He demolished an identity which thousands of people throughout America regarded as their source of moral authority. Bob Moses had become Bob Parris; he would never again head an organization but would work in some lonely corner of Alabama— and we were alone. I got very drunk the night I heard about his decision. He was lost to people like me, that was instantly clear, and I knew that I would feel his absence even more keenly than I felt the absence of John Kennedy. His act, however noble, seemed an admission that the hopes he had felt at the start of the decade, during those nights in New York when he listened to Odetta sing of her people and brooded on injustice in Mississippi, were unattainable in America. He had not stepped aside to make room for new leaders; the destruction of his identity seemed a naked admission that Bob Moses had failed. At least Kennedy was trying to bring change when he was murdered; Bob Moses, whose energy and dedication were much greater, was now asserting that no important changes could be inspired in America by people like himself. America had destroyed the politician who had sent our generation into action; now it was defeating the man who had supplied us with our courage and our vision. Bob renounced his identity, he said, to free others to find their own; but somehow his act merged with the mood of sad, weary resignation in some of us and produced something akin to despair. There was no longer much love in the civil-rights movement, and it seemed that Bob's resignation meant that the remains of that quality would quickly drain away. Men like Stokely Carmichael, who had always maintained confidence in Bob and let their actions be influenced by his example, would soon reject their belief in nonviolence and reasoned conversation between the powerful and the powerless. They would entirely reject the hope that had sustained the movement since the earliest sit-ins—that poor Negro communities could be organized into America, and that their example would redeem the country. Soon they would begin to talk to black America as if it were a separate nation.

When Bob erased his image, they knew—as Bob must first have feared, then reluctantly, despairingly accepted during the summer in Mississippi—that the only way to change America was to threaten it, to preach self-defense and not nonviolence, to demand revolution and scorn reconciliation.

One evening late that spring Al Lowenstein was in Chicago to give a speech. Bob's renunciation, the escalation of the war in Vietnam, the invasion of the Dominican Republic, the rebellion at Berkeley, and the assassination of Malcolm X were all part of our history now. After Al spoke, a group of us gathered in a graduate student's apartment to talk with him. He was beginning to weave his thesis of the far-left conspiracy for us, somehow connecting the Mississippi movement to the Free Speech movement and the Free Speech movement to the protest against the war which SDS was organizing. As usual, he argued that the far left was conspiratorial, nihilistic, intent on destroying a great nation. Finally, I said—mildly, I thought—that I found myself losing confidence in the American government, too, and that Al's criticisms of the new protests made me wonder whether he had thought carefully about the tragedies that had occurred in the country over the past years. He answered me immediately: "You're the sort of person who wants to believe that America is a Fascist society. That will help you to tear this country down."

Clearly he wasn't speaking to me as much as to the other people in the room, using me to recruit them in the same way as he had used SNCC to recruit me just a few months before. At first I was pained by his comment. I thought that I had organized my life around my love for my country's potential. But the more I thought about it, the more I realized I should feel flattered.

Epithets like Al's, charges of disloyalty and un-Americanism, were beginning to seem like compliments.

PART TWO

1

In the spring of 1965 it was deceptively easy for a white radical to denounce America.

In the midst of a controversial war abroad, an uneasy peace at home, social protest had become an industry. Dissenters became celebrities very quickly, often before they had time to consider the consequences of their ideas. They seemed to be protected by a communications industry that instantly transformed their most daring statements into cocktail-party clichés. The tension between the momentary respectability that so many radicals enjoyed and the apocalyptic rhetoric in which we all indulged was constant. It was almost impossible to judge, in those shifting, crazy years, whether one's friends were about to inherit unprecedented amounts of power or to become political outcasts. To judge from our wild speculations, the point that we stood at in America was about equidistant from the White House and from those legendary concentration camps which the McCarran Act had legalized.

The truth was that, although our rhetoric was nearly as angry as the rhetoric of the black militants who were about to expel us from their movement, our protests were still protected to a degree that they could not imagine. Nor did we really have the same desire to destroy American institutions as did the blacks with whom we had worked in Mississippi, no matter how passionately we sometimes raged. We were, after all, our parents' children, and as a group our parents possessed a great deal of power in the country we told them we wanted to dismantle. The graduates of the elite universities who comprised most of the radical student movement in those early days would have to do more than issue militant proclamations to lose the protection of an establishment that trained them. So those years were a time of constant testing, son challenging father.

For all the criticism that people like Lowenstein were directing at us, for all the harsh statements we made in response, ours was still, for the most part, a movement of model citizens. The New Left's motto that year, enunciated by Paul Booth, a national officer of SDS, was "build, don't burn." Thousands of the same sorts of people who worked in Mississippi in 1964 were now eager to join SDS projects in urban ghettos like the one Tom Hayden helped organize in Newark. Almost reflexively we still tried to emphasize the values that our elders had been most careful to transmit to our generation: courageous behavior and rational thought. We had already proved our courage in the civil-rights movement—no one could tell a young man who had been willing to die in Mississippi that his reluctance to fight in Vietnam was the result of physical cowardice. Now we were demonstrating our commitment to reason in the teach-in movement. No one who sat through those long hours of detailed debate in uncomfortable college lecture halls could argue seriously that the opponents of the war were ignorant of its causes.

We called ourselves radicals, but the truth was that in those days—when Bobby Kennedy, Richard Goodwin, and Arthur Schlesinger all still favored the war provided that the pacification program was intensified—we were almost the only loyal opposition in the country. We joined a few Senators like Fulbright, Gruening, Morse in questioning the assumptions behind the United States' intervention in Vietnam. But our questions, which outraged so many of our elders, usually fell well inside the framework of America's global interests. Most of us still wanted to help run the country, not to become revolutionaries.

For each of us, privately, the draft threatened to interrupt that delicate balance, for it would put an end to the comfortable life we all enjoyed while we protested a war we agreed was immoral. But even after the first major escalation, in February 1965, it was still a danger that could be outmaneuvered. Marriage meant a deferment, so did graduate school, the Peace Corps, most forms of government work, the slightest physical or psychological defect; and even if you were single, healthy, and self-employed, you would probably not be called.

Rachel and I were married in June. We planned to move to New York the next fall, where I would work as a reporter for the *Village Voice* and she would take a job at the Hudson Guild Settlement House. A few days after our wedding, a friend of mine, who was just beginning his Ph.D. thesis, asked me whether I was worried about the draft.

I had spent most of my adult life trying to avoid it, with complete success so far. "I just can't believe that the government wants us to spend our youths that way," I answered. "They're not so crazy that they'd draft married men and graduate students and make enemies out of a generation whose loyalties they need."

I couldn't understand why my friend looked so skeptical.

John Kennedy probably wouldn't have been that crazy: A month later Lyndon Johnson announced a substantial increase in the troops that would be sent to Vietnam. Draft calls nearly doubled. The married man's deferment was ended. Not quite twenty-five, just married, still childless, done with graduate school forever, I was as vulnerable as anyone in the country. For the first time in my life I felt genuinely endangered. I could always have fled from the segregationists in Maryland and Mississippi, but I couldn't flee from the army. The nation that had protected me until July suddenly seemed to have vanished. I had planned to remain inside America, writing about it, working on the fringes of its political system, relying on courage and reason to correct injustice. Now I would be ordered by America to travel abroad as part of its political system, relying on force to defend it. It was as if I had become a citizen of a new, more hostile land.

II

WHEN I joined the staff of the Voice I wanted to create a sort of journalism that would be like Pete Seeger's folk music, or Phil Ochs', or Judy Collins'. Then, as I grew angrier about the war, increasingly bitter about the government that was waging it, my fantasy was that I'd write the sort of essays Albert Camus would have published if he'd been an American and my age.

During my first weeks at the Voice I used to imagine our office on Sheridan Square as the equivalent of the Combat office in Paris. In my most romantic moods I would think of our readers as members of the underground in France, ready to display the same élan in their efforts to win the war against the war in Vietnam as the French intelligentsia had when it fought the Vichy regime.

I remember walking down Fourth Street toward the Voice with Jack Newfield one day, listening to him tell me that he wouldn't change his job on the newspaper for any other in the world. A community that included Norman Mailer, Mike Harrington, Bob Dylan, and Tom Hayden seemed to him ideal. At the time, I was impressed with the revolutionary potential of the anonymous people I used to see on those streets whose names were so thrilling and evocative. (Bleecker Street, Christopher Street, Houston Street; John Reed, Emma Goldman, John Dos Passos, A. J. Muste.) So, high on hope, stoned by history, I answered Jack eagerly that if a civil war ever broke out in America the Village would be the left's main stronghold. He and Mailer and Hayden would have to take their place among the hippies, the junkies, the dykes, the fags, the thousands of thwarted artists: they would all use every weapon the streets provided to keep the cops and straightlifers off their turf.

I assumed, too, that the radical intellectuals I was beginning to meet would resemble the best of the characters in Simone de Beauvoir's *The Mandarins*. So many stirring essays against the war had appeared in the *Voice*, in the *New York Review of Books*, there had been such serious, persuasive analysis of America's accelerating decay, so many highly publicized protest demonstrations involving people who lived in the literary world, that I was sure the community's life would contain some of the committed austerity that I associated with wartime London or Paris. After a month in New York, I was embarrassed when I remembered the kid who had brought such naïve expectations to the city. I had learned what everyone else must always have assumed: that literary people lived as luxuriously in 1965 as the rest of America's middle class. They seemed eager to spend the money that had been loosed by recent, huge investments in the communications industry as quickly as possible, purchasing new pleasures with the words and pictures they created; even the radicals who loudly proclaimed their willingness to make any sacrifice that would end the slaughter in Vietnam.

The New York literary world was a Big Fiesta that year. Y'all come. Not only were there large sums of quick money to be earned. There seemed a limitless supply of free sex, free drugs, wonderful food, excellent liquor; constant travel and brilliant talk; the opportunity to meet famous people and the chance that one might obtain quick celebrity oneself. The measure of a skillful journalist in New York, I began to think, was his ability to gain entry into the roaring, thrilling world that one associated with names like Norman Mailer, Bobby Kennedy, George Plimpton. The committed life that Camus had described, that Bob Moses had exemplified, seemed to me monkish, even priggish, from the vantage point of the Big Fiesta.

The corridor to the celebrity parties was clearly marked, and I was more anxious to enter it than I wanted to admit. One had to be the frequent subject of living-room gossip, occasionally mentioned in the mass media. The star system dominated New York just as it had dominated Hollywood, and brashness was as important as raw talent to a man who wanted to get ahead. The magazines and publishing houses were as eager to create new celebrities as the great studios had been. Their main job, it often seemed, was to find writers who could sell large numbers of books, and to an increasing extent that meant writers with the capacity to create sensations, provoke brief, loud controversies, rather than the ability to inspire thought.

A young novelist came to New York hoping to find his Maxwell Perkins, a contemporary version of that great editor whose first commitment was to his writers' work; instead, he usually found himself dealing with Ivy League replicas of Cecil B. DeMille or Samuel Goldwyn.

At parties, at shops in the village, I began to mention my name to see if anyone at all would recognize it. Few people ever did. New York was not my new Cambridge. I began to wonder if anyone ever read anything I wrote.

Several months after I started to work for the *Voice*, an editor at *Esquire* called to tell me that he wanted me to write an article. I had known him slightly at Harvard and seen him at a few parties around New York. It was exciting to realize that he had thought of me for an assignment. It meant that someone with taste had liked the articles I had been writing.

I was excited—until I heard the editor's proposition. He wanted me to interview as many sons of famous men as I could find, and then do an article describing their attitudes toward their fathers. As he talked to me, I became convinced that he had never read a word I'd written. But he was interested in my connections. Because I had graduated from Choate and Harvard, I was part of the same old-boy network as many of the people whose names he thought should be mentioned. The civil-rights movement had given me access to the few eccentrics he hoped to include. Then he mentioned the most disturbing feature of his idea: I was supposed to interview contemporaries of mine—and his—whose parents had become notorious as a result of the anti-Communist witchhunts in the 1950s.

He didn't seem to feel any reservations about converting the tragedy of a life that had been spoiled by America's obsessive anti-Communism into a campy tidbit of gossip for *Esquire*'s readers, many of whom had probably supported Joseph McCarthy's crusade against intelligence in the first place. And when we began to discuss the civil-rights movement, about which I said I might be willing to write an article, I realized that his idea of relevant information was a direct contradiction of the values for which my friends and I had risked our lives. He seemed eager to hear any amusing stories I might know that revealed foolish, excessive behavior on the part of militant black leaders—yarns that would make Bob Moses sound like Kingfish on *Amos 'n Andy*—but not the slightest bit interested in my description of the pressures that were forcing men like Bob and Stokely Carmichael to adopt increasingly radical positions. He could not believe that the black militants were as important to America as he was; therefore he couldn't regard them as serious political figures. It seemed that the point of their activities, so far as he was concerned, was to provide material for *Esquire:* a new idea for an establishment chart, a new face in the 100 Best People awards, a new fool whose picture could be displayed in the annual Dubious Achievements section.

He reminded me of the undergraduates I had known at Harvard whose emotional paralysis had made them totally cynical. I was sure that they thought the subjects that writers like Orwell and Camus and even James Agee had chosen as their themes were intrinsically very dull. For they lacked the energy to look past their own dreary fears and frustrations. They could assert their humanity only by swapping signs of status—dropping names or juicy tidbits of gossip, mentioning hip places they'd visited—or by making brittle, elitist jokes about the world they were afraid to confront. How could such a person understand what I was trying to write about, let alone edit my copy?

Of course I refused his offer. But then, for some reason, I was suddenly filled with a missionary's zeal to convert him. I began to lecture him, priest to sinner. He was wasting his life devising little gimmicks that would keep *Esquire's* circulation in range of *Playboy's*, my sermon began. Why did he want to spend his time converting serious ideas and genuine emotions into parlor games that would afford a few hours of entertainment to the new, rich class of half-educated Americans who had transferred their childhood awe of movie stars and sports heroes into a new fascination with gossip about politicians, artists, activists, intellectuals. Sure, there were always some good articles in *Esquire*, but the over-all effect of the magazine, of its snotty little contests, its instant profiles, its gross covers and misleading headlines, was a pernicious one. The magazine filled its readers' minds full of surfaces and sensations, damaged their capacity to make discriminating judgments about complex problems in the real, gritty world—so unpleasantly different from the jet-set America on which one could spy by reading *Esquire's* glossy pages.

When I finished my outburst, he reminded me that he had called, in the first place, to find out whether I would write one rather inconsequential article. By his tone of voice he told me that he had no interest in my general appraisal of *Esquire*—or of the way he conducted his life. But coffee was still to come; it would be ungentlemanly to part abruptly. So the editor, now chuckling, began to tell me amusing stories about mutual acquaintances from Harvard. Soon I was so interested that my anger vanished. When we separated we promised that we'd get back in touch as soon as possible.

I was certain that if I had gone straight from Harvard to New York, without my three-year detour in the movement and in Israel, I would have had no trouble dealing with the *Esquire* editor. Certainly I had known people like him on the *Crimson*, and some of them had even been my friends. But the new attitudes I'd half-consciously absorbed in the South, the changes in my personality that I'd deliberately set out to make after the Summer Project, made it impossible for me to be diplomatic with him. As long as I retained a lively memory of Bob Moses, or even Papa Doc, and imagined that they were participants in conversations like the one I had had with the editor, I could not include people like him in-side my psychic plurality. He insisted on insulting people to whom I owed great loyalty.

But I was not yet a skillful enough radical to confront him ef-fectively. I was still clumsy and a little timid, something of a buf-foon, like Pierre in *War and Peace*, not nearly as calm or calculat-ing as I was beginning to think I'd have to become.

During the months I worked on the *Voice* staff I never felt free enough to use the first person. I never dropped the journalist's façade of detachment to let the reader see me sweat and frown and wince and smile. As a result, most of my articles were neither good folk journalism nor effective radical polemic. They were the work of a promising minor-league ballplayer who had come along when the leagues were expanding and broken into the majors a couple of seasons too early.

Dan Wolf, the editor of the *Voice*, a master psychologist who edits character rather than copy, did me an enormous favor by tell-ing me frankly the reasons he thought my writing was somewhat dull and tight. My articles sounded as if I was still back at Har-vard, he said, still writing to please intellectually intimidating peo-ple who knew more about books and ideas than they did about life.

It seemed to him that many Harvard graduates were spoiled by the kind of small triumphs that I had achieved when I won the Dana Reed prize for writing. They have succeeded in a highly competitive atmosphere when they were still young and assured themselves of interesting, rather glamorous work in academia or New York or Washington. They no longer feel much need to test themselves or expand themselves.

Nor were most Harvard people ever forced to open themselves up to new experiences, he continued. If we were cool enough we could proceed from our undergraduate successes through our pleas-ant lives as young adults to positions of considerable power in our professions or in government without ever venturing very far from our self-enclosed world of prep-school and college friends. But that sort of security is disastrous for a writer, he warned. Why should one struggle with life, and develop a distinctive, personal style in the process, when one knows that a certain sort of victory is preordained?

But I fight myself, my class, and my country every fucking day I kept thinking as I listened. Nevertheless, Dan's words underscored a complaint I'd heard from a few good friends, that something human was missing from my writing. Certainly I wasn't able to admit my private feelings as openly as Jack Newfield, whose articles, often written in the first person, comprised a sustained dialogue between himself and experience. When I remembered how unthinkingly cautious I'd been on the *Choate News*, how reluctant I'd been to express my unpopular views during my first three years on the *Crimson*, I realized that in a way I'd always regarded newspapers as places of refuge, where I could share absorbing work with other intellectuals, not as outlets for ideas I'd acquired in more dangerous settings.

Perhaps Dan had overlooked the most devastating criticism of my writing: that I was even more constrained by my concern for my own safety than by class biases. For example, I had just written an article about an interview I'd had with General Hershey without once indicating that the draft (which wasn't yet recognized as an important political issue) was the source of my deepest anxiety, that it was forcing me to ask questions about my own loyalty to America which were even more disturbing than those which had haunted me after the Summer Project. I suppose I was scared that readers would be able to mock my clumsy quest for a way to live in a country that seemed to me increasingly evil, that politicians who were as intolerant of genuine dissent as the people who ran Choate would read my articles and somehow make trouble for me.

I didn't want to argue about my personality with Dan, though I knew that I felt far more isolated from my past and from my friends than he realized. I didn't want to argue because I knew that he was right about the thing I cared about most, my writing.

He didn't exactly fire me from the *Voice*. But he suggested that I leave the paper, that Rachel and I leave New York, and that I try to expand myself, deepen my responses, in an environment that was totally unfamiliar.

His good advice awoke an older memory:

> Times are getting hard, boys, money's getting scarce.
> If times don't get no better, boys, I'm going to leave this place.
> There's a lonesome freight at six-oh-eight running through this town . . .
> And I feel like I've gotta travel on.

Two Pete Seeger songs that throbbed through my mind the spring of my freshman year at college. I was the Vagabond, who would spend his life movin' on.

III

In a way, though, Dan's advice was superfluous, since I had to get out of New York anyway. Old Man Draft had finally trapped me.

The irony is that in almost any other period of American history the impulse that Dan's words reawoke might have guided me toward the army. In Stephen Crane's generation, in Hemingway's, in Norman Mailer's, writers my age had been able to prove their manhood and discover their country in battle. But if I let myself be sent to Vietnam, where the battle was, I would have already lost my manhood, betrayed the country I believed in.

"The great war novel of this decade will be written by a draft dodger," my friend Jacob Brachman said one day.

I was reluctant to trick the army: to bluff a medical or a psychological ailment, or fake a return to graduate school. Nor was I willing to apply for a C.O. deferment. I wasn't really a pacifist (I would have fought for Israel in its war of independence in 1948);

and, though I hate to admit it now, in 1965 I feared that a former conscientious objector might have trouble if he wanted to enter politics. No modern candidate I knew of had ever boasted of his peace record in order to win an election.

Besides, I could not quite argue myself out of my belief that a citizen owed a portion of his life to his country. It was not unlike the sentiment that had caused Al Lowenstein to force his way into the army despite his bad ankles and weak eyes; or, for that matter, the argument that Socrates used when he told Crito that he would die in Athens rather than escape into exile.

IV

I REMEMBER telling the English girl I had failed in London and lived with in Washington that I would marry only the sort of woman who would willingly volunteer for the Peace Corps.

It was in December 1963, just a month after President Kennedy's assassination, in the middle of a night full of tangled, boozy conversation. Clumsily, I was seeking delicate, painless arguments that would extract me from the dilemma that the writer in me wanted very much to prolong. She wanted me to remain single, I wanted to marry Rachel—excellent material for a novel that has been written many times. Just two years before I had been frantically worried about impotence; now I was cockily confident that I could win any woman I wanted. Radical politics and wandering sex. Norman Mailer goes to Mississippi. Clancy Sigal comes home.

But Rachel meant more to me than any knowledge I might gain from secretive, interwoven love affairs. The book I wanted to write, the life I wanted to live, was about creation, not decay—about loving stability won from a chaotic world.

But why did I choose willingness to join the Peace Corps as a symbol of the qualities I was seeking in my mate? Rachel and I had worked in Cambridge, Maryland, we were already planning to go to Mississippi: in conversations with other integrationists we even used the Peace Corps as a symbol of the patronizing attitude toward poor people we were all trying to love.

But I had always felt a special respect for my contemporaries who volunteered for the organization. Though I mocked them in front of my radical friends, I thought secretly that they might be more dedicated and compassionate than I was. John McAuliffe, a friend who had worked with me in Mississippi, entered training for a community-development project the next fall, and whenever I thought of him I felt a disturbing moral tension. While I kept shuttling back and forth between the powerful North and the romantic South—occasionally making headlines, always involved in activities that seemed historic—that other invisible corps of secondary-school teachers, rural-electrification workers, community developers, foresters, and nurses was doing the same work under much more difficult circumstances: in silence.

Tom Hayden had once dismissed them as a group of 4-H graduates, and I partly agreed. But only partly. For the fact was that most of them stayed in their foreign villages for two years. And too many of the self-proclaimed radicals I knew—though certainly not Hayden himself—had remained in their rural towns or urban ghettos for only a few months, or never tried to work with poor people at all. Actions seemed to me more important than attitudes: salvation by works a far more sensible doctrine than salvation by grace.

As the war began to escalate, and the protest movement along with it, the Peace Corps had inaugurated a recruiting drive aimed at the campus activists whose feelings were captured by the slogan "build, don't burn." When I was feeling cynical I likened the agency's campaign to Theodor Herzl's early efforts to direct the Zionist movement away from the Holy Land, which he for a time thought was unobtainable, toward Uganda, which the British might be willing to cede to the Jews. But I was too harried to explore the implications of that thought. I let the doubts I had be eased by the fact that many Peace Corps staff members seemed to understand the reasons behind the movement's protest, to share some of our emotions. That was more than one could say for most people who were too old to be drafted in 1965. Most adults saw us as a bunch of trouble-making kids who opposed the war because we were too soft to fight.

Two of the Peace Corps senior staff members, Frank Mankiewicz and Harris Wofford, seemed especially eager to incorporate the ideas and convictions that had given the New Left its special character into the agency's programs. The clearest symbolic expression of their attitude came when they invited Tom Hayden to head a project in Peru. They flew him to Washington for a meeting that lasted an entire afternoon. Afterward, Tom seemed to modify his criticisms of the organization. At least he did not regard Mankiewicz and Wofford as the sort of men who could comfortably administer the Boy Scouts or the Future Farmers of America. Their actual offer left Tom a little amused, though.

"They told me that I could run my region any way I wanted," he said later. "Oh, of course they're convinced that there won't be any revolution in that part of the world for at least a hundred years. But they say they want me to go ahead and try to make one.

"I told them that my work is here and not abroad."

The Peace Corps certainly got more out of the meeting than Hayden did. Neither the content of the conversation nor Tom's refusal to accept the job was as important as the fact that the conversation had been held at all. Within a few weeks thousands of people on the New Left knew that the Peace Corps had offered a job to the most controversial young white radical in the country. The knowledge strengthened one's impression—my impression, certainly—that the Peace Corps really was a unique government agency, permanently protected by the lingering magic of John F. Kennedy's name.

It might give us a final chance to believe in the government that seemed to have betrayed us. Even Hayden seemed to share that feeling. When he described his interview with Wofford and

Mankiewicz he recalled that as an undergraduate at the University of Michigan he had been present at the speech in which Kennedy first proposed the Peace Corps. As he talked about that night in 1960, his tone became genuinely, deeply nostalgic.

But I never quite realized how important the Peace Corps was to many of my friends in the movement until I was actually inside it, on home leave from our training program. During that brief period I kept trying to share my increasingly pessimistic impressions of the organization with other members of the New Left. I suppose I was trying to prove that I was still as radical as they were. Some old friends, like Todd Gitlin and Richie Rothstein, agreed that it had to be a stunt, designed to improve America's image in the world. But I remember a much more typical conversation with a younger SDS member. Just before I started talking he had been telling a new joke based on the idea that Robert McNamara was really Adolf Hitler with brilliantine on his hair. Now he seemed shocked that I thought the Peace Corps might be closer to the State Department than it was to the movement.

"Think of what those volunteers did during the Dominican Republic crisis," he said. "Crossing back and forth between enemy lines to care for the wounded. I wonder whether I would have had that kind of courage.

"You know, I guess I really do trust the Peace Corps a lot. You may have been right to join it, Paul. I guess I'll think of you and the other volunteers as my representatives abroad."

The offer that Mankiewicz and Wofford made to Tom Hayden was just one indication of the direction in which they had been trying to push the Peace Corps since its earliest days. Each of them had his own special constituency. Mankiewicz was to the civil-rights movement as Wofford was to the movement for university reform. They were always writing essays and developing projects that were designed to make the Peace Corps into a more tolerant, better financed version of the angry, charismatic organizations to its left like SNCC and the Free Speech Movement. From the perspective of the New Left, they seemed remarkably effective. So far as an outsider could tell, they were the two most respected members of the organization's senior staff.

Mankiewicz, then head of the Latin-American division, saw volunteers as potential participants in an "international sit-in." He wrote an essay, the subject of considerable controversy within the agency, in which he called the Peace Corps "a revolutionary force" and borrowed heavily from the language of the nonviolent civil-rights movement to define a role for the community-development volunteers it sent abroad: a Peace Corps worker must "function, in the best Christian sense of the word, as a 'witness' to the majority of the [Latin] nation's citizens." After citing Jim Forman's insistence that the people who went to Mississippi in 1964 identify themselves as closely as possible with the poorest people in the state, Mankiewicz wrote: "Forman, of course, was referring to workers in the Summer's civil rights project to register voters in rural Mississippi, but the analogy to the work of the Volunteers in rural Indian towns and Latin American slums is extremely close."

"It may sound strange when I say that our mission is ultimately revolutionary," he wrote elsewhere in the essay, but "the ultimate aim of a community development project is nothing less than complete change, reversal—or revolution if you wish—in the social and economic conditions of the countries to which we are accredited."

As he described those conditions, he sounded like any Northern college student back from a punishing summer in the South.

> Where children are insulted by their teachers and told that their own language is an ugly animal dialect, it is idle to build a school where 20 or more of these children go through that experience and claim that we've done Peace Corps work. That would simply be contributing to the preservation of a system that cannot last and must not last. That's why community development is essentially a revolutionary process and a political process, consisting of helping those outsiders—95 to 98 per cent of a country's population—to get in.

When I read Mankiewicz's essay I decided that I would certainly be willing to spend the two years the army was demanding trying to create the sort of revolution he was talking about. In the process, I might be able to settle some of my questions about the capacity of middle-class Americans to work in alien cultures—questions that had been disturbing me ever since the failure of the Mississippi Summer Project.

Harris Wofford seemed determined to examine the Peace Corps' work much more carefully than we had examined our efforts in Mississippi. I found his ideas even more appealing than Mankiewicz's.

He described some of them in an article called "The Future of the Peace Corps." "Like an Odyssey," he wrote, the organization has "moved from adventure to adventure, crisis to crisis, point to point, with no compass but the imagination of Sargent Shriver and his associates. It was a Socratic seminar writ large, with one rule being to follow the question where it led, the next step known by careful attention to the step just taken."

Wofford had another way of describing the institution he sought to build. "From the beginning of the Peace Corps some of us have seen it as a *University in Dispersion*" (his italics) he told a group of volunteers while he was still Country Director in Ethiopia.

This is like the idea of a straight line which you can never draw. We haven't come close yet to developing the procedures and techniques necessary to make this idea a reality. But the reality of the Peace Corps as a big educational body comes in its learning together. A University in Dispersion is coming into being, just through the confrontation of problems together.

Two years later the Peace Corps Educational Task Force, which Wofford began to direct after he returned from Ethiopia, reiterated the idea in language that made it seem as if a volunteer could spend two years involved in stimulating bull sessions. The Peace Corps, according to the Task Force, would be a "university of seminars, workshops, organized readings, and always and continually a dialogue with the other volunteers and host country friends where the talk would be open, expansive, and long into the night."

Before I decided to apply for the Peace Corps I read as many of the essays Wofford and Mankiewicz had written as I could, as skeptically as my increasing depression about the draft would allow. Then I used the *Voice* as a pretext to interview them both. They were as impressive in person as they were persuasive in print. Mankiewicz, particularly, seemed to know how to charm a young reporter. When I told him that I'd met several returned volunteers who were disgruntled because the Peace Corps had failed to provide them with work, he answered, "That would never happen to someone like you, though. You have too much energy and initiative."

I wanted very much to join an organization whose officials had that kind of confidence in me.

So I managed to persuade myself that the Peace Corps represented the best place to go in America, not a somewhat desperate compromise between a conscience that nagged and an ambition that insisted on safety. That was the point of the last piece I wrote for the *Voice* before I left its staff.

If Mankiewicz and Wofford had actually created the institutions that their rhetoric described, then the Peace Corps might provide a far better training ground than the civil-rights movement had done. It might produce a generation of people equipped, for the first time in America's history, to live as sensitive, generous citizens of a complicated and diverse world.

PART THREE

I

RACHEL was even more relieved to be leaving the Big Fiesta than I was. She had found most of the people we met there pretentious and dull and was depressed by the collective uncertainty which, she felt, forced them to adopt such a hurried, gaudy style of life. And she was worried about the effect that my increasing preoccupation with their world, and my career in it, would have on my personality and our marriage.

As a community organizer at the Hudson Guild Settlement, she had spent most of her time working with Puerto Rican block groups, although she spoke no Spanish. She had grown quite attached to the people she met and to their culture, and was particularly eager to work in Latin America. The Peace Corps told us about several projects in Spanish-speaking countries for which we could train that winter and we decided to try the most experimental of them, a program that was supposed to send community developers and specialists in public administration to Guayaquil, Ecuador, a city of seven hundred thousand, by far the largest population center in that Andean country of five million. The Peace Corps' representative in Guayaquil, Bill Gshwend, was supposed to be a disciple of Frank Mankiewicz's and one of the most imaginative people in the organization.

But nothing about our three-month training program at the University of New Mexico began to suggest the angry humanism that Mankiewicz's call for an "international sit-in" seemed to convey, or to reveal the appetite for honest discussion which was essential to Wofford's "Socratic seminar writ large."

The main purpose of the three-month course was to enable an assortment of psychiatrists, psychologists, and other members of the Peace Corps staff to spot people who seemed unfit to serve abroad: to examine us rather than educate us. Nor did those who ran the training center make any effort to disguise their intentions. They certainly did not follow Washington's lead and state their ideas in the language of the Free Speech Movement or the civil-rights movement. No, they described the rules we would have to follow if we wanted to be accepted into the Peace Corps in the bluntest of terms:

"Trainees must attend all classes and all assigned activities," read a notice we received the day we arrived in Albuquerque (the italics were theirs),

> and are expected to have a sufficient sense of personal responsibility to arrive *on time* to all scheduled meetings. If you are unavoidably late to a class you will be expected to explain your tardiness to the instructor after that class. Should you miss a class, please inform the instructor of the reason at the earliest possible opportunity.
>
> Every one of your instructors will contribute to your total assessment, inasmuch as the training program is part of the selection process which began before you came here and will continue after you leave. Please wear your name tags to all training functions.

Once, in the middle of a meeting with the training center's teachers and administrators, I asked whether any of them had ever considered incorporating Harris Wofford's "Socratic seminar," or his concept of a "University in Dispersion," into the program.

There was silence. Then, a little frustrated, I asked whether any of them had ever heard of Harris Wofford. After all, he was supposed to be one of the main administrators of the branch of the Peace Corps to which the training center was attached.

Finally, Sandra Long, Chief Assessment Officer, began to answer. I was particularly curious about what she would have to say. During those months she was one of the most important figures in our lives. More than anyone else at Albuquerque she had the authority to determine whether or not a trainee was stable enough to represent the Peace Corps abroad. "You know," she said once, "I really admire your ability to live in these slums. I couldn't bear the flies and the quarreling babies." She had offered that compliment to some trainees in Ciudad Juárez, Mexico, while she was assessing their adjustment to the city's poor *colonias* in which we were all living to prepare ourselves for the *barrios suburbanos* of Guayaquil.

"Harris Wofford," she answered. "Of course I know his name. I've known about him since high school. I remember that I thought his ideas were strange back then. You say he's written some essays? I wish he would send them out here. You know, it's so hard to keep up with what's going on back East."

The name of the thing that would happen to a trainee who could not conform to the center's rules was as coldly eerie as the process it described—"deselection." It occurred twice, at "midboards" and "finalboards." Then the trainees whom the psychiatrists and their helpers considered inadequate were declared unpersons, from the Peace Corps' point of view, and were cast back into outer darkness.

We received the news of our futures individually, during long, tense meetings at which Sandra Long presided. She called out our names alphabetically and we would walk, one by one, to the front of the classroom. She handed each trainee a sealed envelope and remained silent until he walked out into the hall. "Don't be ashamed if you're deselected," she comforted us once. "Remember, a man can be fit to be President of the United States and still not qualify to serve in the Peace Corps." (In other words, a deselected trainee was not a felon.) In the hall outside the classroom each of us secured a small, private area where we could compose ourselves in case the strip of thin white paper which the envelope contained should say that we had been rejected.

("We don't want to inflict you on the poor people of the world," Sandra Long told a girl in our group who had asked her, tearfully, why she was considered unworthy.)

On both deselection days I tried to insure myself good luck by wearing some cowboy boots and a string tie that I'd bought in an Albuquerque store. I had not been so superstitious since eighth grade, when I tried to persuade fate to make me the high scorer on our basketball team by touching all the numbers on all the awnings I passed as I walked home from school.

I felt the same sort of grueling fear—acid lining my stomach walls—as I had when we left Oxford, Ohio, by bus to journey to Mississippi. But there was this difference: In the civil-rights movement one was afraid of being murdered. In Peace Corps training one feared that he would be judged inadequate.

II

IT was no secret that Peace Corps training is an absurd ordeal. From the day Rachel and I first decided to apply to the organization we had been told by returned volunteers that if we remained as cool and moderate as possible during those three miserable months, we could do anything we wanted during our two years abroad. After I had heard several similar descriptions of the experience, I even began to do some role-playing to be certain that I could remain judiciously silent when I disagreed with a teacher, a psychiatrist, a member of the Peace Corps staff.

But before we went to Albuquerque we were told by officials in the Peace Corps' Washington office that our program would be unusually free, singularly sophisticated. We were "blue-ribbon trainees" one of the chiefs of the Peace Corps' programing division told a friend of mine; "the brightest, best-qualified group that has ever been here," according to the people who were training us at Albuquerque.

Our special task was to serve as mediators between the administrators who staffed Guayaquil's *municipio* (city hall) and the people who lived in the *barrios suburbanos* (an Ecuadorian term for slum communities), to connect poor people to a powerful institution for the first time in the city's history. To that end, our group was supposed to be composed of skilled technicians—architects, engineers, public administrators—who would serve as advisers to the relevant municipal agencies, and skilled community developers who would teach the slum dwellers how to confront city officials and how to cooperate with them.

Rudolfo Benitez and Bill Gshwend, the AID (Agency for International Development) technician and Peace Corps representative who had designed our program, spoke to us frequently during training, and sometimes as I listened to them I believed the strategy they were proposing was entirely unworkable. Many of their ideas and assertions seemed to violate the lessons I thought I had learned in Mississippi. But the two men had both lived in Guayaquil for two years, and it was obvious that each of them felt a genuine love for the city's people. That love was linked to their expertise. So if I felt some skepticism toward the plans they were outlining, I felt more skepticism toward my own skepticism. Was I revealing the flaw that older people were always locating in the New Left: criticizing opinions and analyses before I had investigated them because they didn't conform to my ideology? Was it an ornery, academic side of my nature that insisted on doubting most of what I heard? Almost every time I found myself disagreeing with Benitez and Gshwend during the training program I decided that I was reacting like a typical radical intellectual, chopping logic to score debater's points instead of listening sympathetically so that I could equip myself to help poor people.

Benitez, an expert in public administration from El Paso who was working in Albuquerque during the months we were training for the Peace Corps, had just spent two years studying Guayaquil's *municipio*, and he described his conclusions for us in a series of lectures. He had been sent there by his employers, a management-consultant firm which the Ecuadorian government and AID had contracted to evaluate the performance of Guayaquil's municipal agencies. A Mexican-American who was as fluent in Spanish as in English, Benitez had quickly developed an affection for the city's poor that was as deep as his disappointment in most of its bureaucrats. By the time his assignment was finished, he was convinced that an efficiently run *municipio* could relieve some of the terrible poverty that afflicted most of the city's seven hundred thousand people.

But he was also certain that the government departments would begin to provide adequate services to Guayaquil's slum dwellers only if they adopted the administrative techniques which have been used successfully in the United States for the past fifty years. In the long report he submitted to AID he suggested many specific measures whose adoption would signal the start of substantial, far-reaching reform: a more comprehensive means of tax assessment, specific laws to insist that the rich actually paid their taxes, a civil-service system based on merit and not political debt, night classes to help government workers perform their jobs more effectively, greater cooperation between the municipal departments.

But Benitez had no illusions that his lonely report could affect a social system that had been entrenched for so long. Worse, he doubted that there were any powerful Ecuadorians who still wanted to hear his ideas. For the popular Mayor who had originally requested the AID study, Asad Bucaram, had been removed from office by a conservative military junta months before Benitez's study was complete.

If only he could find a way of creating conditions that would force Ecuadorians to accept his ideas . . . He was convinced that as soon as a few of his concrete proposals were adopted, the entire plan would have to take effect: it was a bureaucratic process which accumulated its own momentum. The Peace Corps, he realized, could be extremely helpful. He had known the few volunteers who had already been assigned to work in City Hall: they seemed capable enough, but the much more important fact was that they brought a North American background to their work. They were equipped, by their cultural habits, to understand the modern ideas and attitudes that most Latins seemed to find both threatening and confusing. And they seemed able to win the trust of their office mates! Perhaps a Peace Corps project in which their example was replicated on a larger scale could put some of Benitez' proposals into practice.

The hope that North American efficiency would quickly conquer the Latins' more convoluted form of bureaucratic behavior was at the core of most of the lectures that Benitez gave us. It was clear that he felt the conflict especially strongly because of his own mixed heritage. But he seemed to have emerged from a painful private debate with a great respect for the United States. He showed us that attitude when he described his own experiences with prejudice in America (he was dark-brown) and tried to connect them with the feelings the Ecuadorians would have about us:

> I remember once when I was in the service I went into a restaurant in the South with my sparring partner and my wrecking crew—that's what I call my wife and kids, they don't mind—and the owner turned us away because he didn't want to serve any of our kind. Now what kind of a thing is that for children who are supposed to grow up loving their country? But my children do love America, and their father feels the same way. You know, I would be served in that restaurant today. Where else in the world could something like that occur?
>
> And you know there are many Ecuadorians who feel the same way as I do. Of course they resent you. They're right to feel that way. They don't like it when you come in and boss

them around. But deep down they're grateful. Because they also know what America promises, and they believe that our country really cares about them.

Sometimes it seemed as if Benitez had distilled his belief in America into a somewhat mystical faith in our project.

The Peace Corps had not recruited nearly as many technicians as it had promised the Ecuadorians. Only three of the people in our group of twenty-nine had ever been employed by municipal agencies in the United States. No more than half the trainees had even lived for substantial portions of time in cities that were as large as Guayaquil. Our average age was twenty-four. Only four people spoke Spanish. So we asked Benitez how we could expect to have any influence on middle-aged civil servants who spoke no English, who would regard us as illiterates in their native tongue, who had spent most of their adult lives working inside Latin bureaucracies. Wouldn't the mere fact of our physical presence provide a constant threat to them, a reminder that we wanted them to undergo an immediate radical transformation, on our terms?

"None of that is as important as you think," he said.

When you get to Guayaquil you'll realize that your background is the important thing that you're bringing to the *municipio*: the training you have absorbed just from living in the United States—from your high schools and your colleges, your Boy Scout troops and summer camps.

Those people will follow the example you set. Here's an illustration. I always observed when I worked in the *municipio* that if a man had ten pieces of paper on his desk he'd make ten trips to the wastebasket to throw them all out. Now, I know that all of you would only make one trip. That's the kind of efficiency you'll teach, sometimes without knowing it.

Gshwend, the Peace Corps representative in Guayaquil, was as convinced as Benitez that the *municipio* could do a great deal for the *barrios suburbanos* if Peace Corps volunteers were to serve as technical advisers. Our project grew out of a series of conversations the two men carried on while they were still in Ecuador, and out of some meetings between both of them and Joachim Orrantia, the man who had succeeded the man who had succeeded Asad Bucaram (Benitez' original employer) as Mayor of Guayaquil.

Then in his early thirties, Gshwend had finally found the kind of job for which he had been searching during most of his adult life. Before the Peace Corps was formed he had been a slightly dissatisfied social worker in Chicago, married, with one child, who was as nostalgic for the year he had spent as a student and community developer in Mexico City as most of the returned American exiles in the 1930s were for the time they had spent as artists in Paris. He loved Spanish culture and seemed to find few things as rewarding as the feeling that he was helping very poor people. Kennedy's proposal for a Peace Corps seemed to offer him an ideal way to recapture those feelings. When he discovered that married men with children were prohibited from volunteering, he applied for a position on the staff. He was assigned to serve as the second regional representative in Guayaquil, a job that was considered one of the most frustrating and challenging in the entire organization.

He had quickly discovered that he liked the hot, tropical port city. He enjoyed the erratic pace of its life, the warmth and volatility of its people. Guayaquil reminded him of Chicago, only it was much more manageable. Like Benitez, he spent much more time with Ecuadorians than with North Americans, and he made a special point of cultivating some of the bureaucrats who worked in the *municipio*. For example, he was part of an informal club of civil servants who met every Friday afternoon to drink and gossip about the week's work. He must have expected to gain some political return on his investment of time, but he was also filled with an intense, human concern about Guayaquil's life. He was genuinely fascinated by all its gossip, by every nuance of its politics.

Gshwend's plan for our group of volunteers seemed to complement Benitez' perfectly. He placed great emphasis on the role of the community developers who, he thought, should live in as many different *barrios* as possible. He wanted them to link the city's widely scattered slums into a single, durable organization that would be strong enough to force the Mayor and city council to respond to the demands of the poor. "A Saul Alinsky-type organization," Gshwend called it. (Alinsky was then at the peak of his reputation as a radical who knew how to build durable organizations which won substantial gains for their deprived communities through imaginative, nonviolent confrontations.) "Within a year or eighteen months some of you should have your *barrios* well enough organized to march on the *municipio* and demand their rights."

If the community developers were the stick with which the Peace Corps would beat the mulish city government into sharing its resources, the technicians whom Benitez had hoped to recruit were supposed to be the carrot, our way of inducing the *municipio* to transform itself voluntarily. The theory was that, through their skills, the technicians would quickly gain enough influence in the City Hall to assure our success in the *barrios*. At the same time as they were impressing their Ecuadorian counterparts with America's efficient administrative techniques, according to Benitez' plan, they would also be acquiring substantial control over the *municipio*'s resources, according to Gshwend's. Soon they would be powerful enough to direct benefits like land fill, garbage disposal, clean water out to the neighborhoods where the community developers were living.

The process was supposed to be irreversible. The more resources our technicians could direct to the slums, the more likely the poor people would be to realize that they could benefit from the Alinsky type of organization the community-development volunteers were building. It was a nonpolitical kind of machine politics. (". . . a good parallel to the work of community development volunteers in the slums . . . of Guayaquil, Ecuador, is the work of the big-city political machines in the 1900s," Mankiewicz had written in his essay, "A Revolutionary Force.")

In training, the technique Gshwend had in mind was described as "infiltration." The volunteers, more sensitive to the needs of the poor than their Ecuadorian counterparts, would infiltrate the *municipio* and the *barrios suburbanos* with their uniquely North American brand of compassion. With the power they accumulated they would transform the city.

Shortly before we were supposed to leave for Guayaquil, Gshwend told Rachel and me about a special mission which he had reserved for us. Our assignment in the *municipio*, he said, would be to work in the Department of Community Development, the agency that was most closely linked to the slums where we would be living.

Our specific objective should be to win the affection of Jorge Rodriguez, our department's chief, so that we could overthrow him later on.

Gshwend made Rodriguez sound like the Peace Corps' single biggest enemy in Guayaquil. His shortsighted stubbornness was preventing the department from offering substantial assistance to the poor, Bill said. If we were able to dislodge him—perhaps by employing some of the techniques we had learned in the civil-rights movement—we could use his office to establish and control the "Alinsky-type organization."

Gshwend criticized Rodriguez even more harshly than I had criticized Papa Doc in Vicksburg. Some television sets, some books, some money were missing from the community centers which the United States had helped the Ecuadorian to establish, and Bill was convinced that Rodriguez had stolen them. But the Ecuadorian was worse than a thief, Bill said. He was also a hypocritical manipulator. "He'll be very polite to you when you meet him. You may find him extremely charming. But that's exactly why he's so dangerous. I think that at heart he hates our country. I wouldn't be surprised to learn that down deep he's a Communist, or at least that he sympathizes with the Communists."

Though Gshwend's suggestion that Rachel and I scheme to remove Rodriguez from power indicated that he was at least as insensitive to the Ecuadorians with whom the Peace Corps had to work as we'd been to the black organizers who administered us in Mississippi, it was always clear that Bill was motivated by the genuine affection he felt for Guayaquil's poor, not by malice.

The week we arrived in Ecuador he showed Rachel and me how deeply he cared about our project. We were driving back through the center of town from one of the dirtiest, poorest of the endless *barrios suburbanos*. The entire area, where more than three hundred fifty thousand people live, is built on swampland. Though many of the streets have been filled with dirt from the hills that surround the city, the place we visited was a quagmire. People lived in cane shacks above fetid water and could walk from one place to another only over cane bridges. It was a breeding ground for the worst kinds of diseases—typhoid, hepatitis, polio. A child who went outside to play might literally drown in the mud.

There was little relief as we drove back into town. The long, rutted dirt streets, the apartments with their crumbling brick façades, the tiny *tiendas* with their meager supplies, the undernourished children who crowded every block—it was more depressing than anything Rachel or I had ever seen.

Bill must have driven down those streets at least a hundred times during his stay in Guayaquil. But now he seemed to be viewing the scene through our eyes—for the first time once again—and he appeared to be as disturbed as we were.

"You know," he said slowly, "that's why your project is so special. It could mean the difference between peaceful revolution and bloodshed in Guayaquil."

III

THE University of New Mexico should have been the ideal place to prepare us for the program Benitez and Gshwend had designed. As the Peace Corps' main training center for Latin America it was, at that time, readying about a thousand volunteers each year for work throughout the continent. Its department of Latin-American studies was one of the best in the United States. The University attracted students from almost every Latin country, of all political persuasions, most of whom would have been willing to spend some time sharing their ideas with us.

But the courses we were given in Albuquerque were as insubstantial as the psychiatrists' observations of us were rigorous. Most of the people who trained us there were products of the middle America that was just beginning to re-emerge in 1966, and in that country, Nixonia, appearance is far more important than substance. Sandra Long was a typical citizen of Nixonia, and her influence pervaded the training program. Of course, she cared much more about our capacity to make a good impression on the American public than about our ability to work in the *municipio* and the *suburbios*. She and her confederates prepared themselves for the Great Deselection Day by examining us under a microscope of written tests, personal interviews, small group discussions to make sure that no single misfit slipped by. Of course they decided who was fit and who was mis, not Ecuadorians with whom we would work. They were like parents who are so obsessed with examining their children for germs, for dirt, for signs of disease, that they forget to prepare them to live in the world.

A description of one of the psychiatrists' favorite techniques, and of their attitude toward those who questioned it, should suggest something about the atmosphere in which we were living as we prepared ourselves to realize Gshwend's and Benitez's hopes for Guayaquil.

The psychiatrists obtained some of the information they would use during midboards and finalboards through the "peer ratings," an institutionalized buddyfuck. We devoted two full afternoons to filling out long, dittoed questionaires which asked us to predict which members of our group would succeed and which would fail, to list the people we wanted to live with and those we objected to living with. It wasn't like a "T-group"—God forbid that we should have told each other what we thought: the whole exercise was for the psychologists' eyes only. Tell each other what we thought! The process fortified the Willy Loman complex that so many of the group had carried with them to training. We treated each other with the saccharine friendliness of second-rate high-school politicians. A moment's honesty might lose one a crucial vote for the student council.

Once I complained about the system of peer ratings to one of Sandra Long's subordinates, the psychologist who was evaluating the trainees whose names began with A through G. Quite passionately, I argued that a technique that made people so self-conscious, so intent on assimilating themselves to the spirit of a particular group, could not possibly encourage the openness and flexibility that Peace Corps volunteers would have to display abroad. Though I talked heatedly, I really thought I might be able to engage him in a discussion of the nature of the work that we had been assigned. What had convinced him that it would be possible to rely on North American standards of sanity and stability in a foreign culture?

But: "You take life too seriously, Paul. When you mature a little you'll learn to relax and adjust. But now you're too intense, I'm afraid. You can't see the woods for the trees."

To insist on a clear explanation for a dubious technique, then, was to display a juvenile kind of intensity. I realized that he'd transform anything else I said into a piece of data for the selection board, not consider it part of a discussion that can take place between rational people, so I remembered my role-playing and shut up.

"Every one of your instructors will contribute to your total assessment," we had been informed at the beginning of the training session.

There were classes from seven in the morning until ten each night—gym, Spanish, training in community development, an industrial-arts program, a weekly quiz, and the sessions with the psychiatrists and psychologists. For many of the teachers the most important didactic device seemed to be the attendance list.

We had to take four hours of industrial arts each week, a class specifically designed for people whose work in rural areas of Latin America would oblige them to dig wells and build latrines. There was no reason at all why a man who would spend two years working in the Department of Taxation in Guayaquil's *municipio* should have to know how to build a storehouse with a Cinveram machine. But the schedule we received the day we arrived in Albuquerque included those twenty-four hours of industrial arts, and any word from Authority was law. Our teacher, a graduate of Northern State Texas University who was now an associate professor of education, insisted that if anyone failed to attend his classes he would personally make sure that person wasn't sent to Guayaquil. None of us was willing to call his bluff.

Many of our academic instructors were as strict as the people who taught our industrial-arts course. The worst, in my opinion, was the fellow who received about a hundred taxpayers' dollars each week to tell us something about Latin-American history and politics. Often he didn't even show up to lecture us. He would turn his class over to some returned volunteers, Ph.D. candidates, who were his teaching assistants. One afternoon, apparently unable to find anyone who would substitute for him, he spent two hours reading us a United Nations pamphlet that described Ecuador's gross national product, item by item. It was the sort of thing Strom Thurmond might do in the twenty-fifth hour of a filibuster, wonderful material for an Andy Warhol movie. But we were all exhausted that afternoon. We had been attending eighteen hours of classes each day, most of them similarly absurd. Earlier that week, for example, an engineering consultant had spent two hours telling us how to convert feet to meters and then, incredibly, how to convert dollars into all the currencies in Latin America. The same week an ex-Marine finished showing us how to use a compass when he suddenly realized that the entire lesson was inapplicable because Ecuador is on the other side of the equator.

The next time the professor of Latin-American history was supposed to speak only a few of us appeared. He seemed outraged. "I hope you people didn't join the Peace Corps to stay in your rooms sleeping all day. You can tell the rest of the trainees that if there are ever so many absences again I'm going to report all of you to the staff."

Our teachers had a ready justification for the mandatory classes, the boring lectures: "At least this is better than the army." But when they used the army as an analogy—or, rather, as an excuse—they only emphasized a deep flaw in the program's conception. The military involves its recruits in rigorous, arbitrary exercises in order to turn young men into killers who will accept any command their superiors give. But a Peace Corps volunteer, who is on his own in a complex, fluid situation, must be equipped to make the kinds of unorthodox personal decisions that were discouraged in our highly structured training program, where every order was backed by the threat of deselection.

We needed instructors who were willing to treat us as responsible adults, who realized that their primary task was to help us understand the shifting nuances of the culture in which we were supposed to assume such a complicated role. Instead, the people in charge of our courses in Albuquerque were accredited spies for the governing agency of mental health, not so much teachers as psychological secret police.

Of course we all spent a great deal of time complaining to each other about the quality of our classes, the attitude of the psychologists, the schedule that left us little time to sleep and no time to learn. I had never seen such gripers—or griped so much myself: not even in the bad early days of our project in Vicksburg. There was a Papa Doc at training, only now it was an entire bureaucracy and not just a single, jealous project director. One of our main objections was that the people who ran the training center were not willing to consider our opinions.

A few days before midboards we had a meeting with the acting director of the center, an associate professor of psychology. I had assumed that everyone's rage would come gushing out then—as rage had gushed out during the occasional meetings that brought people from various projects in Mississippi together to discuss the future of the civil-rights movement. But the trainees sat stone silent—afraid, I quickly realized, that the mildest expression of discontent or even a constructive suggestion might prove disastrous later that week when the director relayed it to the rest of the people who sat on the selection board. I remained silent too, sharing their fears.

Finally, a girl raised a point which, she insisted, was on everybody's mind. She was a white physical-education major from Birmingham who was famous for the phenomenal memory for names she had acquired at a Dale Carnegie school. The candy machine in the vestibule of the building where we trained had been out of order for a week, she pointed out. Also there was not enough milk for the coffee in the coffee machine.

The director said that he was always glad to speak with a group of trainees because such confrontations enabled him to understand what we were thinking about. If any of us had a personal problem we should be sure to see him privately. His door was always open to us—figuratively, that is.

He promised to study the problem of refreshments. Then he adjourned the meeting.

IV

THE America that the Peace Corps psychologists sought to manufacture for export was a sterile paradise whose ideal representative (in effect, a sales representative) would be as sleek as the wondrous technology that had made the United States the envy of the world. Through mechanisms like the peer rating and the selection process, it was clear, they hoped to produce a standardized volunteer which would be germ free and psychically pure, a walking smile with no self-doubts.

To me, our health lectures were a fit symbol for the entire process, possibly because they affected me more profoundly than they did most of the other trainees. As a confirmed hypochondriac, I paid the closest attention to each warning the doctors issued and heeded their advice throughout most of my time in Ecuador. In a way, I am grateful to the University of New Mexico medical staff, for I never did get seriously sick. Rachel, who was not nearly so cautious, contracted a case of hepatitis which kept her in bed for several weeks. But the price I paid for that rather narrow margin of good health, I sometimes think, was to spend more than a year encased in a sort of emotional cellophane wrapping.

The doctors had told us that a single swallow of unboiled water might give one a serious case of dysentery or hepatitis or typhoid fever, so for about six months I never even accepted a Scotch and water when I went to Ecuadorian parties. (I always asked for beer instead.) Vegetables whose leaves grew close to the ground might contain parasites or some residual manure, so I was always careful to extract the lettuce from sandwiches, even in relatively expensive restaurants. You could ingest amoebas with unpeeled fruits, so I removed sliced tomatoes from my sandwiches, too, until Rachel finally convinced me that I had only to peel off the skins. Under-cooked pork might contain trichinae, and you could get worms from half-cooked beef, so I never bought any meat from street vendors until my last month in the country, when I discovered a pork sandwich too good to resist. But I always felt a little nervous and a little guilty when I ate it.

We had been warned that raw milk carried bovine tuberculosis, and I was never convinced that the milk in Guayaquil was properly purified. There was supposed to be a factory there whose pasteurization process included the addition of formaldehyde to every bottle. So I always drank Coke or Pepsi or Orange Crush. But you had to be careful with those beverages, too, for fear that the local merchant had decided to earn himself some extra money from unsuspecting customers by putting a sweet, germy brew into familiar bottles. For reasons of sheer superstition, which had nothing to do with the specific warnings we had received, I also refrained from drinking Ecuadorian soft drinks, except for a very refreshing brand of mineral water called Guitig.

Dogs and even cats could carry rabies, so I was always hesitant about petting my friends' animals.

The chief medical lecturer at Albuquerque described in the most garish terms the diseases we would contract if we failed to obey his warnings. He behaved as if his duty was to instill Pavlovian responses in all of us that would force us to protect ourselves from anything that seemed alien and therefore germ-ridden. Thus, he not only emphasized the fact that bad water could give a volunteer parasites (though that was bad enough; until your parasites were cured you couldn't get back into the United States—and a friend of mine in Guayaquil used the law to earn a comfortable living by selling clean stool specimens to parasite-ridden Ecuadorians who wanted to get visas to America without undergoing lengthy treatments), but he also defined parasites, which could easily be cured, by the worst case he had ever heard of. He spent a full fifteen minutes telling us about a girl in the Philippines whose entire liver had been infested with worms. He sounded almost voluptuous as he described the symptoms of the tropical diseases to which we'd be exposed—the headaches, the stomach-aches, constant depression, sleepiness, insomnia, diarrhea, constipation, vomiting—and then made sure that the mildest complaint would alarm us terribly by suggesting that symptoms were interchangeable; a slight headache might signal the beginning of malaria, constant vomiting might be a sign of simple flu.

He was very careful to remind us that most of the common tropical sicknesses like parasites, dysentery, or hepatitis might continue to debilitate us for decades. (Most people recover from them very quickly.)

One day he told us about the *chinchorro* bug, an insect which makes its home in the crevices of the cane shacks in Guayaquil. One bite causes a degenerative heart disease for which there is no cure and from which death occurs within twenty years. Because of the *chinchorro* bug, volunteers weren't allowed to live in cane shacks.

"You know, we're taking years off our life by going on this project," a trainee said after listening to the doctor one day. The health lectures turned even the bravest members of our group into hypochondriacs. They nearly convinced me that it would be more dangerous to be a Peace Corps volunteer in Ecuador than a soldier in Vietnam.

Once the doctor told us that the threat of infection in Guayaquil was so serious that we would be safe only if we wore long-sleeved shirts with rubber bands around our cuffs. Of course no one took that kind of advice very seriously. Only a few people followed his instructions even as carefully as I did. Still, the lectures had a powerful effect on all of us. One couldn't help but half-believe that Guayaquil would be as pestilential as anything one had read about in medieval history.

That was our attitude as we set out to help the people there by working alongside them.

During our home leave I bought Defoe's *Journal of a Plague Year* to read when I arrived in Guayaquil. I thought it would be interesting to compare his England to my Ecuador.

Our trainers were as determined to protect our minds from Ecuador's culture as they were to protect our bodies from its germs. Accordingly, the psychiatrists and psychologists took great pains to warn us about something called "culture shock," a sort of mental infection that we would contract from meeting Guayaquil's people even more rapidly than we'd contract parasites and dysentery from eating their foods and drinking their water. "Culture shock" is nothing more than the disorientation every traveler experiences when he finds himself in a society whose customs and ideas differ from his own. But it was described to us in several mental-hygiene lectures as if it were a disease. The symptoms were depression and lethargy (the same as every physical disease the doctors had warned us about). If they became too severe we should talk to our regional representative or to the staff physician, both of whom had been especially trained to deal with the ailment. The psychologists even showed us a graph, taken from studies the Peace Corps had commissioned, which indicated the point in a volunteer's tour of duty when he could anticipate the most severe attacks of culture shock, the points at which he could expect to be free from it.

In a community-development class one day I began to realize how deeply the idea that contact with foreigners produces mental disorders could affect the responses of the volunteers who accepted it. Just as the health lectures had persuaded me to protect my stomach against parasites, so the psychiatrists' warnings might induce others to protect themselves against "culture shock" by acting as if prolonged exposure to any alien influence, people, or customs, might infect their psyches. Thus, wherever they lived they would continue to believe that American behavior was the only form of sanity.

A returned volunteer had been describing the standard method of community development to us. His ideas were new to me—I hadn't realized that the Peace Corps took such a mechanistic view of its work in foreign communities—but Rachel said that she had heard dozens of similar lectures during her two years at the University of Chicago's School of Social Service Administration.

His operating assumption was that the slum dwellers with whom Gshwend and Benitez expected us to work would be totally disorganized. Most of them would be recent immigrants from rural villages who had come to the city in search of work, but found themselves jobless and confused, even more disoriented than people who had remained in the *campo*. To accomplish the project's objectives, then, we would have to act as "catalysts" and teach them to work together harmoniously. We would find a few local people who were "natural leaders," encourage them to create organizations in their *barrios*, and teach their members how to deal with the city officials at the *municipio*.

Then he outlined the formal method most community developers use, whether they work in the city or the country, Latin America or Africa. The first step is to discover a "felt need" in the community where you are living (your "site," as the Peace Corps calls it). The usual example of a "felt need" is water—the people need water, but it hasn't yet occurred to them to dig a well. Or education: they know they need a school, but they haven't gotten together to build one. Next, the volunteer persuades the "natural leader," and through him the rest of the community, to form an organization (a *comité*) which will devise a satisfactory way to resolve the felt need. Often we would have to instruct the Ecuadorians in the most fundamental processes, we were told: show them how to call meetings, devise schedules, appoint delegations, insist on regular progress reports. We would have to explain each step very carefully at the same time as we mediated between factions whose quarrels seemed likely to tear the *comité* apart. But in most cases the tasks which seem impossible at first can be completed within a year or two. Like university students at the end of a complicated course, the townspeople finally understand ideas that once seemed entirely obscure. Now they know a method (and can see an institution which it has produced) which will allow them to progress even more rapidly in the future.

In effect, the process the returned volunteer had outlined was a scientific one: the "catalyst," the outsider, could cause elements that were already present, the local people, to form a new compound, the *comité*. Presumably, in our case, the compounds would eventually come together to form a new mixture, the "Alinsky-like organization." But then he concluded his lecture with a brief story about his own experience as a community developer which provided a sharp, startling contrast to the argument he had been making.

He had been stationed in a small village in Colombia, he told us. After more than a year he had become convinced that its inhabitants felt a deep need for a new road so that they could market their products more efficiently. So he urged some people he trusted to form a *comité*, drew them a surveyor's map of the route that seemed to him ideal, and accompanied them on a trip to the provincial capital. There they persuaded the governor to let them make use of the land the volunteer had marked off.

But then, when the volunteer and his *comité* called a meeting to announce their plan, the standard community-development process began to break down. For the route that had been selected went directly across the village's main graveyard. If the Colombians were to build the road they would have to uproot all their ancestors' remains. The townspeople rejected the volunteer's proposal so vehemently that the Colombians on the *comité* began to disassociate themselves from it. Soon the volunteer was isolated.

It sounded like the night in Mississippi when the two local black men who had seemed to agree with all our plans for the teacher exchange, the food-stamp program, the *Citizens' Appeal* had suddenly sided with Papa Doc and Bob Moses, without a word of explanation. Later, I realized that they had been too intimidated by our collective presence to argue with us. If we had been sensitive to their mood, less eager to believe that they approved of our plans, we might never have tried to impose that enormous structure of unsuitable programs on their community.

The returned volunteer didn't seem to blame himself for his failure. You could see all the anger and frustration he must have felt during that meeting in Colombia return as he told the story. He spent several minutes complaining about peasant superstitions. Then, suddenly, he spoke the sentence that might have served as the motto of the entire training staff:

"Those people are the biggest obstacles to progress."

When I asked him whether that was what he really meant to say, I realized that most of the other trainees in the room could not understand why I sounded so agitated. But I did not know how to explain that such attitudes, which are encouraged by concepts like "culture shock," would make our complicated job in Guayaquil virtually impossible to perform; or, more important, how to show that his short, depressed comment revealed an assumption about America's cultural superiority which, under slightly different conditions, could justify the most brutal kinds of behavior. "Those people are the biggest obstacles to progress." "We burn villages to save them."

His sentence, tacked on at the end of that long, optimistic lecture about community-development techniques, seemed like a contemporary replay of that moment in *Heart of Darkness* when
Kurtz ends his idealistic essay about the Congo's natives with the
scrawled inscription: "Exterminate all the brutes!"

PART FOUR

I

I FELT much closer to Rachel during training than ever before. It was such a rich emotion, so filled with subtleties, such a welcome relief from the preoccupation with my career which had separated us when we lived in New York that for the first several weeks in Albuquerque I spent much more time savoring it than I did worrying about our classes or the other trainees. If anything, our sudden isolation from New York, the skepticism we shared about our work, the desire we nevertheless found ourselves sharing to discover ourselves in its midst, allowed us to explore entire areas of each other, share portions of ourselves, that would have remained tightly closed if we'd remained part of the raucous, ambitious crowd at the Big Fiesta.

In late February 1966 we had taken a train from Chicago to Albuquerque, the first time we had traveled across America, and when we arrived in New Mexico we experienced a strong, lasting sense of physical satisfaction. Once we got used to Albuquerque's altitude of five thousand feet, its climate seemed marvelously clear and refreshing. The simple pleasure of breathing pure air instead of the gray, polluted filth that strangled us in New York was worth a month of dull classes and daily indignities.

We were living in a motel at the edge of the university campus. Our room was like an enlarged closet with a bathroom so tiny that one could shower and shit at the same time. The training program forced us to accept a discipline that we would have considered puritanical in New York. We had to get up at six-thirty every morning in time for gym. While we were dressing we would listen to Albuquerque's version of the WMCA "good guys," disk jockeys who were popular in New York that year. They would always play Sgt. Barry Sadler's "Ballad of the Green Berets" to inspire the city's citizens to another hard day of patriotic labor. I confess that I felt virtuous, too, as Rachel and I walked through Albuquerque's glistening sunrise, down its broad, open streets, toward the gym: like an American who had finally come home, not a colonialist in training.

I lost ten pounds that month, and cut down from three packs to fifteen cigarettes a day; Rachel gave up smoking altogether. There was an immediate incentive to get in shape. The only part of training besides Spanish that made sense to me was called Outward Bound. It took us up to the high Sandia Mountains one weekend to practice rappelling and then rock climbing. Rachel caught on immediately. She rappelled gracefully and scurried up the highest rocks with no trouble at all. I still carry small scars on my wrists as proof of my clumsiness. People who mounted the jagged cliffs after me told me that I left bloodstains in the crevices. Afterward, I was so jealous of Rachel's success that I accused her of deliberately embarrassing me. But she forgave me quickly, and within a day I felt more pride in my physical condition than I did shame at my atavistic outburst of jealousy.

During that short period the trainees seemed to accept us completely. Rachel is blond and beautiful, gentle but a little reserved. "I've always been the sort of person grandmothers trust," she told me a few days after we met. It is not a quality she particularly admires in herself. In fact, she is every bit as angry as I am, and perhaps a little tougher in her proud, patrician way. But in the Peace

Corps appearance is nearly everything. She looks like she might have been a cheerleader or a prom queen if she had gone to a state university instead of Bryn Mawr; or, if she had seemed too mature and serious for those bouncy, peppy jobs, she would certainly have been elected to the student council or the dorm committee. She is just cool enough, friendly but self-contained, to be the sort whom boys form strong but hopeless crushes on, whom girls idolize.

A visitor to the University of New Mexico training site seeing us together might have classified us as the kind of volunteers who believe in the Boy Scout troop and the fresh-air camp, not as members of the New Left. We might have passed, for a short while, as the cheerful, faithful young missionary types that the Peace Corps has in mind when it recruits what it calls "married couples" to lend the organization stability.

II

IN late April 1966, six weeks after our group arrived at training we spent five days living with poor Mexican-Americans in the *barrios* of Albuquerque. During the debriefing session afterward Rachel wrote to a friend from the Mississippi Summer Project:

> One girl just told me that she had not enjoyed herself at all. She says she doesn't like poor people—how's that? But she isn't alone. Last week another girl said, "You can take the person out of the slum, but you can't take the slum out of the person." Another time in a community-development class a boy named Sid Raschi interrupted Paul, who was trying to explain why Bob Moses and Stokely Carmichael are so bitter against white liberals, to say that he doesn't see how anyone in this country can feel that way. "You know, we are the most

generous people in the world. America is the only country in the history of mankind that has ever tried to solve the problem of poverty."

There are twenty-nine of us here, and it is rare to find such a smug, complacent, and unperceptive group of people. They are mostly all quite pleasant and agreeable, but very few of them seem to have heard of discussing ideas, and they all have so little experience outside their own culture that they keep coming up with astonishing viewpoints and theories in class, as you can see. Paul and I get outraged and struck with disbelief, but we try to suppress our feelings. People seem to like us well enough, though they think that Paul is a little too intellectual and that we are all in all an unusual pair, although I am something of a mother figure. The girls arouse all my emancipated woman's ire because they are so sheeplike, cute, and helpless.

Certainly it was hard to understand how Frank Mankiewicz could have believed that Americans like those in our "blue-ribbon group" would be willing participants in an "international sit-in." Most of them had barely heard of the civil-rights movement from which his strategy was drawn. If almost all of them did know that there had been some kind of big freedom march in Washington in 1963, that there had been some incidents near a bridge in Selma, Alabama, a few years later, they had only the faintest recollection of Medgar Evers' assassination or the autumn day in Birmingham when four little black kids were blown to bits in the midst of their Sunday-school class. They knew virtually nothing about the other events that had been America to Rachel and me: Cambridge, Maryland; Danville, Virginia; Albany, Georgia; even the 1964 Convention Challenge. Almost all of them seemed to be persuaded that the Negro had made considerable progress under Lyndon Johnson. They found it impossible to understand why black militants were so strident in their demands for more.

Of the twenty-nine trainees in our group there were seven, including Rachel and me, who had spent any time at all doing volunteer work in deprived communities in America. Gerald Erlham had been part of a church-sponsored voter-registration project in Kansas City. Ralph Craft had spent two summers in Quaker work camps. Nick Zydycrn had tutored some black children in San Francisco. Sammy Bernstein had marched in some open-housing demonstrations. Jane Snider had been attached to a tutorial project in St. Louis.

Even fewer of the trainees in our group would have volunteered to work with poor people overseas if there hadn't been a war on; just six, I estimated—three single men and the three single girls. That doesn't exactly mean that the rest of us were draft dodgers, for the Peace Corps was certainly not the easiest alternative to military service that a young man could find. There was still some of the robust desire to "help people" that seems to have characterized most of the earliest groups that went abroad, a lingering echo of the missionary's belief that God's universe contains a fixed amount of suffering, that one man's sacrifice insures another man's relief. And some of the trainees would have joined me in arguing that the Peace Corps was the only government institution in which one could "build not burn," that we were therefore engaged in an act of affirmation. But all those strains, which had given the Peace Corps its initial aura of purity, were somewhat diluted now. Even the trainees who believed in America most devoutly seemed to feel a little guilty about the fact that they were living a lie: their parents and friends at home viewed them as generous college graduates who wanted to use their good fortune to serve mankind, but they knew—we knew—that finally we weren't affirming a belief so much as we were fleeing a war that had frightened and confused our generation. And we felt especially guilty because we were hesitant to mention our true motives in case the staff should find out that we weren't so altruistic after all, and send us home and then off to fight.

But although it seemed to me natural that most trainees had been pushed into the Peace Corps by the draft, still I was surprised to realize that once they were on the inside they began to view the organization as a poor black or white views the army: it offered them a chance to broaden themselves by traveling, to transcend restrictions that had been imposed by class and education. In a few cases their goals were rather specific. Gerald Erlham thought that he might want to go to the Columbia School of Social Work but doubted that he could get accepted immediately. He hoped that the admissions office would be impressed that he had lived for two years in a Latin slum. Hank Dawson believed that a good recommendation from the Peace Corps might help him to land a more attractive job with the State Department than most new recruits to the Foreign Service receive. Another man I met when we got to Ecuador wanted to work for AID, but had been told by a friend in the agency that he would have a better chance of getting a job there if he trained for two years in the Peace Corps.

But most of the trainees were not so settled in their ambitions. They were just anxious to make the best of a situation that had seemed quite bleak at first: drifting, hoping. Maybe the Peace Corps was better than going right to work for one's Dad, a Ford dealer in Phoenix, or enrolling for another dull year at UCLA's School of Public Administration, than working in an engineering firm in Dallas, than settling down in Fairfax County, Virginia, at the age of twenty-five and beginning to raise a family. Maybe two years in Guayaquil, the ability to speak Spanish, some knowledge of municipal government in Latin America, some ability to work with poor foreigners, would mean four thousand dollars more as a starting salary in an international company like Grace Lines or the Bank of America.

At their most honest, most optimistic, many trainees would have sounded like Dan Stringer, Bill Gshwend's successor in Guayaquil, when he told us why he accepted a job as Peace Corps representative:

This is the best springboard in all of Washington. It's a great thing to have on your record if you want to get ahead in business or politics. Look at all the young men around Bobby Kennedy and Lyndon Johnson, and you'll see that a surprising number of them were with the Peace Corps once.

Harris Wofford argued that the political assumptions and professional motivations that encouraged people to join the Peace Corps were relatively unimportant since the experience abroad transformed so many of the volunteers who underwent it. In training it was impossible to tell whether that assertion was based on evidence or faith. But it was immediately clear that few of the members of our group had the kind of intellectual energy that Wofford's invocation of a "University in Dispersion" suggested.

When I first read the phrase in New York I was pleasantly certain that most of the volunteers would be as open-minded and curious as my friends in the civil-rights movement. I never visited a Freedom House in Maryland or Mississippi, Newark or Chicago, that wasn't littered with dog-eared copies of paperback books. James Baldwin, Ralph Ellison, LeRoi Jones—Norman Mailer, George Orwell, Paul Goodman—Camus, Fanon, Che Guevara: at our "Socratic seminar writ large" we were always studying their writings and debating their ideas. But only a few of the people I met in the Peace Corps read the contemporary thinkers who had influenced us so much—whose reputations, I had assumed while I was still at the Big Fiesta, spanned the entire middle class. Once, after we arrived in Ecuador, an editor at *Commentary* asked me to review Paul Goodman's book, *Five Years,* and I mentioned the assignment to another member of my group. Although he read every issue of the *New Republic* and *Newsweek*—much more carefully than I did—he'd never heard of *Commentary* nor did he know Goodman's name. That scrap of ignorance surprised me so much that I decided to survey as many people as I could find. Just three of the thirty volunteers I spoke to could tell me who Goodman was, although he was at the peak of his career as youth's spokesman in the adult world. I tried Norman Mailer. Most of them, if they'd heard of Mailer at all, knew him only as the author of *The Naked and the Dead,* or at best, they had gathered from college teachers and the literary gossip of Nixonia that he'd declined as a writer ever since he had published his first novel. Only five of the volunteers I talked to had ever heard of Lawrence Durrell. I couldn't find anyone in Guayaquil who had a copy of *The*

Wretched of the Earth on his bookshelves, though one could rarely walk through Greenwich Village or Berkeley that year without seeing at least one young person carrying Fanon's tract.

In training and in Ecuador the staff sought to discourage us from reading. Though the Peace Corps provided each of us with book lockers, we were frequently warned that to make extensive use of them was to abdicate our responsibility as volunteers. The assumption was that books were a device that allowed one to escape experience, not to understand it or enrich it.

Early in training I realized that most of the people in our group were as unaware of contemporary affairs as they were of contemporary writers. The Peace Corps furnished us weekly issues of the *News of the Week in Review* section of the *New York Times,* and each week our current-events teacher would give us a ten-question short-answer quiz which was taken almost directly from the previous edition of the *News of the Week in Review.* Most of the issues he discussed had been in the news for weeks and even months before we arrived in Albuquerque, so the trainees' average score of forty per cent could not be attributed to our temporary isolation or our demanding schedule. About one-third of them didn't know the name of the Chairman of the Senate Foreign Relations Committee, though Senator Fulbright's hearings into the war in Vietnam had been televised nationally throughout the winter. Most of them failed to identify the United States Ambassador to South Vietnam or the South Vietnamese Premier. Almost none of them knew the name of the Rhodesian Prime Minister who had just withdrawn his country from the British Commonwealth, or of the two candidates who were then seeking election as President of the Dominican Republic.

Their appetite for the news did not increase appreciably after we arrived in Guayaquil. Although most of them read *Time* and *Newsweek,* they did so mostly for information about American books, movies, fashions, sports. Inside the small clique to which Rachel and I belonged, which read *Newsweek* more carefully than *Time,* the small bits of speculation that are published in the Periscope section became the substance of inside-dopester's gossip, even though we knew that we were all reading the same magazine on the same day. But we could rarely sustain conversations about the 1966 elections, the war between the Arabs and the Israelis, the United States' wavering policies toward Latin America with most of the other volunteers. And it was even harder to interest them in the nuances of Ecuadorian affairs. During our first months in Guayaquil a few of us sought to organize a series of meetings at which local intellectuals, politicians, and professional people would speak to Peace Corpsmen, and any students from the two universities in town who were willing to attend. But it soon became apparent that so few volunteers were willing to participate that the sessions would be insulting to the Ecuadorians. We dropped the idea after most of our peers joined the staff in arguing that our attempts to learn about the city represented an evasion of our real work in the *barrios*.

Most of the volunteers preferred *Playboy* to any other magazine. They worked out an elaborate system for sharing that expensive publication as widely as possible. Of course they liked to look at the photographs of nudes, the suggestive cartoons, but I think that what really attracted them to the magazine was the voluptuous sense of Space Age luxury they found in its fashion sections, its advertisements: sex as an expensive stereo, love as a split-level home whose bars display the most exotic liquors in the world. I began to think that the most ambitious of them perceived the Peace Corps as an entree into the *Playboy* reader's dream world. Within a few years, if their records were good enough, they would be international civil servants (employed by private businesses or the U.S. government to jet around the world), James Bonds who took no risks, with Pussy Galore in every country.

The difference between most of the people I knew in the civil-rights movement and those in the Peace Corps was not so much of social as of intellectual class. (Of course, that is a journalist's generalization, and I could produce a dozen exceptions on demand. And it also represented a phenomenon that was more transient than I realized then. In the mid-sixties students at schools like Stanford, Yale, and Swarthmore, from which most integrationists came, had been exposed to liberating political and cultural influences that would begin to reach responsive undergraduates at the University of Arizona, Grinnel, and Lake Forest College, the common denominator of our Peace Corps group, a few years later. Radicals would continue to be a relatively small minority at such schools, but in 1969 left-wing organizations would have at least as much of an impact on Kent State and Purdue as their counterparts had on Yale and Columbia.)

Bookishness, cosmopolitan knowledge, characterized the families that had produced the movement's participants much more than did relative wealth. Many parents of integrationists earned several thousand dollars less each year than the Ford dealer from Phoenix or the hardware-store owner from Waukeegan, Illinois, whose children were in my Peace Corps group. But they were usually involved in professions that demanded broader educations and more catholic tastes: they were union organizers or teachers or ministers or magazine writers. Some time in the 1930s or 1940s the parents of many of the integrationists had flirted with socialism, and many of them had remained deeply committed to reform politics. They were proudly, sometimes boastfully, in favor of free speech, of peace, of integration. They believed that their country could be gravely, sinfully wrong, as it had been during the McCarthy years or the war in Vietnam. And they discussed those ideas with their children—the events, the books, the people that interested them. Often dinner was a time when talk was more important than food: the dinner table was a forum. Such parents believed, almost religiously, that the strongest families were those that practiced democracy at home.

They sent their young to colleges and universities like Stanford and Swarthmore not so much to acquire technical skills or make wide contacts immediately as to take real advantage of great professors, vast libraries, brilliant peers: to train themselves to think more creatively and carefully. To succeed, in their terms, was not so much to make money as to be recognized as an equal by the country's leading professionals and intellectuals.

To the parents of many Peace Corps people success meant rapid promotions inside conventional bureaucracies. They sent their children to college principally because a man with a B.A. could command a higher salary than a high-school graduate. Their dinner tables were places where Dad talked business or described the latest Rotary meeting, where Mom gossiped about the neighbors or talked about bridge, where you planned what kind of car you were going to buy next year, where you would take the next vacation. The Ford dealer and hardware-store owner had worked all their lives to expand their businesses, to develop a reputation for industry in their communities, and they were much more reluctant than the magazine writers, ministers, university professors whose children went to Mississippi to waste time by speculating on the country's strengths and weaknesses, by evaluating its role in the world. Indeed, the kind of self-criticism in which intellectuals indulge threatens them directly.

To put it crudely: most of the integrationists came from that small group of American intellectuals who insist that free speech and intellectual curiosity are the most important ingredients in what they still call the American experience, as if it has been some kind of especially rewarding adventure: the country for which J. William Fulbright speaks, or Eugene McCarthy. Most Peace Corps volunteers come from the much larger middle class to whom democracy and freedom mean the sacred right to buy a second car or build a new home: for whom America is the sterile paradise, and Richard Nixon its perfect leader.

III

A book like this should be a prism, not a beacon. But when you are trying not only to describe, but also to compare, numerous slices of society, not to mention distinct cultures, you cannot help but overstate yourself, if only to make certain paragraphs and passages more clear than ambiguous.

I know that the intellectual class is not so admirable nor Nixonia necessarily so terrible as I may have suggested in the last chapter. And now I am worried that as I continue to criticize Peace Corps volunteers according to standards very much like those to which the intellectuals claim to adhere I will encourage the liberal members of the educated elite who are reading this book, and their brothers, the radicals whose commitment to the abstraction they call revolution is mainly verbal, to maintain their comfortable disdain for the citizens of Nixonia while they continue to ignore their own complicated prejudices.

In fact, I have even less confidence in the intellectual class now than I did just before the Democratic Convention of 1968, when I first wrote the draft that turned into the previous chapter. In July of that year, when the McCarthy campaign was at its height, when you saw small paper peace daisies stuck to automobiles all over America, it seemed possible that the New Politics might, miraculously, release the decency that one hoped one had seen in this country during the best days of the civil-rights movement. But that illusion ended quickly: even before the Democratic Convention many pro-McCarthy organizations, which had seemed so dedicated to ending the war throughout the spring, began to dissolve amid vicious internecine fighting. For the most part, the combatants (student leaders who had urged their contemporaries to give the political system another chance by working for McCarthy's nomination) were the children of the intellectual class, fresh from Harvard and Swarthmore and Stanford, who had discovered to their great surprise that their idealism and youth, which had seemed like liabilities when the primary campaign began, could be used as a means of accumulating power quite quickly. Soon many of them became as crafty, as personally ambitious, as the old politicians they continued to oppose. Instead of cooperating to change the country, they conspired, group against group, to win small scraps of prestige and authority within their own organizations.

They were, it turned out, as careless of ideas, perhaps because they had been brought up among them, as many rich men's children are of inherited wealth. They transformed what they had learned from their great professors, brilliant peers, inside the vast libraries, into slogans and strategies that would help them win internal battles, used ideas as vehicles to power. Although they maintained their intellectuals' manner—casual dress, hip talk, bookish tastes—it was now largely a disguise, self-deception at best. They might have planned to read Toqueville or McLuhan as they jetted across the country from conference to conference (sometimes bearded, sometimes in jeans), but they usually found their minds distracted by tactical questions, or by reveries that were really masturbatory of the stunning political arguments with which they would impress their peers during the conferences' heated sessions.

The press reported that they were practicing the New Politics, but in fact they were the new politicians, no purer than the old (no less pure), considerably less reliable, who would continue to use the bold language they had learned when the war in Vietnam radicalized them into a fraternity of expense-account revolutionaries only as long as they depended on youth and blacks for their support.

Meanwhile, their parents, so skilled at practicing democracy at home, have been forced to confront an intimate challenge to their ideals in public events like the campus insurrections and the New York City school strike; sometimes, now, they sound more virulent, more narrow-minded, than the Ford dealer from Phoenix, whose Goldwater conservatism would have made them laugh just a few years ago.

The people I trust are those who view life as a constant dialogue with experience, not an attempt to shape ideas so that they fit intellectual abstractions, or to manipulate events so that they suit professional ambitions. Most of the members of our Peace Corps group who shared that quality with so many civil-rights workers were born on the fringes of Nixonia. Partly for that reason, people like Nick Zydycrn (from Riverside, California, his father a mechanic) and Ed Fagerlund (from Jackson, Michigan, his father an employee of the public-utilities company) made me even more conscious than I had been before I joined the Peace Corps of the condescending attitudes I had acquired with my Ivy League education and my left-wing politics.

I scarcely knew Ed until the few hectic months before we left Guayaquil. Still, during our first year there he was my private symbol for all the volunteers who believed so deeply in the Peace Corps' creed that our dissent sounded like an effort to evade our responsibility to help the poor by complaining instead of working. Though he sometimes seemed anxious to talk about a point I had raised in a meeting, the difference in our perspectives would usually cause the conversation to turn into a tedious, obscure argument. Then, suddenly, Ed became our ally. Later he told me that he had actually begun to move leftward when he took a summer job in Holland and began to debate the war in Vietnam with European students, and then during his training program, when he became a regular reader of the *New Republic*, the first liberal magazine to which he had ever been exposed. He had come to Guayaquil as part of a group assigned to organize credit cooperatives, and he spent a great deal of time trying to figure out ways of improving the Peace Corps' approach. But the other volunteers didn't seem interested in the points he raised. Then he discovered that the nature of his program was political, not economic. There was a board of Ecuadorians who were supposed to control the cooperative movement in the country, but they were thoroughly manipulated by AID, which selected projects according to the intensity of the threat of Communism in a given area, or the importance of transportation routes, not the demands of the local people. But no one on the Peace Corps staff seemed very interested in that information. So Ed began to discuss his findings with us, deepening our analysis of the United States' role in Ecuador with his remarkable ability to explore complicated questions down to their smallest details.

However, that happened long after we arrived in Guayaquil. Throughout most of this book Ed will be a silent presence: watching, listening, pondering the conflicting ideas and actions that surround him.

From the day I met Nick he made me feel somewhat guilty. As we discussed our reactions to the draft, very early in the training session, I discovered, as I frequently would in Guayaquil, that he was often able to act at times when I preferred to cling to the safety of continued discussions. Though he had joined the Peace Corps to stay out of the army, too, he had been defying his local board throughout the previous fall—the period when I decided to publish an objective article about General Hershey in the *Voice* instead of using that interview as an opening into a more risky exploration of my own tangled objections to the draft and the war. When Nick had been ordered to take his preinduction physical in San Francisco he refused to sign the oath asserting that he had never belonged to any of the organizations on the Attorney General's list. "They had no right to ask me a question like that," he said. For several months thereafter the FBI pursued him, both by letter and through interviews with his friends. Whenever he received a correspondence from them he underlined it, wrote sarcastic comments in the margins, and sent it back without complying with any particular request. Finally, the FBI asked him whether he had worked with Communists. He answered frankly that he didn't know. "What I believe in doing I do, without asking who my allies are."

But Nick didn't confuse particular beliefs with ideological certainties. He felt somewhat uncomfortable in the peace movement because many of the radicals he met there seemed as unquestioningly committed to unexamined points of view as his neighbors had been in Riverside, California. Their intolerance often offended him.

Nick and Ed have earned the ideas that many members of the intellectual class inherit.

I was never forced to brawl with my family over fundamental assumptions. We fight, of course, but usually over issues that are more stylistic than substantial. My parents object when I dress sloppily or use four-letter words in print or insist on expressing my ideas so angrily that I insult their friends and can't function inside the institutions in which they still believe. But they supported Geoff and me when we went to Mississippi, would have understood if we had resisted the draft, listened very sympathetically to Rachel and me when we began to describe the Peace Corps as an arm of U.S. imperialism. They are always eager to discuss our ideas and activities, and to help us whenever they can. In a way, their generosity has spoiled me, made me intolerant of people who are less open-minded.

Ed and Nick are forced to quarrel with their families over substantive issues. Their disagreements with their parents and many of the schoolmates they have known for fifteen or twenty years are fundamental, but they continue to love the people who reject their new beliefs. In order to express their loyalty, to protect shared emotions which they cherish, they have evolved a style which is much gentler than mine. They converse with people I dismiss, seek reconciliation where I am tempted to rupture a relationship. The man I mock as a Babbitt Nick perceives as the friendly Shriner who used to live next door to him in California, his Dad's good friend who took him hunting on dozens of happy Sunday mornings. I tend to denounce his ideas a little testily; Nick will spend hours talking with him, human to human, exchange personal reminiscences, gently force him to question assumptions he has never before considered.

I am very much a product of the intellectual class, of course, and many of the ideas I reject in this book, the instincts I seek to deny in my life, have been deeply etched into my personality. Perhaps it was this limitation, and the effort of will I was making to overcome it, that made my feelings about the Peace Corps staff and many of the volunteers so very intense. Certainly there are times when I was as intolerant of them as they, in my opinion, were intolerant of Ecuadorians. Luckily, Rachel is an extremely loving, gentle woman; she and friends like Nick and Ed restrained me somewhat, reminding me by their example that men aren't composed of ideas alone, of the attitudes they express in heated meetings, but of feelings, too, and fears and limitations which they want to transcend as much as I want to transcend my own.

IV

NEVERTHELESS, there were many ways in which the trainees in our Peace Corps group reminded me of the boys I had known at Choate. They were as convinced as the wealthy WASPs who had tormented me in prep school that America was the natural, just climax of the world's history (the sterile paradise was the end of the rainbow), and that anything different had to be worse. Accordingly, they were as narrow as most of the Choaties had been, as insensitive to the feelings of anyone they considered strange.

In addition, most of the trainees were very frightened. For many of them the Peace Corps was the first real test of a safe lifetime: strange people would be their superiors, an alien culture their home. Throughout training they waged a primal fight, against the tide of experience, to cling to the familiar world they understood.

They used nasty jokes, outright insults, to weld themselves together as a group and banish the unknown. As a result, the insensitivity many of them had absorbed from their families, friends, teachers, which they might have been able to control while they were still safe in Nixonia, began to seem like brutality when it was mixed in with their new fantasies and their new fears. In many cases, as the trainees passed through the looking glass of culture their ugliest features became the most prominent. Sometimes their behavior was silly, sometimes it was cruel. Always, their actions were rooted in their persistent, deepening desire to diminish the importance of anything unusual so that they could reassert their own superiority, or their manhood at least.

Their first obvious target was the trainee they nicknamed Batman because he had gone to a party in Albuquerque the week after we arrived disguised as the television hero. For nearly two months, until Batman was deselected, the group managed to maintain a kind of unity by defining itself against his peculiarity.

Batman was born to play the role that so many hippies spend years creating for themselves. He had an intelligence that was purely visual. Because he could express himself in sketches and charts much better than in words, he always carried a variety of colored pencils with him in a small sack that reminded most people in our group of a woman's handbag. During class he would spread the pencils over his desk so that he could take notes as graphically as possible. That act alone was terribly disturbing to most of the trainees. They would joke with each other about his behavior, or make fun of him directly, or even, when they were feeling frisky, swipe his pencils and hide them. The men had an even better chance to express their feeling toward him in gym. Then they would mincingly imitate the way he looked in soccer shorts (which was not the slightest bit effeminate) or try as hard as they could to knock him over during soccer practice. But he often made them look silly. He was one of the best players in our group.

His idea for organizing children in Guayaquil (and thus reaching their parents) seemed to me far more imaginative than anything I had heard from our community-development teachers. He would become a magician and win their interest and their confidence by performing tricks. He used to practice shuffling a rigged deck of cards in class or trying to make some trick balls he had bought vanish. When he heard of a hermit who lived in a cave near Albuquerque—half-mystic, half-magician, he was told—he disappeared from training for several days and served a short apprenticeship to the man.

Sometimes Batman would cut class to search through Albuquerque's stores for new magic tricks or stay in his room and try to invent his own. After a while, when he decided that there were no faculty members worth listening to, he began to spend entire afternoons in the Mexican section of the city or at Spanish movies to learn the language better.

I suppose that the trainees and staff resented Batman so deeply because he mocked the dull, stupid classes and rules they took seriously and did it without even realizing that he was offending anyone. Because he was living the way he chose, he assumed that they were living the way they had chosen, too. He was a free man who could not imagine that his peers were in psychic bondage.

One afternoon the Peace Corps had organized us into an expedition to go downtown and buy some shoes. It was an officially scheduled event. The bus was supposed to pick us up at one o'clock, drop us at the boot store at one-fifteen, return us to the campus bv two-thirty. By one-five all the trainees except Batman were on the bus. Five minutes later, as some of them were urging the driver to leave without him, he suddenly came running toward us, his bag of colored pencils wobbling from his belt.

Only a few people started the chant. "Kill Batman." But within a few seconds nearly everybody had joined in. "Kill Batman." Their voices nearly screamed as he approached the bus. "KILL BATMAN."

He came into the cabin and they were silent. Totally silent. He sat down alone in the front seat of the bus and gazed out the window. Then, a few blocks before the boot store, he got off the bus to spend the next hour searching for some art equipment.

If he was offended by what the trainees had done he never revealed his emotions, not even to Rachel and me after we had become his good friends.

I prefer to think that he remained oblivious to their hostile feelings, even after he was deselected at midboards.

I kept remembering my classmates at Choate who used to flatter each other with the phrase "That's mighty white of you" or ask "How far did you chase a nigger" for a particularly gaudy item of clothing? Some of them must be running the country again, high up in the Nixon Administration, those boys named Skip and Bunt and Biff and Kip and Cam and Bus.

One day at Albuquerque we were shown a film the British had made to show that their colonial system was benevolent. It was part of a smorgasbord of methods we were offered in our community-development course. The idea was that once we'd mastered the basic approach we might want to add our own wrinkles, like those pilots who wear gaily colored scarves on their bombing missions. So members of our group reported on a variety of theories, from SDS's to the British Foreign Office's.

The movie was about some Africans who were building themselves a maternity ward under the fond supervision of their British administrator, and one long scene was devoted to the process of construction. It showed an African carpenter hammering some boards together. He kept the nails in his hair and removed them one at a time as needed.

The trainees made as much noise laughing at the carpenter as they had shouting, "Kill Batman." Suddenly, it was as if the community-development class had turned into a Saturday-morning movie show for pre-teens, as if the African on the screen was Stepin Fetchit or a member of a minstrel troop which the director had filmed on location in darkest Africa for the special pleasure of his white audience.

Now, I don't know, maybe it's better for people to laugh at the aspects of foreign cultures which they consider strange instead of suppressing their amusement, as the prissy liberalism of the fortys and fiftys would have insisted. But one doesn't have to be unusually worldly to put one's amusement into some sort of perspective. Is the African who pulls the nail from his hair any funnier than the American storekeeper who pulls a pencil from behind his ear to total up some figures—or the American carpenter who holds his reserve nails between his teeth, and swallows them sometimes?

In Guayaquil the little Ecuadorian kids found the presence of the large, sweaty *gringos* who walked back and forth on their streets at least as funny as the trainees found the African carpenter. They would laugh at us frequently and delight each other with imitations of our language, which seemed so weird to them ("Wisheewasheewisheewasheewoo, meester?"). But in Guayaquil the volunteers who laughed at the African would get furious at the children who mocked them: try to swat shoeshine boys away from the tables where they were drinking beer, gesture as if to hit kids who stopped them on the street, chase them for blocks, and even slug them once in a while.

If a returned volunteer, a teacher, a psychiatrist had questioned the trainees' response to the movie he might have lodged a thought in their minds that would have helped them to understand the Ecuadorians. The sort of remark a Bob Moses would have made might have traveled straight to the heart of their insecurity, for despite all their bluster they really did not know how to construct the identities that would allow them to survive in the dangerous world they were about to enter. I wished that something would happen at Albuquerque like the episode during that other training program in Oxford, Ohio, when a group of black SNCC workers walked out on some Northern students who laughed during a movie about voter registration in Hattiesburg, Mississippi. Their anger, the subject of hundreds of discussions throughout the summer, finally helped us to understand our relationships with people like Papa Doc.

But there wasn't anyone in authority at the University of New Mexico who was critical of prejudices like those the trainees revealed when they saw the African carpenter. For the group's laughter fit in perfectly with the lessons we had been taught from the day we arrived at Albuquerque.

And I thought frequently of Choaties like Wade Eastbrook, the boy who had written FUCK YOU, YOU KIKE in my math book. In a way, I was grateful to the Peace Corps for giving me a chance to confront Wade again. Perhaps I would find a way to avenge that frightened, gawky, muzzy-ridden Fifth Former, myself.

Not that the trainees were anti-Semitic in the same sense as Wade must have been, but the gentiles in our group were certainly conscious of the fact that six of us were Jewish and were clumsily, often insultingly, unable to deal with that fact. Never, not even at Choate, have I been made to feel as conscious of my origin as in the Peace Corps—by staff members as well as volunteers—nor have I ever felt so keenly aware of biased remarks directed at other Jews.

Passover fell while our group was still in Albuquerque, and the three most religious Jews decided to show their gentile friends what the festival means. It was the kind of impulse that produces Brotherhood Weeks and Interfaith Councils. They bought matzoth and Mogen David wine, borrowed several copies of the Haggadah from the University of New Mexico Hillel House, found enough *yarmulkahs* to cover the heads of all the Jewish men. Then they gave a sort of guided tour of the ceremony, pausing at famous passages as if they were historic landmarks. The gentiles listened with a curiosity that was more than polite, and asked observant questions about points they didn't understand. If you regarded the ceremony as a prelude to similar experiences in Ecuador, when local people would explain their customs to the people who had gathered at the Seder, then for once you could feel optimistic about the trainees' prospects for success. They seemed interested. They made a good impression.

The service had been over for several minutes. As Rachel and I were about to leave, we walked into the range of a conversation between Hank Dawson, the most popular member of our group, its best athlete, its recognized wit (the perfect fraternity president), and Barney Ableman, the most devout Jew. The two trainees were supposed to be good friends.

"Man, that sure was boring," Hank said. "Now I know why Hitler put all you people in gas chambers."

I knew from experience that if I interrupted their conversation it would deepen whatever pain Barney felt. One day at Choate some Christian boys were teasing me—imitating the sort of accent that the character Mr. Kitzel used to use on the old Jack Benny show, calling me a "mocky"—and I was laughing to hide my confusion and my fear. Another classmate overheard the conversation and told them to shut up. Later on he asked me why I hadn't fought back. But his question hurt me more than their insults had. I wished he had never seen my embarrassment, had refrained from protecting me, would be obliterated now, and with him my shame. But I couldn't let him see such unmanly emotions. "Oh, we were just kidding around," I said. "Those guys are some of my best buddies, you know." From then on I always tried to avoid the boy who had protected me, as I feared Barney would avoid me.

But a few days later I did tell Hank that I resented his remark. At first he looked quite insulted. Then he told me that I had no appreciation for friendly chatter and implied that I had to make a political point out of every joke.

I'm sure that Hank really did intend his remark to be more affectionate than cruel. In his terms, it was a manly response to a situation that made him feel a little uneasy. To him the remark about the concentration camp was like the jokes Spiro Agnew made during his Vice-Presidential campaign about the "fat Jap" and "Polacks," out of the country-club locker room, that knots friends together even more closely than before. But so far as I was concerned, Hank's idea of friendly humor was especially disturbing.

For he could always excuse an insensitivity so profound as to be a form of racism by insisting on his good intentions.

Remarks like Hank's were produced not only by unusual situations like the Seder; often they were unexpectedly introduced into normal conversations.

Once, shortly after midboards, I went into Sandra Long's office to discuss the process of deselection. Batman was the only member of our group who had been sent home that early, and the decision seemed unjust to me. At least he should have been given a chance to prove himself during our month-long field experience in Juárez, as all the other borderline cases would be. Instead of discussing the issue she discussed my personality. I was "abrasive," she said, a "big-city type": that must be the reason I was so fond of protesting. I heard myself and other Jews described in those terms often enough to realize that they were code words, like "pushy."

The night before we were supposed to leave Ciudad Juárez I had a particularly curious conversation with a director of the field trip, a returned volunteer. The Mexican organization which had found us housing was giving a party for us, and by midnight we were all quite drunk. Nick Zydycrn and Rachel and I began to argue with some of the other trainees about the war in Vietnam.

"I agree with you that we should get out of there," the returned volunteer said, "but where I think you're wrong is when you say our real mistake was entering that war. No, our real mistake was entering World War II. That was when this country began to fall apart. We should never have intervened in Hitler's internal affairs."

Then I asked, "What about his treatment of the Jews?"

"Oh, I know all that," he answered. I had the impression he was slightly hurt because I seemed to be talking down to him. "But don't you see, that was Hitler's personal prejudice. What right did we have to change his mind by force?"

Now, I do not want these examples to suggest that there is institutionalized bias against Jews in the Peace Corps. During the time I was in the organization I encountered at least twenty or thirty people with "big-city personalities." I never heard of anyone who failed to become a volunteer or gain an appointment to the staff specifically because he was Jewish.

Nevertheless, in Peace Corps training, and then in Ecuador, I had dozens of conversations like the ones I've just described with volunteers, with members of the country staff, with officials from Washington. I rarely initiated them, although once in a while I would ask volunteers to quit using phrases like "jew him down," or tell them that it was not a mark of affection to call someone a "silly little yid," an epithet Hank Dawson once applied to Sam Bernstein, one of the most insecure members of the training group.

Long after we'd arrived in Guayaquil, Dan Stringer, Gshwend's replacement as field representative, gave me one reason that I made Peace Corps people so conscious of the fact that I am Jewish. He said that I got angry at the insults the volunteers frequently directed at Ecuadorians because, as a member of a minority group, I am "hypersensitive to such things."

The more I protested the more Jewish I seemed.

Apparently, by America's standards, to have a healthy regard for other people's feelings is to be "hypersensitive."

V

THERE was no single event that encouraged Rachel and me to drop the roles we had been playing since training began. Nor were we always even conscious of the fact that during those three months we were drifting toward a new, more dangerous definition of ourselves and our relationship to America.

If anything, we always tried to keep the protests we felt obliged to make as moderate as possible, even after we realized that we had a much wider margin for dissent than we'd imagined when training began. Though we continued to act like average, frightened trainees, we also began to feel that we were especially protected by Mankiewicz and Wofford. Letters from friends who were working in Washington gave us the impression that, although we were not at all famous, still we had enough of a reputation in the New Left to make the Peace Corps worry that its appeal to campus activists might be slightly diluted if we were deselected. Besides (it was not irrelevant), even if the members of the selection board felt that we were too contentious in class, they could not deny that we had the potential to become excellent volunteers or that we seemed better equipped than most other people in our group to refine and accomplish the objectives which Gshwend and Benitez had established for our project. In the slums of Albuquerque, and especially in the *colonias* of Ciudad

Juárez, where we spent the last month of training preparing ourselves for the *barrios suburbanos,* we formed close, lasting friendships with our neighbors which we were sure we could reproduce
in Guayaquil. (Rachel's Spanish was excellent, and though mine
was clumsy and ungrammatical, I could still understand and communicate virtually anything.)

In a very short while we began to feel comfortable with the habits and the customs of the Latin communities, eager to share in
their lives. When we got back to the training center we spent more
time trying to apply our experiences in the field to our futures in
Ecuador than we did debating the abstract theory of community
development. By the end of training we were percolating with
ideas for programs on which our entire group could cooperate.

If we had been entirely honest with ourselves, we would have realized that the frustration we felt with the trainees and the staff
was a more accurate indication of the mood that would persist for
two years than was the satisfaction which filled us when we lived
in the *colonias.* The idea of a team approach, which Rachel's so-
cial-work training and my pleasant memories of relations among
white volunteers in Vicksburg encouraged us to advocate as the
only way Gshwend's and Benitez' objectives could be realized,
was in fact a relic of our American past. How could we cooperate
with Hank Dawson, with the side of Benitez that wanted us to
teach Ecuadorians to throw paper into trash baskets, with Gshwend's desire to overthrow Jorge Rodriguez?

Those three months of training were the first time I had been
able to attain any perspective on myself since I left Israel, and I
suppose I should have realized how much I was changing. Certainly
as I thought about Hank Dawson's comment to Barney Ableman,
about the trainees' laughter at the African carpenter, their ignorance of the emotions behind the civil-rights movement, their
faith that the America which I partly saw through the eyes of a
Mississippi Negro was the most generous country in the history of
the world, I felt new deposits of anger collecting inside me, and I
welcomed them.

For I was becoming convinced, too, that I'd made myself go

limp at the Big Fiesta, had rid myself of strong, active emotions because of my well-bred belief that a radical should communicate his ideas rationally. If you are dispassionate you persuade people. Dress well on demonstrations, that's the way to influence Congressmen. Talk politely in living rooms, that's the way to convert moderates. Write thoroughly researched, carefully reasoned articles so that you can convince influential intellectuals that the New Left makes more sense than the Social Democrats. But the lesson I had learned from my months at the Big Fiesta is that you cannot reach other people by constricting your own personality. You might flatter the process with terms like "self-restraint," "belief in rationality," "desire for respectability"; you might condemn it with terms like "self-repression," "hypocrisy," "dishonesty." Yet whatever value judgment you made, one thing was clear: it didn't work. In the America of the 1960s when someone told you to "be reasonable" or to "think through your arguments more carefully" he usually meant either "accept my terms" or, simply, "be quiet." There were very few people who wanted to listen patiently and review their ideas. It was a time when people were moved by passions, not persuaded by calm words.

Those were not conclusions yet, just sensations in my pores; I was trying to feel my way to the point where barely related experiences in America might connect; thus, the ideas I projected back on my past in New York were also the product of my present experience in Albuquerque. I couldn't really see it then, but slowly, imperceptibly, my words and actions were becoming more passionate, less conventionally rational, at least in response to certain specific frustrations.

At first, when trainees made remarks like "you can take a poor person out of the slum, but you can't take the slum out of a poor person," Rachel or I would try to answer as politely and patiently as we could, explaining that such remarks offended millions of poor people in the United States, dozens of our personal friends. We would try to illustrate our explanations with descriptions of some blacks we had known in the South and the movement, trying to let people like Mrs. Hamer or Papa Doc or my partner

Bill in Chestertown communicate with the rest of our group through us. But the medium was the message. Trainees like Hank Dawson heard two "activists" (he used the word as if it was almost synonymous with "extremist") talk about an experience that was reserved for the elite (most of the trainees had worked during the summers we went South), boasting of their bravery, arrogantly implying that they were uniquely suited to survive in Guayaquil, too. Soon they developed increasingly strong, complicated feelings about Rachel and me, which obscured the people we were trying to describe.

We must have had twenty such discussions by the time we saw the movie about the African carpenter. But our group's reaction convinced Rachel and me that we hadn't communicated anything at all. I was angry enough to give a speech, too moved to converse when I asked them to "Imagine that he was in this room right now. Would you be laughing like that?"

Those words, I realized, had been stored up in my mind for two years, in search of a definition: ever since December 1964, when I had gone to an SDS meeting in New York and heard Tom Hayden denounce some white campus-based radicals who were trying to devise a strategy for the poor. "You don't know how arrogant you sound," Tom had shouted. "Can't you see that the people you're talking about aren't here?" I was then still a protégé of Al Lowenstein's, still accepted the idea that the main purpose of a SNCC project in Mississippi, or an SDS project in Newark, was to achieve certain obvious local goals and prod a friendly Democratic administration to pass broader legislation. Tom often infuriated me. He seemed intent on making his permanent home beyond the boundaries of what I considered reason and good taste. That day I could not figure out why he was so angry; I thought he might not be entirely sane.

Now I knew that Tom had been talking about something far more complicated and important than politics as I understood it, but I could not explain it to the other volunteers, even though I used a set of terms that Hayden would have scorned as reformist: "Please try to understand that when you do things like laugh at that movie you're revealing the exact attitude that Bob Moses and Fidel Castro have in mind when they use words like 'colonialism' or 'imperialism.' "

The trainees would have listened to a staff member who said something like that, but not to one of their peers. They must have seen me as an unusually intense young man, something of a prig, determined to chastise them for the most incidental human reactions, and with words like "colonialist" and "imperialist" that obviously came out of the left-wing textbooks used at Harvard and in the movement. So, soon they began to explain Rachel and me to themselves by attacking our personalities instead of discussing our ideas. But they still liked us too much, and feared us too much, to be as consistently cruel as they'd been to Batman.

Sometimes they did try to make me into a joke. They laughed at the sloppy way I wore my clothes, at the bookish references I made in class (especially once when I said that the *Odyssey* and T. E. Lawrence's *Seven Pillars of Wisdom* provided a perspective for the emotional experience I expected to have in Guayaquil), at my clumsiness in sports, at my huge appetite and my terrible table manners. And they tried to dull the effect of my criticisms by incorporating some of my pet phrases into the sharp, ironic language (Hank Dawson's invention) they used to push back experience when they talked to one another. (If you wanted to do something you were "up for it"; any problem was a "bind"; a worried man was "psyched.") "Old Cowan is really psyched. Archie the Activist, goll-ee. He's up for another group discussion. Let's talk about how bad we are. Prattling Pablo, what a bind."

But that kind of sarcasm came in flashes, and never lasted very long. Then most members of the group would accept us as willingly as they had when training began. They didn't seem able to find any set of terms that made us fully comprehensible to them. Sometimes after our heated discussions in class they would join us for dinner or for drinks at Oakie Joe's, the campus hangout, and confide their problems to Rachel or recount their experiences and review their ideas for both of us. On free nights I sometimes spent time with Hank Dawson and his friends playing basketball (I was only fair: too fat at first, too slow throughout) and poker (I usually won). The part of me that still suffered at the thought of being called a "weanie" at Choate was genuinely grateful to be accepted by the jocks.

But that kind of contact was too superficial: it did not begin to touch the part of the trainees' psyches that had been conditioned in Nixonia to believe that America is the most generous country in the history of the world. Nor did our careful classroom descriptions of the blacks we had known in the South, our reasoned interpretations of people like Bob Moses. By the end of training Rachel and I had decided that the only way we could push past the flabby complacency we had found in so many members of our group, even enter the shell of cruel humor that encased it, was to direct sharp, crude, honest statements straight to the heart of their personalities. And I was willing (much more willing than Rachel) to use the radical words that still antagonized my liberal friends in New York, that had antagonized me before I came to Peace Corps training. For I was very tired of qualifying words like "colonialist," "imperialist," "racist," or disguising my belief in their accuracy by attributing them to people like Bob Moses or Fidel. To my surprise, I had become too proud to apologize for perfectly legitimate words just because they set off bad vibrations in the American psyche.

But I don't want to simplify complicated feelings, lie about divided loyalties. Our enemies were our friends; our friends were our enemies. I might have gotten angry when Hank Dawson joked about the Jews or about me, but I also found him a very funny and engaging person and admired him because he had joined the Peace Corps even though he was exempt from the draft. I would rather spend an evening drinking and playing cards with Hank than with Papa Doc, and more: I'm almost certain that Hank will never harbor the same hatred for me that the black man I have spent so many pages defending did from the day we met.

Nor do I want to suggest that Rachel and I were fighting a solitary battle. From the day training began Nick Zydycrn was our very good friend. In Guayaquil we met Ed Fagerlund and Margot Jones, with whom I would be eager to share any experience. We were always very close to Bill and Joyce Dodge. Bill, who at twenty-five was auditing low-cost housing legislation at the Bureau of the Buget, has an athlete's sure sense of an organization's strengths and weaknesses and is one of the few thoroughly humane technicians I have ever met.

We wanted very much to share with the other volunteers the same kinship we had with Nick and Margot, Ed and Bill and Joyce. In a way, of course, we already did. Even when we censured people like Hank Dawson most angrily, fought the staff members as craftily as we knew how, we always knew that there were some hidden levels on which we were extremely close. So when we used words like "colonialist" (usually in a more personal context than I have placed it here) it was with as much love and hope as anger. We were begging them to enlarge themselves through their experiences: to join us as we attempted to grow beyond America, to become citizens of the world.

PART FIVE

I

FROM the day we arrived at training, our field experience in Ciudad Juárez had been described as the *summa* of our special program. We would live with poor Mexicans and observe their relations to the city government and to local self-help organizations. The month-long experience would help us synthesize all of the lessons about community development we'd learned in Albuquerque and provide a dress rehearsal for our years in Guayaquil.

By the time we were actually supposed to leave for Juárez, the Peace Corps bureaucracy had developed a guilty fear that the Mexican government would cause an international incident if it discovered that a bunch of trainees were living on its soil. Those people had so much pride, we were told by our superiors, that they refused to cooperate with the Peace Corps in any way. It was the Latin *macho* complex, a pride that amounted almost to paranoia: to associate with a foreign organization like ours would be to make a public admission of their inability to help themselves.

So the training-center staff provided us a cover. We were told to pose as a group of graduate students from the University of New

Mexico who had been assigned to live with the poorest people in Juárez in order to study the Spanish language and Mexican culture.

They couldn't have invented a more ridiculous disguise. The few people in the *colonias* who could imagine that a university student might get credit for spending time away from both his campus and his country were even more suspicious of us than the majority of Mexicans we met, to whom no set of words would explain why a group of North Americans would want to cross the border and spend time with them. What kind of people would live in the *colonias* to learn the Spanish language? The sophisticates connected us to the FBI, the CIA, the Border Patrol. Most people just thought we were crazy.

The fact that we were forbidden to reveal our identities gave us a peculiarly suspicious sense of ourselves: there must be something shameful about an identity which has to be hidden. The emotion, instilled in us so carelessly, would persist for two years, alienating the most conformist, most conventionally ambitious members of our group from the organization they had wanted to serve.

It turned out that the precautions were unnecessary. A week before we left Juárez one of the trip's codirectors told an El Paso television announcer that a Peace Corps project was training in the area. Apparently, he didn't realize that television signals can cross borders without passports: when the item was carried on the evening newscast it was seen in both El Paso and Juárez. The Mexicans realized what we were doing in their city, and for a day the Peace Corps was panicked. But soon it became clear that no one in Juárez, except the silly *gringos* who administered us, cared enough about us to ask us to stay or to leave.

When we got back to Albuquerque we learned that Peace Corps groups had been training in Mexico for years. The training-center staff, the desk officers in Washington, hadn't been efficient enough to ask the simple question of some coworkers that would uncover that fact. So they built a castle of fear from their false information.

For most of the month Rachel and I were able to maintain some distance from the Peace Corps staff. We were far more interested in Colonia Emiliano Zapata, where we lived, than in the organization that had deposited us there. The people we were staying with were so kind, so generous that despite their confusion about our role in the community they allowed us to enter freely into their lives.

It was the richest experience I had enjoyed in years. For the first time since I left Chestertown I felt as if I was part of a new, exciting culture, not of a movement composed of my peers whose avowed intent was to change a way of life it barely understood. And I lost some of my left-wing preconceptions as I realized that the America I was beginning to despise still seemed the land of promise to many of my Mexican neighbors, would seem a land of promise to many poor Ecuadorians, as Rudolfo Benitez had said. My disappointment in my country became a far more complicated emotion.

I kept a diary during that good month, and I want to include a portion of it here:

April 26, 1966

In the center of this town you see the terrible effects of American tourism. This is a backdoor culture—Americans treat the Mexicans here the same way many white Southerners treat their nigger maids—and the culture is composed of whores, of drugs, cheap liquor, gaudy wares, divorce courts, abortionists. Sometimes the Juárez that exists for *gringos* seems to have choked out the local Mexican life. The street cries you hear, and even the stereotyped accents in which the hawkers advertise their wares, provide a constant, grating reminder of the extent to which the United States controls its nearest non-Aryan neighbor.

Of course hawkers are the same all over the world—men with ambitions too large for their shrunken souls. At any moment thousands of them are at work on tourists everywhere, standing in port towns, border towns, the side streets of major cities, in front of bazaars and market places: asking "Johnny" if he wants a cheap lay, a cut-rate camera, some filthy pictures, a cheap tour of the city.

But back in the hills of Juárez, in the *colonia* where Rachel and I are living, you see traces of the same attitude the hawkers display in the tourists' city below. It seems depressingly necessary for people who live in this city to be parasites. A slum child's first reaction to a *gringo*, perhaps everywhere in the world, is to beg for money: "penny, meester?" But as you learn about the lives of their parents, people who are not beggers, you begin to realize how much of their existence depends on the willingness of the United States to heed similarly desperate pleas: to let them cross the border and work in the *gringos'* factories. That, for example, is the biggest problem that confronts our host, Domingo Guzmán. His wife, Paula, can visit El Paso to shop, but neither he nor his nephew can cross the bridge over the Rio Grande to earn the penny's multiple.

But it would be wrong to conclude that people here feel exploited exactly, that they consciously resent the United States for turning them into cheap labor. Indeed, the Americans they resent most are the liberals and labor leaders who finally persuaded Congress to pass laws restricting the number of *braceros* who can cross the border and travel from state to state picking fruits at low wages during harvest season. There are thousands of men here who pray for the time when they will be able to return to their old, exploited routines. Certainly the toothless old owner of the tiny *tienda* near the Guzmán house feels that way. He even seemed rather proud when he told Rachel and me that he had spent most of his life as a *bracero*. If he had been able to work in the United States for just a few more years he could have retired comfortably instead of running this fly-specked store. Of course his life as a *bracero* had been hard, he said, but from the vantage point of a *tienda* notched into a dusty hill in an insulated *colonia*, it seemed in retrospect almost a time of splendor.

In a house near by we talked to another man who has always been a migrant laborer. For more than a decade, in over twenty states, he has "chased the big dollar," but managed "to save only a few small ones." He would have settled in California, he said, but he couldn't get resident visas for his wife and his children. I asked him whether he had really wanted to spend the rest of his life in the United States. "Of course. Your country does much more for poor people than ours does. Just look around you. All the unhealthy, all the unemployed, all the hungry people. And what has our government done for them? Nothing. But in the United States your Congress always finds ways of helping poor people get richer."

Afterward, Rachel and I watched some kids play baseball and chatted with a few of them in our flawed Spanish. We met one boy who spoke English almost fluently. Where had he learned it? we asked.

"In an institution near El Paso."

"A school?"

"No, a jail."

"Well," I said, "you must prefer this neighborhood to that place."

"No," he answered quite seriously, "I wish I was back there. At least we ate regularly."

April 27, 1966

Don Pedro Martinez, a grizzled old man who is said to be one of the *colonia's* two most important leaders, came over to the Guzmáns' house this afternoon to meet us. It was clear that Paula has great respect for him. She was complaining about the poverty that pervades this community: "It's the government's fault," she claimed. "They never provide enough money to help us." Don Pedro rebuked her, sounding like a teacher or a priest. "Don't think only of the government," he insisted. "Think of the rich people who have your money. That is the enemy our fathers fought in the revolution."

He looked content when Paula obediently changed her mind to suit his views.

He had come to her house, he said, because he wanted us

to teach English to his twenty-year-old son. "He will need to know your language if he is to do anything useful with his life. Once I knew it myself"—he had lived in the United States for six years, working on railroad construction crews in Chicago, St. Louis, Los Angeles—"but a man forgets a lot in thirty years. I try to teach the boy what I know, but I want him to learn so well that he will never forget."

We went to Don Pedro's home, and while Rachel spent an hour teaching Chencho a few words and a handful of grammatical rules, Don Pedro and I conversed. Our talk was the real reason for his flowery request for an English lesson, I'm sure. He needed a polite excuse to learn something about the unusual *gringos* who are living near by. Can we help him? Do we threaten him at all? Were we placed in his neighborhood as the agents of some power that dislikes him?

It was a very formal occasion. Don Pedro made a ritual out of preparing to talk. First he carried two of his family's few wooden chairs—the kind one finds in first-grade classrooms—out to the little table on the scrubby front lawn where we would converse. Then, very carefully, he put his chair on one side of the table, mine on the other. Very graciously, he offered me refreshments. Did I want a Coca-Cola? Some cigarettes? Some matches, perhaps. "Pepe," he commanded his grandson before I could answer, "run down to the *tienda* and buy Don Pablo . . ." "No, Don Pedro," I interrupted him. "I am content just to talk with you."

I was teasing myself by imagining that we were a couple of professional diplomats negotiating the futures of our respective countries: Stalin or Churchill or Roosevelt at Yalta, dividing the world from the comfort of our wicker chairs. The fantasy seemed somehow appropriate, despite the actual setting. While we conferred about Don Pedro's adventures in the United States and his ideas about Juárez, his wife, an aging, shapeless woman with a plain brown face and black braided hair, stood off to one side, grinding out the family's laundry over a simple metal tub.

We sparred for a time, Don Pedro judging my Spanish (and

therefore my intelligence) while I tried to figure out his position in the community, one of the first steps in the community-development technique we learned in training. My Spanish, I gathered, was considerably worse than he had expected, which was a boon to our friendship: it meant that I was a little stupid, probably not the agent of a crafty government like that of the United States. His power, I gathered, is considerable.

When we talked about the United States he spoke English, both to impress me and to make the conversation easier for me. Then he was like a spic, a wetback, the hawker in the center of Juárez who insists that you chase a little fuckee-fuckee in his taxicab. His expressions seemed cunning: eager to add whatever money or material he could negotiate away from a naïve *gringo* to his meager supply of objects and wealth.

But when we spoke Spanish, discussing Mexico, local politics, the *colonia*, the revolution, he was an altogether different person. His face was straight and stern, his eyes were sad. He told me about the community's intense poverty and insisted that neither the government nor the private organizations in Juárez would ever be able to relieve it. Now his eyes, which earlier had seemed to be assessing my wealth, measuring the extent of my power, were examining my face to make sure that I understood every nuance of his Spanish. Did my blank expression suggest that I had failed to grasp an idea, that I had misjudged a word? He would repeat it, then, reshape it with his mouth and his hands and literally seek to lodge it in my brain.

The old man was both bitter and gentle, as proud as he was kind. The longer we talked, the more clearly he displayed his ambivalence toward me as an American and toward America as a country. Of course he wanted to live there, he said early in the conversation, when he still thought that I might be an agent or a powerful Mr. Charlie, but none of your people cares about a man like me, he complained later on, when he trusted me more. "We are the Mexican poor. Your government doesn't want us now." Years ago it had been much easier to enter the United States. "I know how to read and write. That was all that mattered then. Now you make us fill out all those papers, and you never accept us anyway."

Of course he has no illusions about the way foreigners are treated once they enter the United States. The years he spent there must have been the least pleasant of his life. "I never made a single *gringo* friend," he said. "Your people refused to help me, even when I was tired or hungry or lost. Once in Chicago I was with a Mexican who got into a knife fight. He cut another man all over his body. By the time the police came, he was gone but I was still there, trying to help. As soon as they saw me, a Mexican, they handcuffed me, strapped me by the waist, and took me to jail. Two days later I was tried in court, in English, and I had no lawyer. So I was sentenced to five years. They took me away to the city of prisons. Only a few people there could speak Spanish. I was very frightened because I was so helpless. Then, suddenly, two months later a man called me into his office and told me to go back to Mexico and never return to the United States. They took my picture and said that they would send it to police stations all over the country. Then they released me. I still remember how disappointed my family was when I came back to Mexico with no money at all."

I could see how "Pete Martinez" (as he would have been called in Chicago) might have looked like a "Mex" to most Americans: sleeping under the trees, awakening to talk about women, about liquor, about the pettiest kinds of thievery in his funny, slow, open-consonanted English. Generous, willing to work at times, but never able to follow instructions. And dangerous. Crazy when drunk or angry! But now, in his small community in Juárez, he was Don Pedro, a distinguished man, a person with more poise and dignity than most American mayors.

Toward the end of the conversation I asked whom he had worked with on the railroads. "We were all Mexicans," he answered. "Until the Negroes came along," I suggested, assuming that ethnic groups had fought for jobs. "No, I never worked in the same gangs as Negroes—or Irishers or Polacks or Swedes." (He was speaking Spanish, but he used the English slang.) "None of them. But I have watched many people work"—he was serious now, his eyes so concentrated that they nearly seemed fierce—"and I know that no one works as hard as a Mexican. The Polack doesn't like to work. When the Italian starts to hammer you see that he is lazy. He talks all day. But my people like to work and we are the best. I am telling you the truth. You will see."

April 29, 1966

I feel uneasy about my relations with Domingo Guzmán, my host. How can he really accept us?

He is such a shy man and so patient with his children—those qualities draw me to him. He sits silently at dinner listening to his *novellas*, the Mexican soap operas. He holds the baby Teresita in his arms, sometimes kissing her, occasionally cooing. The setting always seems a little eerie at that hour. The only light by nine o'clock, when Mingo eats, is the jet of flame from the kerosene stove and the flickering of a single petroleum lamp. The room is colored entirely in grays and smells intensely of kerosene and dust. We can hardly see Mingo's face as he eats his *frijoles* flavored with chile, drinks his three sodas, releases loud burp after loud burp. His head forms a swollen shadow on the chipped, peeling wall.

Sometimes, after he has finished eating, he begins to tease me in his hesitating, indistinct voice. Do I remember the Spanish word for "saw," for "apron," for "plane"? (He is as amused by my thick American accent as my countrymen must have been by Don Pedro's odd way of speaking English, but friendlier in his laughter.) Do I want chile on my beans, he asks, and before I can answer the question he and his two nephews are laughing hard. They remember the last time I tried to douse my food with the hot spice. I became almost uncontrollable. For nearly five minutes I could do nothing but sneeze and sweat and cry.

My weaknesses must please Domingo, for they allow him to feel that in some ways he is superior to a *gringo*. In a way, that makes me happy. It must help to afford him a new, more ample view of himself.

Is it the kerosene that weakens his eyes and makes them water so frequently? His face always seems to me a little unfocused: not plodding and deliberate like so many peasants, but permanently displaced and a trifle weak. Suppose sorrow or fatigue, not kerosene, makes his eyes tear? Each day he must get up at six-thirty, walk downtown and search for a day's labor, like loading ice on trucks, which he rarely finds. How can the man avoid worrying almost obsessively about his failure to earn money? Until two years ago Mingo drank steadily, too, wasting such a large part of his meager earnings that, despite having five children to care for, Paula had to go downtown every day and sell fruit. Now he usually abstains. At least she is free to take care of the kids.

They operate two tiny businesses out of their house. There is a shabby, rectangular box in the room where Rachel and I sleep. The box is almost covered by two slabs, one of wood, the other of stone. Inside, irregularly placed, are flaking, faintly dusty cakes of ice which chill the two crates of soda pop which Paula and Mingo empty into the box every day. Until very recently, when the ex-*bracero* opened his *tienda* on the corner, the family quickly sold all it bought. The profits, even then, were very slight. Now the business hardly seems worth maintaining.

On days when Mingo fails to find work in town he pursues a second private enterprise. Every afternoon at siesta time he and his nephew Mundo and his tiny son Pepe, walk to the fringe of the commercial city to rummage around in some of the wood shops there. They know the exact length of the board for which they are searching, and Mingo is willing to pay five *pesos* (nearly fifty cents) for the right kind. After he has carried the lumber home (a half-hour trip), he must walk another half mile to borrow a saw and a plane from his slightly wealthier brother who lives in a nearby *colonia*. Then, as a ritual, he draws several diagonal lines and drills a few holes. After some sawing, some planing, some hammering, the wood will have been shaped into a slightly knotty ironing board.

The task takes Mingo about six hours. If he is lucky, if the board sells within a month or so, before it begins to rot, he will earn ten *pesos*, a little more than a dollar.

The shop where Mingo buys his wood belongs to Los Hermanos Guzmán, no kin to him. But he and his brothers have acquired aprons with the store's name inscribed on them, which they wear when they work. Clearly these *hermanos* Guzmán dream of owning a wood shop one day, too. But they probably won't.

Mingo must think about such things every night, behind the half-focused blue eyes that tear and blur in the smoke and the kerosene. How does he feel about the fact that God has brought him five children he can hardly support? That his wife, at thirty-six, is tired and almost used up? Now Paula is pregnant again. One night Mingo told me that he loves to dance and his wife does not. I had the feeling that he was confessing something important. He must long for the pleasures, and the material goods, that are so evident whenever he enters the tourists' city. But he will never possess them, and his family is no substitute for his peasant's dream of luxury. There is so little relief. Perhaps he takes another woman occasionally, but he is too responsible now that he's quit drinking, too worried about the future, to escape the dreary problems of poverty for long.

Now, enter Pablo the *gringo*. Thank God I am a bit of a fool, for that makes my presence more bearable. But I am also a *yanqui* fool with *yanqui* possessions—two expensive suitcases, a flashlight, some expensive glasses—and some sort of rich *yanqui* organization behind me. And I have a beautiful *yanqui* wife besides. Whenever Mingo looks at Rachel he must think of Paula, of the youth he has spent and the pleasures he will never enjoy, and feel some envy of us.

My relationship with Mingo makes me wonder even more than usual about the Peace Corps' strategy. For, as a community developer committed to peaceful change, I am in a position to offer him only a slow, limited form of progress. But I know that he has the moral right to reject my offer and take much of what I possess—to make a revolution. It was that conflict, though with men fifteen years younger than Mingo, that tore the civil-rights movement apart.

May 2, 1966

Sounds of the *colonia*: children crying, dogs barking, the Pepsi man chanting, the fruit vendor hawking, angry mother scolding, carts clanking, cars starting. The noises resound through the dust, through the heat, as if they were all concentrated in a single small dry tunnel.

There are no rich colors here, no soft smells. The sun parches the skin on your arms. Its rays intensify the smells of human shit, animal shit, of dust, the choking vapors of kerosene.

Sometimes, walking up one of the hills along a rough, tilted road, I feel as if I am back in the desert behind Beersheba. Each rise is a crater, and all it seems to shield is more sand. Then the presence of a house is a wonder.

The houses are sunk, piled, placed at all angles on the dusty brown hills, and the community straggles on for miles and miles —running up steep slopes that appear almost mountainous, dipping down inside rocky valleys.

Layer upon layer of cactus, of rock, of desert flower have been scraped from these hills in the past decade as thousands of people fled the decaying towns in the interior of Mexico and settled here, wretched family after wretched family.

First they built one-room shacks of tarpaper and mud, but by now, a generation after the first migration, almost all those hovels have been replaced by firmer structures: houses with adobe walls, with hard-packed roofs of mud and dirt, with floors of concentrated earth or even concrete. In every yard there is an animal or two: hens to provide cheap breakfasts, perhaps a pig, dogs and cats.

Then there are the kids, so tiny, so ragged, so brown by birth and from the sun that they blend perfectly with the parched land: each the product of a cramped, lonely night, of a man and a woman, a Paula and a Mingo, with normal animal capacities for pleasures of all sorts, and nothing, nothing to do—except listen to soap operas on the radio and make new children so silently that the others, products of earlier lonely nights, are not disturbed.

How can the few *pesos* that Mingo scratches from his skimpy jobs that satisfy the most peripheral human needs—for ironing boards, for soda pop—ever provide Teresita and Pepe and Maela and Socorro and Cuca what they need to push beyond this community?

But maybe the kids will go in a direction their parents can't imagine. Yesterday Rachel was talking with Maela, Mingo's eleven-year-old daughter, about her studies. She knew a lot about Mexican history and a little about her country's literature. Then they talked about studying foreign languages.

"I don't want to learn English," she insisted. "I'm a Mexican, and Spanish is my language. I'm proud of that."

May 3, 1966

Perhaps Don Pedro was right when he boasted last week that Mexicans were the hardest workers he had seen during his years in the States. I have never seen such energetic people, not even in Israel. They struggle at least as hard as the fabled frontier Americans to improve themselves, make their kids' lives more comfortable, even though the odds against them are at least as high as the odds against those hardy New Englanders who traveled to Oregon by wagon train.

Most of them seem to care more about their houses than anything else. Every day, at any hour of the morning or afternoon, you can find dozens of old men busily trying to transform their old homes into more comfortable dwellings. They even work during siesta, when the sun here is as hot as in Mississippi or Beersheba, hours when our American legends insist that every Mexican male is sound asleep. They grind their adobe bricks and use cement as plaster, shaping their materials so that the houses look as if they are made out of stucco; they strengthen their tarpaper roofs with mud and sand; they use rejected, secondhand lumber, for which they scavenge everywhere, and mud, adobe, and even cloth, to build new homes which will provide their children and parents space to sleep comfortably.

But there are disturbing ways in which this community already resembles suburban America: its people are prejudiced against Negroes and against Jews.

This evening Rachel and I paid Don Pedro a brief visit. Now that Pedro realizes we are not here to challenge his authority in any way, he has become rather fond of us and acts as our patron. I think he enjoys talking with me, although our conversations may seem a little tedious to him, especially at night, when my Spanish collapses. Or maybe he gets satisfaction out of my being so dependent on his help with a foreign language. Sometimes his guesses about the amount of Spanish I know insult me. "*Yo creo en mi Dios, Pablo,*" he told me last night in what was to be an argument about the Jews and Jesus Christ. "*¿Sabe usted que quiere decir 'Dios'?*"

Don Pedro had served Rachel and me coffee in the austere little bedroom which is also his entire house. I have never understood why Pedro, who is clearly the patriarch of his large family, voluntarily lives in quarters that are the most primitive on the property. His room is littered with clothes, dusty, without electricity; he and his wife must sleep on a narrow single bed. His oldest son Roberto has electricity and a television set; Pedro has only a single kerosene lamp. Chencho, who doesn't work, has a gas stove and refrigerator in his small portion of the house; Pedro has only a kerosene stove. The single object that makes his room seem at all modern is a tennis racket that hangs gracefully off a nail on the wall. It looks like a champion's souvenir. Don Pedro has never played a game in his life.

He wanted to talk about religion. Perhaps he suspected that since Rachel and I have no clear political mission here we are really undercover religious missionaries. There are already Jehovah's Witnesses, Seventh Day Adventists, and a Baptist sect in this small Catholic community, so I don't blame people for wondering if we have some special brand of God we want to sell them.

But I think that the old man was genuinely astonished when I told him that I am Jewish and Rachel is a Unitarian. "*No me diga, Pablo. Esta tomandome el pelo.*" He couldn't believe that I am Jewish. And if I was Jewish, he couldn't understand why a beautiful gentile like Rachel had married me.

For he was absolutely convinced that my people had murdered Jesus Christ. That was what he had learned in school, and his sons and daughters after him. He tried to rebut my arguments by quoting papal encyclicals, biblical scriptures, half-remembered grade-school textbooks. Since I had never been forced to argue the point before, I must have sounded particularly stupid: I didn't know what to say and was unable to put my sputtering objections into decent Spanish. But finally, after trying to communicate the version of Jesus's trial and the Crucifixion that I have always believed, the one that emphasizes Rome's guilt, I did manage to negotiate a concession from Don Pedro. "I like you too much to believe that you killed Christ, Pablo," he said. "It all happened a very long time ago. Perhaps you Jews have changed since then. But you have to admit that it was one of your people who did it in the first place."

If I had been listening to Hank Dawson, I would have been outraged. Nor am I sure that I should expect greater tolerance, greater sophistication from Hank, or the other trainees, than from a wise old Mexican like Don Pedro. All I know is that I like Pedro better than most of the *gringos* I've met lately. He seems to have survived hardships they can't imagine. In fact, he reminds me of many of the old European Jews I knew in Israel who seem to have won their wisdom in the concentration camps.

I let the argument drop in order to sustain our friendship.

Later on Chencho and his brother Roberto invited us to watch television with them. They had tuned to a variety show from California and had already transformed the fact that one of the chorus girls was a Negro into an in-group joke. Every time she appeared on camera they would laugh and hoot. After a few minutes Chencho asked Rachel and me one of those gentle, cross-cultural questions Peace Corps volunteers are supposed to answer gracefully. "How come you people let those savages appear on television?" Now, what do you say to a remark like that, especially in a strange language? *"Pues, a mi ellos no parecen salvajes."* Well, to me they don't seem to be savages. *"Yo tengo muchos amigos negros."* Some of my best friends are Negroes.

Rachel tried to explain that we had spent three years working in the civil-rights movement in order to discredit arguments like Chencho's. *"Ustedes son gringos locos,"* he answered, but rather affectionately. Then: "The black people are apes. Even your American soldiers who come over here to sleep with our women. The black ones always get arrested first and stay in jail the longest. Would you marry one?" he asked Rachel directly.

"If I loved him."

"And would you let your daughter marry one?" he asked me.

"Of course."

"Gringos locos."

People are the same all over the world—they despise one another.

May 5, 1966

A pencil sketch:

Lucho Hernandez—The old man who sits, every afternoon, on a wooden chair that occupies the full width of his newly shaded front porch, hungrily reading the thick brown-and-white comic books that are the printed equivalents to the radio *novellas* Mingo enjoys so much. A twelve-year-old girl runs across the rocky dirt road to exchange her latest buy, a particularly sexy story, for his mystery thriller.

His face is bisected by a long white patch of skin that is exactly the same color as the sombrero he is always wearing. On his chin there is always a bristle, almost thick enough to clutch, which neither grows nor vanishes. His teeth, which slant in all directions, are chipped and yellow, stained by the cheap, thin cigar-smelling cigarettes he is always sucking. When you see this odd, angular array of brown whiskers and tooth stumps slowly separate into a smile you get the feeling that their owner is an unusually disoriented human being. The impression is heightened when you hear him talk. His rapid, murmured Spanish, splintering along his tongue, is made even harder to follow by the fact that the old, liver-marked hand nearly always obscures his mouth.

I have spent enough time with Lucho to know that he is dominated by his wife, the massive La Chepa, and by his four rather ugly daughters.

But if you look into his eyes you see a somewhat different man. Not that they are wise, exactly, for they do not watch you intelligently or suggest much mental activity when he talks. But they do reveal a man whose capacity to endure has endowed him with a kind of strength that I barely understand. How many strange, distant states has Lucho journeyed to in search of a winter's wages during his twenty years as a *bracero*? Followed how many half-understood commands? Sat smothering in how many stench-ridden boxcars as he was shipped, like a rusting old plow, from one harvest to the next? Been caught by the law how often, forced home, then sneaked back to America?

They are eyes that have grown accustomed to peering out over vast, rich, ripening fields—the eyes of a poor, drifting Mexican picker, always lonely, never able to win from life more than his tiny wage.

Watch him now as, grudging the time away from his comic book, he helps to build a fence in front of his house. How slowly he moves the shovel. Surely a younger man could compress a minute's work into his ten seconds. But somehow the pile of dirt vanishes, more rapidly than if I had shoveled it, and Lucho feels no fatigue at all.

Two years ago Lucho and La Chepa moved into one of the most luxurious houses in Emiliano Zapata. It was built and furnished by one of Lucho's brothers, apparently the most ambitious member of the family, who thirty years ago left his ancestral *pueblo* in the interior to become a jockey. Now he works as a horse trainer near Los Angeles, earning nine thousand dollars a year.

An entire family can live inside the Hernandez house, not scattered in individual cabins as people are at Don Pedro's. There are four separate rooms, and they all open onto an ample hallway. The walls between them are much sturdier than those inside the Guzmáns' or Don Pedro's houses, and they seem to contain either stucco or some kind of concrete as well as the more flimsy adobe brick. In the largest room, where the grandparents sleep, there is a double bed covered by a rather modern, fluffy pink spread. It looks not only solidly comfortable but positively haughty when you compare it to the sagging frames, torn mattresses, and shredded sheets on which the Guzmáns sleep, four to a bed. A few feet away, against the smooth green walls, there are two long couches, made slightly showy by their bright-red exteriors. In the home of a Southern Negro one would respond to such furnishings with slight aesthetic distaste. But here, where poverty is more extensive and more concentrated than in Mississippi, the naked fact of a possession, any object that eases this burdensome life, is its own justification.

La Chepa's two oldest daughters are in their early twenties. They can find work in the States much more easily than their father and his friends. The harsh laws that restrict the ex-*braceros* cannot be enforced on their daughters, who cross borders to work as maids for some of El Paso's richest families. They are illegally employed, of course, but the Border Patrol can rarely penetrate the subtle conspiracies between the Mexican poor and the wealthy Anglo women. The girls demand such low wages: it is worth it for their American *patronas* to learn how to evade the Border Patrol and to learn enough Spanish to evade the language barrier. That way they can save themselves hundreds of dollars each year.

La Chepa's oldest daughter is already married and has a three-year-old girl—*una blanca*, she boasts. Her husband is light-skinned, too, and so is she: as long as the two of them earn a little money and don't dissipate themselves in drink and infidelity, they are assured of a degree of respectability. Their ambition, La Chepa says, is to move to El Paso when the children are old enough and enroll them in the best public schools.

The second daughter is the source of great sorrow for the family.

Her *novio* (fiancé) was the first Mexican national to be killed in Vietnam.

A poor boy from a small village in the interior, he had been lucky enough to enroll in a bilingual school immediately after his family arrived in Juárez. His English quickly became fluent, and he acquired a working knowledge of electronics. Immediately after his graduation he went to El Paso to find a job. He hoped to earn enough money to matriculate at a business school and to provide for La Chepa's daughter, to whom he was already engaged. She was doing domestic work in El Paso, so they saw each other nearly every night. Even though they were not yet married, they began to pool their money, to save for the American future of which they dreamed.

But after a year the Texas border authorities discovered that he had crossed over from Juárez without the proper papers. They threatened to deport him. Of course he was desperate. He had solemnly promised La Chepa that if he married her daughter she would become an American, too.

So when someone told him that any foreign national who serves in the United States army can become an American citizen he realized that he had no choice but to enlist. After all, it was only two years. Within six months he was in Vietnam.

This afternoon Rachel and I visited the bereaved woman. She showed us the newspaper accounts of her *novio's* death and the letters he had sent her. He seems to have been a cheerful fellow. At least he never complained in his letters. And he said that he was quite grateful for the things the army was teaching him.

Neither Rachel nor I knew what to say to her. Should we apologize for our country because it enforced a law too harshly? Insist, as of course we both believe, that the war is both unjust and pointless? But statements like that would rob her *novio's* death of the little meaning it has. For a moment both of us were tempted to praise the war, or at least to say that we were grateful that her fiancé had died to preserve our freedom. But we couldn't lie so grossly either.

As she wept, we stumbled to find the appropriate words, not because our Spanish was inadequate but because there was no way to express to the Mexican woman our horror at the fact that another foreigner had been murdered in our government's ghoulish war. After all, he didn't think that the American government was ghoulish. He was willing to risk his life to live under it.

If you go shopping in El Paso with a poor person from Juárez, the nature of the relationship between the cities becomes even clearer. To a *gringo* Juárez is a city where sex, sin, liquor, divorce, abortions can be bought cheap. To a Mexican man El Paso means a good job; to his wife it is a town of bargains. Luxuries are cheap in Juárez, necessities in El Paso.

May 7, 1966

An entire section of El Paso is devoted to Mexican trade. Near the border the Southwestern city looks almost Eastern. A few blocks thick with warehouses fringe off into some shabby apartments, some small Spanish stores, and then the whole area explodes into a quarter mile of Spanish-language department stores, five-and-ten cent stores, clothing stores, grocery stores. Everything material in El Paso has a resonant, lasting quality that is absent from the *tiendas* and tourist dives of Juárez. In shops like Newberry's, Woolworth's, Jenson's the goods seem to form their own horizon, to span onward for miles. Even the labels on the products give one a sense of ampleness, for they suggest that no matter how much is bought more will always remain.

A small town in Utah furnishes penknives—one night La Chepa's husband might have passed through there on his way to a job picking apples. Detroit, Cleveland, Cincinnati, New York—those cities, names on the product labels, are all dream worlds that inspire the most opulent fantasies in the imagination of the Mexican shoppers. A job in the factory that produces the cheapest, shabbiest item on the rack would provide Domingo Guzmán's family with conveniences it now can scarcely imagine.

As you walk through the stores in El Paso, your imagination begins to transplant wares that seem so common on the shelves in front of you into the shabby houses in the *colonia*. The three candy bars you can buy for a dime would give Paula's children a treat they would happily remember for a week. The gaudy green-and-red fabric that sells for a quarter a yard would allow Paula to make herself some curtains that the entire neighborhood would envy, even Don Pedro and La Chepa. The toy soldiers, toy houses, toy medical sets—thirty-nine cents at the most—would excite the Guzmán children for months.

But those are not products that Paula can afford. She has come to buy school clothes for her kids, no more. She must search for the very cheapest cloth in all of El Paso, remnants, certain to wear out within a year. She must test it with her fingers and evaluate it in her mind, and finally, when she buys the material from which she will make all her children's clothes, reckon the expense of only eighty cents into her over-all budget for the next month.

If she buys the material to dress her children for school, she will probably have to deprive them of meat for a week.

In the El Paso stores all clothing and small household items are described in Spanish. Furniture and large appliances are called by their English names.

As you cross the bridge from Juárez to El Paso, entering the gateway to North America, the climate suddenly begins to seem a little brisker. The illusion is produced by the slight wind that drifts upward from the murky, trickling Rio Grande. But it heightens one's sense that one is leaving a land of gentle, leisurely politeness for another of violent efficiency.

May 11, 1966

Some theoretical notes—on a bitter afternoon:
Several assumptions about the communities where we will be living in Ecuador are thrown into question by our experiences in Juárez.

The returned volunteers keep talking about a newly urbanized peasantry which has absolutely no sense of organization. The Peace Corps volunteer, it has appeared, will only have to lend his presence and the right set of tactics for the new organization to materialize. This theory of political behavior has been supported by the medical staff's remarks on hygiene and food, Benitez' on public administration. The over-all impression one gets is of people just one remove from animals, for whom any civilized activity is miraculous. So Jane Snider can tell a community-development class, with total seriousness, that if she teaches one woman in Guayaquil to embroider flowered doilies her years in the Peace Corps will have been worthwhile.

Yet the *colonias* of Juárez, which consist almost exclusively of the newly urbanized, are surprisingly well organized. In virtually every one of them there are political party organizations, self-help organizations, church organizations. However irregularly these groups meet, and however far their practice falls behind their rhetoric, they do assist the poor.

And the poor themselves do not seem so unsophisticated. The Guzmáns have less money than almost any family in Emiliano Zapata. But one night Domingo was talking about an organization in the *colonia* which is supporting poor people against a city that requires them to pay unjustly high taxes, and his ideas were very much like those which SDS organizers like Tom Hayden and Richie Rothstein try to communicate to American poor people. I asked him whether local leaders like Don Pedro were much help in the organization. "Some," he answered, "but there are things that we must do for ourselves. There must be an organization, but inside it we must act on our own." If people in Guayaquil have ideas like that, then they are actually one step ahead of the Peace Corps volunteers—they should be organizing us.

The staff at the training center kept insisting that the slum dwellers would be ignorant of their political situation. But most of the people we have talked to here, however poor or recently arrived, have a pretty thorough knowledge of the *colonia's* six-year history, and are very conscious of the differences between the federal and municipal political parties. Everyone we have talked to seems to know, for example, about the fight that preceded the *municipio*'s acquisition of the rich man Ramos's land. They can describe the part that Lopez Mateos (who was then President of Mexico) played in the transaction, and the reasons that he and they were betrayed. Thus, they understand why they must pay the city for their land now, and Mingo's group has even gone so far as to analyze alternate ways of protesting.

Moreover, all of the poor people we have talked to—and they live in different parts of the *colonia*—know the names of past and present political leaders and the history of interparty warfare. They can date the changes in their living conditions—tell you when the road was introduced, for example—and some can tell you who was responsible for the improvements. (I doubt that people in Chicago know as much about their block leaders, their ward captains, their aldermen.) Furthermore, the Guzmáns and Don Pedro and Lucho and La Chepa all can name the men who have been President of Mexico since the revolution, can gossip about them, can describe what they did for poor people. They know the name of Juárez' Mayor and something about the city's bureaucracy.

And they know, both personally and organizationally, exactly where to go to petition for better government service. Mingo now has a better sense of whom to talk to and what office the bureaucrat resides in than a Peace Corps volunteer like me could acquire in a year. It's hard to see how I could really be of much help to him.

May 12, 1966

It gets hotter in Juárez, the *colonia* stuffier. No longer do Rachel and I spend all night fighting over our single blanket. The heat intensifies the odors, too: our room is never free of the smell of kerosene now. The family's room smells thickly, cloyingly of all the bodies that sleep there in shifts, around the clock, depending on the hour one must go to work or to school. "In the summer we spend all night outside," Paula says. Their beds: dry, rickety wooden chairs, lined three together, balancing uncertainly on the sloping, tumbling dirt terrain.

Summer or winter, though, Sunday is the day when working-men feel free: yesterday, for the first time since we came, Mingo was drunk. Rachel came home from Don Pedro's before I did and soon left again to visit La Chepa, a bit frightened. As I was walking down the path to the house, I realized that the children were not coming out to greet me as they usually do. Then I saw them standing together on the patch of dirt in front of the house, looking very worried.

"*No entras, Pablo*," Pepe said to me. "*Papi borracho*." (Don't go in. Daddy's drunk.) But just as the others were echoing Pepe's advice, I heard Mingo calling me. He was standing outside the kitchen, leaning heavily on its rickety door while he pinched Paula's ass and her thigh. The message she had for me was that Rachel had gone next door. Then, with great good humor, Paula asked me whether I had eaten a *perro caliente* for lunch. Until Rachel told her what a hot dog was, several days ago, she had imagined me running up and down the streets of Juárez trying to catch the dog I would later fry.

I didn't yet realize the contrast between the stereotype before my eyes—a lurching husband who was trying to pinch some sex into his pregnant wife—and the real people who were talking to me. Still a *yanqui*, I was frightened and embarrassed for the moment, so I retreated to the other side of the house. The kids were there and I thought they were frightened, too. I remember the stories my father tells about the nights my grandfather used to come home and beat him. I wanted to join Rachel at La Chepa's. But then I decided that I should be available to help Paula and the kids in case Mingo went out of control.

He called me into their stuffy bedroom, where he was sprawled out on the bed that he and Paula share with Teresa and Cuca. He looked more disarrayed than dangerous, his shirt unbuttoned, scattered bits of sawdust (remains of the week's ironing boards) fleck-ing his hair. "*Vamos al centro, Pablo*," he said, his voice on a crutch, hobbling along despite its incessant hiccups. If I said no, I didn't want to go downtown with him, I wondered, would he be insulted? Maybe he'd think that *gringos* go drinking only with their own kind, not with the likes of him. But how could I say yes? I just didn't want to spend the rest of the day drinking cheap whisky—the smell, as it came off him, was of wild, desperate parties, of deathly hangovers. So I told Mingo I wouldn't go with him *"¿Pues, tienes miedo, Pablo?"* (Well, are you afraid, Paul?) Was my nervousness that close to the surface, then? *"Vamos al centro, Pablo."* The entire routine repeated itself two or three times, with Paula interrupting to translate my noes into more fluent Spanish or to coax an even sharper negative out of me. The children were all in the room, too, and Maela kept trying to mouth an answer for me. But I certainly can't read lips in Spanish.

Finally, Mingo broke the cycle with an addition to his constant question. *"¿Tienes miedo de Raquel, Pablo?"* He thought I was hesitating for the same reason he was: because the old lady would get angry. Suddenly the whole thing seemed quite funny to me. A drunken man trying to use me, sober and *gringo*, to get free from his wife and go on a spree. I was able to smile, and I sat down on the bed. Mingo grinned, too, and then, to make this abstract spree of ours particular enough to be tempting, he started listing streets that were popular with *gringo* tourists to which we would *vamos*. There was no way I could show him how profoundly I hate the *gringo* tourists or how mortified I would feel making the rounds of all the tourist dives while towing around a drunken Mexican who would seem to be my factotum. So I refused his invitation again. He asked me if I was scared again.

By now all the children except Socorro were with us in the narrow, musty room. Mingo had begun to tone down a bit. But to remind me of our rendezvous he would describe a cross with his fingers and then stick a thumb in his mouth to suggest a slug of whisky. The kids seemed to find him as funny as I did. Soon our conversation shifted, though, all the way from going downtown to various peculiar animals whose names I didn't know. Then Mingo asked me, *"¿Que quiere decir 'chici'?"* and from his gestures I realized that the word meant "tit." He took off his shirt and pointed at his nipple, then touched Paula's breast. Soon she and I had begun one of our frequent cross-cultural conversations, this time about whether more American women or Mexican women breast-fed their young.

But Mingo had no interest in that subject. Had I ever heard of Cantinflas? he asked. Yes. "What is the comic's real name?" I didn't know. Mingo told me, and then he began to stiffen his arms and legs and thrust them about in a pantomime of uncoordination. The effort had made him hungry despite the fact that he'd just vomited a large lunch, and he kept sending the children to the corner *tienda* for bags of pork rind. He would eat part of the flaky food but lose most of the bagful on his pants and on the floor. All the while he kept telling Paula how hungry he was, and she would answer—patiently, lovingly, but in the somewhat whiny tone she sometimes uses—that no, Mingo, you shouldn't eat, you have to go to work. Rebuffed again, he would lie back on the bed, scattering pork rind on his stomach, shut his eyes, and almost fade off into sleep.

Once Cuca came over to the bed to hear some request that Mingo was making. He pulled his hand way back, as if he was cocking a bow, and then let fly at her rear. It was meant as a love tap. She started to cry. With more grace than he had displayed all afternoon Mingo hurried over to the corner where his daughter was now cringing, picked her up, and held her in his cradled arms. For a few minutes they stood like that: Mingo, completely sober, totally serious, rocking the whimpering child.

A few minutes later, drunk once again, he lurched out to the kitchen, where he hoped to find a decent meal. But before he got there he fell to his knees and then toppled face downward, and almost instantly went to sleep amid the family's six chickens. He had put an old, dirty towel around his head to muffle the noise of the flies and the kids.

Mingo has one of the most resonant belches I have ever heard. After each meal he releases it, more of an eruption than a level human sound. Rocks might be sliding down the burp, or great quantities of dirt shooting upward. Of course it embarrasses no one.

Tonight I told Paula that I had learned some words of the Indian dialect that La Chepa's parents spoke when they lived in the interior. She didn't know what I meant so I had to explain to her that Indians were still a separate people, their dialect wholly different from hers. She still didn't understand. As I explained again— my Spanish was clear enough—Mingo began to laugh at his wife's ignorance. With a bit of gentleness, a bit of savagery, he kept teasing her for twenty minutes.

May 17, 1966

Don Pedro, after weeks of daily conversations, a few days before we are scheduled to leave:

"I want you to remember how much I love America. I lived there for six years, and would never say evil things about it. But you know, across the border there are men who think that we Mexicans are no better than beasts.

"I was mistreated often in your country. In small towns, when I was traveling and had no work, I would visit families hoping to exchange a few hours labor for a meal and perhaps a bed. I don't know how many people called the police when they saw me, expecting that a Mexican would do them harm.

"When I was working on the railroad an American foreman used to say to me every day the few words of Spanish he knew: 'Fuck your mother.' When I asked him to stop he threatened to have me fired, or to beat me up himself."

Tonight, as Rachel and I were walking down the road toward the large PEPSI sign that divides Emiliano Zapata from *colonia* Lopez Mateos, we heard somebody calling us. At first I thought it was Chencho, so I answered jokingly. But it was Don Pedro, dressed only in his pants and a T shirt, looking as dignified as he does in his best clothes. He wanted to warn us about the danger of walking too far down the road alone. "There might be robbers up there and criminals who sell marijuana," he said.

He seems to see himself as the community's watchman. "Mingo left your house just fifteen minutes ago, and you two walked down the road in the other direction before you came here," he said, visibly proud of his ability to tell us our whereabouts. But it is not an act. Don Pedro got Socorro the doctor who treated her dysentery, he is helping to form a new political party in the *colonia*, he was responsible for bringing the main road up this far.

Everyone we talk to in Emiliano Zapata mentions his name, and never with malice. That is what he wants from life. Once he described his desire to help the poor as "my profession, now that I am old."

II

TRAINING ended a week after we got back from Juárez.

Before the final boards, Bill and Joyce Dodge, Nick, Rachel, and I organized a meeting with the faculty in which we evaluated our program quite unfavorably and made some suggestions for the training center's future. I remembered our timid discussion with the acting director at the beginning of the program. Now at least we were talking about more controversial matters than the amount of milk in the coffee machine. It had demanded a little courage. There was always the chance that they'd retaliate by deselecting us.

But we all survived the final boards, though it took another week for the government to give Nick and Rachel and me our security clearance.

The day before our home leave we had a meeting with Bill Gshwend, who had come from Guayaquil to participate in the selection process. It was designed mainly to answer our last-minute questions. What clothes should we bring? Would there be typewriters? What was the climate at this time of year?

Then someone asked Bill to describe the rest of the Peace Corps staff in Ecuador. Throughout training, the returned volunteers had been telling us not to worry about the restrictions placed on us in Albuquerque because we'd have plenty of freedom once we got into the field. We had all assumed that was true. This was the first time anyone had thought to wonder about the men who would administer us.

"Oh, you'll like the Country Director," Bill said. His name is Erich Hofmann. Actually, you won't meet him until August. He's on home leave right now, visiting Germany. He was born there and served in the Luftwaffe during World War II."

We all laughed.

"No, he really did. But you'll like him. He's already been Deputy Director in Ecuador for two years. He's a very nice fellow. A little short on imagination, but a very good administrator."

PART SIX

I

JAMES MEREDITH was shot the day before we were supposed to leave for Guayaquil.

Throughout the evening the Associated Press reported that he'd been murdered, and those bulletins added urgency to the questions Rachel and I had been asking one another since the beginning of training. How could we work for something called a Peace Corps when there was virtual civil war at home?

Within a few hours the crisis seemed to ease. The eleven-o'clock news reported that Meredith's wounds were superficial and that leaders of all the civil-rights organizations in the country were flying to his hospital in Memphis, where they would unite to organize a mass march along the route he had mapped for himself. Perhaps, we thought on that nervous night, the sniper's bullet had really been a good-luck charm. Soon the movement would come together again.

But we wouldn't be around to witness the process. The question we had asked one another was just part of an elaborate ritual, designed to prove that we were still more radical and open-minded than the organization we had joined. But we had been seized by the rhythm of the new adventure and were eager to learn the lessons it would teach. It was too late to withdraw.

The night we left Kennedy Airport in New York Stokely Carmichael must have been planning SNCC's role in the march to Jackson. Two days later, after we had arrived in Ecuador, he would issue the simple demand that catalyzed the anger that so many black people had felt for so long.

"Black power": the term soon became a doctrine, the doctrine part of a fight that was too deep, too emotional, to be resolved without violence and repression. It was the formal beginning of the tragic drama that Bob Moses had foreseen so clearly. Mississippi, where just two summers earlier blacks and whites had been convinced that they could save America with their wit, their energy, and their love, was now the setting for the permanent dissolution of the movement that had once seemed to promise our redemption.

I never felt so close to the other trainees as I did that night, flying toward Guayaquil on our Braniff jet. A soldier heading for Vietnam must feel that way too; suddenly, briefly, the people with whom he might die seem his only friends, the only family he has in the world. The war is one thing, horrible; one's platoon is another thing altogether, beloved.

Nine members of our original group had been deselected or had quit; for the twenty of us who remained the act of crossing continents seemed irrevocable. Nobody had very much confidence in himself that night, or in our special project either. As we traveled from New York to Miami, to the shocking heat of Panama, and then on through the tropical sunrise to Guayaquil, each of us was trying to wrest firm pledges, almost blood pledges, from our peers. "You really will leave if you don't like it, Nick?" Rachel asked. "I mean the worst thing would be to stay around for two years on an assignment that didn't make any sense." Most of the voices that murmured in the darkened cabin were posing the same tense question.

Shortly before we arrived in Guayaquil Rachel asked one of the stewardesses to describe the city.

"Oh, I've never left the airport to go into town. It's too hot for me, and I don't think I would like the way it smells."

"Do many people get off there?"

"A few each week. Believe me, it's not a very popular stop at all."

A day later Rachel wrote a letter describing her first reaction to Guayaquil:

The thing that seems really funny is to arrive here in this city which I could never really believe existed and to find that it looks just like all the pictures we have seen. It really is a city, too, where people live; not the inferno we heard about in training, where the only human activity is to suffer and decay. It is much bigger, much more bustling, much cooler and fuller of smaller people than I had imagined. The streets are filled with honking cars—many Anglias, Fiats, and Fords—between which the pedestrians usually pass to the accompaniment of squalling brakes. Ice-cream vendors clang their bells under our windows. The arcades which have been placed under every building as defense against the tropical rains are lined with small shops and stalls. Few of the buildings downtown are higher than five stories; they are built over the arcades, with balconies and high ceilings. It is the kind of city that makes you curious to know it well.

Until we find housing, we are staying at the Pensión Helbig, a clean, friendly place which serves good food and seems to be a regular Peace Corps hangout. So far, our activities have not had much to do with Guayaquil, but with getting orientation from the Peace Corps staff. . . .

II

OUR first days in Guayaquil were not at all like our first days in Juárez. The strongest impressions Rachel and I received were not of the city itself but of the Peace Corps as an organization and of the volunteers and staff members it employed. The orientation sessions mentioned in Rachel's letter were designed to introduce us to our organization and its rules, not to discuss our difficult job or to acquaint us with the strange and complicated society in which we were supposed to perform it. It was soon clear that the organization would be far more important to us than we had imagined before we left Albuquerque. From our formal meetings, from informal talks with volunteers, with staff people, and with Ecuadorians, we learned that the Peace Corps in the field had a set of regulations every bit as strict as those that had governed us in New Mexico, that its ties to the State Department were at least as strong as its ties to the agencies in Guayaquil's *municipio*, and that the volunteer who felt closer to his neighbors in the *barrios* than to his fellow North Americans and worked with them to achieve a successful community-development project was nowhere near as typical as we had been led to believe.

Orientation I: Courtesy of the Peace Corps.

Erich Hofmann, the Director, was still in Germany, so our formal orientation was conducted by his deputy, Caleb Roehrig.

He was the sort of man the Peace Corps is proud to attract. Until very recently he had been an executive of the Land-Polaroid Corporation near Boston, and his presence in Ecuador suggested that another soul had been rescued from American capitalism and put at the disposal of the world's poor. But his reason for leaving his high-paying job seemed to have more to do with his attitude toward living in the United States than with his desire to help the poor people of Latin America.

He told Rachel and me that one morning, after he and his wife had been living in the suburbs of Boston for more than a decade, they suddenly began a discussion about their common hatred of the sound of power motors. The conversation twisted and turned and finally they realized that they were bored with the life that a middle-class executive must lead. Neither of them had spent much time outside the country. They began to wonder how they could travel around the world, do useful work, receive a steady salary, and decided that they preferred government service to private business. First Caleb had talked with AID officials, but he found them too stuffy and resolved to apply for the Peace Corps. When we met him he had been in Ecuador for three months.

The orientation session was held the day after we arrived, in the depressing auditorium of the Ecuadorian-North American Cultural Center. As soon as we were seated—at ten o'clock of the same morning that Stokely Carmichael was planning to demand "black power" on that dusty road near Greenwood—each of us was given a manila envelope containing Peace Corps rules.

Volunteers were not supposed to carry firearms ("The Peace Corps' mission is one of peace," the message began); we were not supposed to drive cars (two volunteers, both of them passengers, had been killed in auto accidents several years before); we were not supposed to climb difficult mountains unless we received permission from the Director several days in advance; we were never supposed to be away from our sites without authorization from the staff (so a staff member could refuse to give Rachel and me permission to go to the beach on a Sunday afternoon); we were supposed to clear all articles we wrote with our regional representative before we submitted them for publication lest they contain comments about Ecuador that would reflect badly on the Peace Corps (eighteen months later that restriction would involve me in two serious confrontations with the senior staff in Washington, but until then I obeyed it completely. I should add, though, that every staff man

I ever talked to, in training and in Guayaquil, assured me that volunteers could say or write whatever they pleased about American politics and policies).

Then Caleb announced two new rules that had not yet been mimeographed and distributed to the volunteers. First he told us that we could not eat at the expensive Hotel Quito in the country's capital.

Then, just as blandly, he told us that volunteers were forbidden to marry Ecuadorians. (The rule had been made in the Quito office, not at the Peace Corps' headquarters in Washington, but I later learned that there was legislation resembling it in most countries where the Peace Corps worked. Sometimes the laws were more lenient than in Ecuador—volunteers might be able to marry after their first year in the field, or if they obtained the permission of the Country Director. But in virtually all cases the Peace Corps tried to discourage cross-cultural union. For example, one girl who served in Guinea later told me that in her training program love affairs with Africans were explained as a form of "culture shock.")

When I asked the reason for the rule Bill Gshwend and Dan Stringer, his replacement, joined Caleb in telling us that many local people were eager to trap the first North American they met in order to obtain an American passport. Lonely volunteers, suffering from culture shock, were supposed to be especially vulnerable to the wily Latins. But even if the Ecuadorian was in love with the volunteer, and not with his or her nationality or possessions, the marriage would diminish capacity to do Peace Corps work. We had to be realistic and understand that the typical host-country national did not feel the same commitment to helping poor people as did most volunteers.

Though I tried to sound moderate, the fact that I insisted on pursuing the issue must have seemed incomprehensible to Caleb, a New Englander used to the restrained behavior of business relationships. Besides, my appearance almost always makes me seem militant, no matter what mood I try to convey through language or tone of voice.

In our community-development classes during training we had
been advised that the best way to gain the confidence of the men
in our *barrio* was to go whoring with them. Now, dripping with
sweat, gulping huge drags of smoke from my cigarette, I told
Caleb that that strategy made the Peace Corps' marriage policy
sound somewhat racist: we were encouraged to sleep with Ecuadorian women but forbidden to marry them. As I spoke, I had a
memory so sharp that it was nearly tactile of an angry black
woman I had met in Cambridge, Maryland, the morning of a
demonstration that nearly caused the city to erupt into a civil war.
She had spent several minutes yelling at me about the white man's
attitude toward sex. "We take care of your children, let you lay us
in the bushes, bear your little mulatto bastards. You sneak over to
our part of town or sneak us over to yours when you get tired of
your wives and want to have yourselves a good time. The Muslims
are right. Your people are hypocrites. They're blue-eyed devils.
You'd better believe that's what this whole mess is all about."

I wanted to find a way to make her fury real to the volunteers
and staff members in Guayaquil, to make them see that their insensitivity could anger Ecuadorian women just as deeply.

I suppose that Caleb thought that I was either a little crazy or
an agitator who had selected an irrelevant issue for its demagogic
value, so that I could reduce the company's efficiency, damage
its morale.

Certainly he was quite exasperated when I finished talking.
What he wondered, he said, was whether I planned to spend my
two years as a volunteer arguing this way over every small organizational detail.

Orientation II: Courtesy of an Experienced Volunteer.

Margot Jones had already lived in Guayaquil for nine months by
the time we had arrived there. But she was not happy with herself
or her work, and you could see signs of her constant tension on
her face. She is a tall, slender blonde with wonderfully etched high
cheekbones and green eyes that slant wittily, a little wickedly.

When she is content she looks like Nefretete, but when she is depressed her skin seems to draw tightly over her face and she begins to appear pale, parched, even bitchy.

She had been assigned to live in a distant *barrio*, about thirty minutes from the city by bus. Throughout the rainy season Margot had spent most of her time traveling back and forth between that community and the crowded municipal offices, where she would sit for hours until the minor civil servant who might help her neighbors procure land fill was ready to talk with her. If she flirted with him, she knew, she could get the material more quickly than the Ecuadorians or the male Peace Corps volunteers; but that was the part of her job she disliked most. It made her feel phony, and Margot, more than almost anyone I have met in my life, is a person determined to discover the truth about herself and live by it.

For that reason she felt almost as out of place in the *barrio* where she lived as in the municipal agencies. There was only one Ecuadorian with whom she could talk at all, and even he had no way of understanding the complicated, contradictory impulses and passions that filled a high-strung, highly educated American girl who had almost joined SDS instead of the Peace Corps, who had finally decided to work with poor Ecuadorians because there seemed no better way of fulfilling the ideals she had acquired at high school in Westport, Connecticut, and then at the University of Wisconsin. Most local people saw Margot through the lens of their own assumptions and probably considered her a little mad. Why else would such a pretty woman, still single at the advanced age of twenty-three, want to spend two years living in the marshy *barrio*? Her skewed relationship with the community made her feel so incomplete that sometimes she hid from her neighbors at night. Their problems, which she confronted all day, had nothing to do with the things that bothered her most deeply. One afternoon, for example, she received a letter telling her that a high-school classmate was now dead in Vietnam and that night, door locked, she worked until sunrise creating a bitter collage as his memorial.

But she was reluctant to complain to the Peace Corps staff. In training, and from more experienced volunteers in Guayaquil, she had learned that Ecuador was like a wilderness, and the Peace Corps experience was actually a test of one's cunning and one's stamina. It was the new frontier. "We always talked as if it was us versus the *Guayaquileños*," she says, "and we always told each other not to let them get us down. We had to prove that we were tougher than they were." So if she failed, if she felt depressed or unsuccessful in her work, she blamed herself. And the Ecuadorians.

Still, she was always doing things that alarmed people on the staff. For example, when her group of volunteers was asked to recite an oath that all government employees must affirm, she remained silent while everyone else said "so help me God." The ceremony took place at Hofmann's house in Quito, and afterward the Director's wife asked Margot to explain her action. "I don't believe in God," she said, "and besides, that sentence might be unconstitutional." "I think that attitude is going to get you in a lot of trouble here," Mrs. Hofmann hold her.

But it hadn't yet. Until she met Nick (with whom she lived for a year) and Rachel and me, she never quite let her independence take her to the conclusion that the barriers between her work and the ideals she wanted to fulfill had been built by her organization and her government, not by herself or her neighbors.

Once she told us a story that seemed to summarize a large part of her experience:

She had been eating dinner at the Pensión Helbig. There was a loud noise several tables away, and when she looked around she saw another volunteer shouting at the Ecuadorian waiter to bring some food he had ordered. But apparently the cook hadn't finished preparing the meal, so the waiter was forced to delay a little longer. Suddenly the volunteer stood up, lunged toward the Ecuadorian, grabbed him, and carried him toward the window. For more than a minute he pretended that he was going to hurl the terrified man down to the street three stories below.

"And you know," Margot said, "the terrible thing is that I didn't react very strongly at all. Oh, I was annoyed and I told him that he looked stupid. But I wasn't *really* angry, you know what I mean? I guess I knew that he wouldn't really throw the waiter out of the window, and that satisfied me. I didn't think about the real horror of what I was seeing. I guess I was too caught up in my own problems, a little numb."

Orientation III: Conversation with a Volunteer on His Way Home.

During those first days in Ecuador I was so curious to know how the Peace Corps experience affected people that I acted more like a sociologist than a volunteer and questioned everyone who seemed half-willing to talk with me. I suppose I must have seemed overly intense to most of the departing veterans. But I don't think that the man who told me the following story on my third day in the country was putting me on.

He had been stationed in a small town near Guayaquil, the sort of rural community where the Peace Corps is supposed to be most effective and had lived there throughout his tour of duty. After about a year, he persuaded the local people to accept his plan for a playground. "That really felt good," he said. "At least I'd have something to show for those years of my life."

But the townspeople kept procrastinating. "There wasn't much time left until I had to go home. I kept pleading with them to hurry up." Finally, a month before he was supposed to terminate (in the Peace Corps' cancerous jargon), the money that had been raised for the playground disappeared. Now the project would never be completed. He was sure that he knew which members of the *comité* he had catalyzed stole the money.

"I can't wait until I get home and into the army," he told me. "I want to go over there to Vietnam and shoot some of those Viet Cong. It will sure feel good to pretend that they're the Ecuadorian *campesinos* I've been working with."

Orientation IV: We Meet a Supervolunteer.

In nearly every Peace Corps group there is one person whose apparent success with host-country nationals becomes legendary, a fantasy for his peers that sometimes carries them through their own relative failures. He is the Supervolunteer: the Peace Corps' Kit Carson, uniquely equipped to find his way through the alien territory.

The Supervolunteer in Guayaquil was the only member of his group who expressly refrained from adopting the *macho* attitudes that most community developers believed were essential in Latin America. A devout Catholic, he rarely got drunk and refused to go out whoring. We met him the night before he was supposed to return to the States, and he gave me the same impression of slightly grubby self-confident toughness that I found among city-born Israelis who had lived on a kibbutz for several years and convinced themselves that they really could survive under physically taxing circumstances.

He spoke gently, and very honestly, about his relations with the Ecuadorians in his *barrio*. It was clear that he had forced himself to accept the fact that they would never change as rapidly as he thought they could, forced himself to accept their traditions and customs although he did not particularly enjoy them. But he was a simpler person than Margot and therefore able to accept relationships that left her feeling thoroughly dissatisfied; and he was much kinder than the volunteer who wanted to shoot surrogate Ecuadorians in Vietnam. He was as patient as a man can be, and I'm sure that no other quality was so important to his success.

The community where he lived was even farther from the center of town than Margot's, about forty-five minutes by bus, and when its people got sick they were often unable to journey all the way to the city's hospitals. Anyway, most of them were too poor to pay for medical treatment. So the Supervolunteer encouraged them to build a health center where they would be examined gratis by doctors who would commute to the *barrios* several times a week.

The Supervolunteer had organized the labor in a way that in theory made great sense. The people, directed by their *comité* would build the structure for the health center; the Peace Corps would devise a regular schedule the doctors could follow; AID would furnish the roof.

But it turned out that the Supervolunteer had to hold the entire project together by the force of his own personality. The *comité* was so torn by quarrels and jealousies that, without his presence, his constant manipulation, it would have dissolved long ago. The Ecuadorians distrusted each other so much, he said, that they had finally appointed him to serve as the *comité's* treasurer because he was the only person whom the community felt it could trust with the funds.

He had even more trouble sustaining the doctors' commitment to the project than his neighbors'. Each afternoon he would make the long bus ride into town, hire a taxi, stop at their offices, and shepherd them out to the *barrio* in time for their appointments. The doctors never traveled out there alone, and they were very reluctant to use the bus.

Finally, AID had not yet delivered the roof it promised. The Supervolunteer felt that the Peace Corps would have to keep badgering her sister organization until the day when its officials felt so guilty that they would organize a big public ceremony, invite the press, and dedicate the health center in the name of the Alliance for Progress and Ecuadorian-American friendship. But AID was a big bureaucracy, and guilt, even self-interested guilt, was not an emotion many of its employees developed very quickly.

The Supervolunteer was an artist: he had done a masterful job of harmonizing many divergent interests. But community development was supposed to be an applied science, a technique that any reasonably intelligent person could learn in two months. Could Sid Raschi, the less talented, less dedicated volunteer who would move into his community, sustain the enthusiasm that Supervolunteer had created? It sounded, rather, as if the flimsy structure of human relationships he had been propping up would collapse before the health center was completed.

And if successful community-development projects required the sustained presence of Supervolunteers then how could the rest of us—or the Ecuadorians themselves—hope to accomplish even the tasks that had sounded relatively simple in training, let alone the special jobs that we had been assigned to do?

Orientation V: From Supervolunteer to Supercop.

One of the volunteers stationed in Guayaquil had majored in police science at the University of Montana. Though he had joined the Peace Corps as part of a rural community-development project, when he got to Ecuador he quickly returned to his chosen profession. By the time we arrived in Guayaquil he was serving as an adviser to the local police force. Next to Supervolunteer, Supercop was supposed to be the hardest working Peace Corps person in the city.

In a way, I liked him quite a bit. He was always honest in his relations with other volunteers, helpful to us, and frank about his attitudes toward the Ecuadorians. He liked the country well enough to feel especially dedicated to the job of eradicating all its criminals.

If I had somehow wound up in Vietnam rather than Guayaquil, I would have been happy (and relieved) to have Supercop as my buddy. But I couldn't believe, in those early days, that a man with his ideas could be part of the Peace Corps, let alone be regarded as one of its model volunteers.

Before we arrived he had been mugged in the *barrio* where he lived. Immediately, he had telephoned Gshwend and begged permission to carry a gun. When Gshwend cited the firearm rule he fashioned himself a balanced nightstick which he carried everywhere until the Guayaquil police force gave him a sturdier one as a sign of their appreciation for his help.

He was protected, but that still didn't solve the general problem of mugging. So he adapted a strategy he had learned at the University of Montana to conditions in Guayaquil. When we first met him he was still annoyed because his superiors on the police force had turned down his plan.

He had wanted about sixty plainclothesmen to dress up as derelicts and go out to the slums, where they would pretend to be drunks. Whenever a criminal seemed likely to roll one of the disguised policemen he would be shot. "A few hundred killings would stop them from committing crimes for a few years at least."

Orientation VI: What the Ambassador Said.

Wymberley Coerr, who had been Undersecretary of State for Latin-American Affairs during the Kennedy Administration, was now Ambassador to Ecuador. Although the post is not so attractive as, say, Ambassador to Brazil, still it is a rather important one. If one is worried about subversion in Latin America, it is unwise to discount even the littlest countries (Ecuador is the smallest country on the continent and, next to Paraguay and Bolivia, the poorest).

Shortly after we arrived in Guayaquil we had an orientation session with Coerr. He seemed very impressive that day, the model of the professional diplomat. He was a slim, blondish man who carried himself very coolly. Even in Guayaquil's most tropical weather he looked ready to play several sets of tennis at the country club. He dressed as neatly, talked as politely, as any prep-school dean of admissions. I was still at the point where anyone who pronounced Spanish words with an accurate accent seemed fluent in the language, so when *"barrio," "jefe," "presidente"* rolled out of that patrician mouth with the proper r's, j's, and t's I was convinced that we had an ambassador who could communicate with the Ecuadorians.

He didn't do so well with the Peace Corps volunteers.

He began his speech with a statement that was particularly surprising after all the emphasis Mankiewicz and Wofford had placed on the independent nature of the Peace Corps and Gshwend had placed on the radical nature of our project. There were about three hundred Peace Corps volunteers in Ecuador, he told us, one hundred and eighty AID employees, sixty members of the State Department, forty scientists from the National Space Agency (who manned an observatory near Quito), eighty-seven members of the military service. "All representatives of the American government here must have the same purpose," he said. (We later learned that the Peace Corps Director—along with officials from AID, the State Department, and the military—was part of the "country team" which held policy meetings once or twice each week in the American Embassy in Quito. In Guayaquil the Peace Corps representative was supposed to participate in similar weekly meetings at the American Consulate.) "The purpose is to help Ecuador maintain its independence," the Ambassador explained.

"Some of the private American money that is at work in this country is for humanitarian purposes, *but most of the aid the United States gives Ecuador is justified by our country's interests.*

"The problem here, of course, is the lack of technical and economic development. If there is too much inequity, there is a lack of development. *But we have to work with the power structure that exists, and there is not much we can do about inequity there.* Credit cooperatives may be one remedy. They are a very peaceful way of bringing about progress, but very slow." (My italics.)

Then Coerr began to talk about left-wing groups in Ecuador. "Communists—or any good demagogues—can exploit issues like poverty and use them to force violence.

"But the main danger here is not from organizations influenced by the Communist Chinese which want revolution now. The Russians worry us more because they are working through parliamentary means. They hope to obtain power by getting their men into cabinet jobs or by winning local elections. We call that technique supervision instead of subversion."

I was surprised to hear Coerr express such ideas so frankly in front of our group. Had no one told him that a few of us, at least, had joined the Peace Corps partly because Frank Mankiewicz had called it "A Revolutionary Force"? But he wasn't warning us. There was nothing in his tone that said, "This is the way it works in Ecuador, men. You're in my shop now, and if you don't like it you'd better get out fast." No, his ideas about American young people were probably as dated as his ideas about Communism— perhaps that is the price of remaining in the Foreign Service, remote from the currents of contemporary opinion. He talked to us as if he had no doubt at all that we shared his point of view: as if all Americans would agree that the interests of the State Department, the Green Berets, and the Peace Corps were compatible. Clearly no one on the Peace Corps staff had been courageous enough to describe our project to him as it had been described to us.

After the speech some of us questioned his remarks, quite mildly compared to the way we questioned the Peace Corps officials. His calm, precise answers reiterated the points he had made, and he seemed extremely self-assured. But afterward he told a subordinate in the State Department that he had never been put through such an exercise by any volunteers. "I've never seen a group with such a chip on its shoulder," is the way he is reported to have put it.

Orientation VII: Jorge Rodriguez' View.

Four days after we arrived in Ecuador, with Gshwend's description of Rodriguez still vivid in her memory, Rachel wrote her parents that "he has the reputation of being two-faced and a manipulator, and full of hot air. Dealing with such a person will at least be a new experience for me, and his office should be a good place from which to learn about this city."

But during our first week in Guayaquil he seemed much more interested than any Peace Corps volunteer or staff member in the work that Rachel and I had been assigned. He seemed genuinely glad that we had come to the country. We went on tours of the city with him, attended his meetings (including some where he was severely criticized by people from the *barrios*), spent hours in his office or in local cafés listening to him tell us about the city's history and its problems as well as his own shortcomings as he tried to deal with them. He was either an excellent actor (and why should he have been putting on a show for Rachel and me, volunteers with no special status except that we'd been assigned to his office?), or he was very much more dedicated to his work and the city's poor than Gshwend had implied. After we had been in Ecuador for ten days Rachel described Jorge as "a very shrewd, ambitious man whom we find quite likable at the moment, although we have been warned that he doesn't like Peace Corps volunteers and can't be trusted."

Two weeks later she described our boss, and our job, in more detail:

> Our work in his office is interesting, but so far it has mainly consisted of sitting around while nobody else does anything: One man draws a line on a piece of paper—he may be tabulating. The secretary has a giggly tantrum when Jorge gives her work to do, although she always does it. Another man is there to bring chairs, hand out note paper to conferees, fetch Coca-Cola or packs of cigarettes. The office is full of people wanting help for their communities, or more equipment, or pay for the teachers in the centers Jorge runs. We sit around a table making inflated plans with Jorge which will never be realized unless we carry them out. The other day I got extremely depressed about the gap between planning and performance, but Paul has since persuaded me that I shouldn't take the plans so seriously.
>
> Jorge is a very smart man and we like him, and he certainly has enormous problems to cope with. This morning he took us along on a tour of one of the *barrios* which he had arranged for the new Vice-Mayor. He plans to build a community center there, and needs the *municipio*'s permission to construct the building on a lot that belongs to the city. This Vice-Mayor has been in office for only a week: Jorge has had to tell him the same things he's already told nine other Vice-Mayors (the turnover is amazing), explain what community development is, and what the department has been doing. But in a town that is full of rival factions, he seems to have done a very good job of remaining apolitical in his department's work.

One statement Jorge made the week we went to work for him provided a new context for the view of him that Gshwend had expressed during training. "Of all the community-development workers the Peace Corps has sent to Guayaquil, only two have continued to work in my office for more than two months," he said. "But forty of them were assigned to me at first.

"They weren't very well prepared anyway. You Americans think that you can send us college graduates who know nothing of our culture, our language, or our professional fields to instruct us in solving our problems. You send us people who think that we're so unimportant that they can leave our offices at any time. It makes you look very foolish to us. But the effect is really much worse. You can't imagine how much your carelessness insults us."

Perhaps Gshwend was correct, and Jorge was a shrewd diplomat who always said what he knew the North Americans wanted to hear while he plotted to use us for his own ends (the technique Gshwend had employed to get us into the *municipio*). But if so, Jorge was more than shrewd; he was remarkable. For by making a few unsolicited statements about the sloppiness of *gringo* technicians—statements that would have convinced someone like Gshwend that he was anti-American and therefore unreliable—he won a far deeper emotional commitment from Rachel and me than the Peace Corps would ever be able to sustain.

Orientation VIII: The Staff and the Volunteers at Play.

(From a letter I sent home about two weeks after we arrived in Ecuador):

Dan Stringer [who had formally replaced Gshwend as rep] arranged a party for the volunteers and a large chunk of the American community here. Of the twenty diplomats and businessmen he invited, only five showed up. The formal party lasted several hours and was pleasant enough. I spent the afternoon talking with George High, who is second in command at the Consulate, about his last assignment in Portuguese Africa.

All the non-Peace Corps people left at nine, and Rachel and I went home at ten. At one-thirty we heard some members of our group coming into the hotel roaring drunk, making so much noise that we all would have been kicked out of here if the Peace Corps weren't the Pensión Helbig's main source of revenue. The next day details of the party began to filter through to us. By midnight, several people told us, it had begun to seem like a fraternity house during a football week-

end: most of the volunteers were squirting beer at Stringer's
ceiling and at one another.

III

In many ways, Ecuador seems to be two separate countries, the
Sierra and the Coast, which are almost always at war with each
other. Both politically and religiously, the Andean towns and cities, of which Quito is the biggest, are much more conservative
than Guayaquil and the settlements that surround it. Most of Ecuador's two million Indians, by far the largest ethnic group, are
much too intimidated by the government's power to make much
trouble for the aristocrats who own most of the land there. They
haunt the regions like ghosts. Though they call themselves Catho-
lics and believe in the religion out of deference to the rich Spanish
families who stole the land from their Inca ancestors, their style of
life still seems rooted in their pre-Columbian past. Most of them
still speak their ancient dialect, Quechua, still wear ponchos instead of Western clothes, still wear their hair in one long braid,
still humble themselves before their *patrons*, who treat them like
animals. They are the poorest caste in the country and have practically no rights (most of them are not even permitted to vote); but
no group in Ecuador seems less ready to make a revolution.

The wealthy *Serranos* (Sierra peoples) are trying to exploit all
of Ecuador in the same way as they exploit the Indians, according
to most people who live on the coast. The *costeños* are convinced
that the government, which is located in Quito, levies unduly high
taxes on Guayaquil's businesses but rarely uses federal money to
solve the Coast's problems. Occasionally the entire city of Guayaquil goes out on strike to protest some outrage that has been com-

mitted against their institutions. Shortly before we arrived in the country, the tension which is always present erupted into a civil war, as unusual as it was brief. Coastal commercial interests, led by Guayaquil's Chamber of Commerce, managed to channel the hostility that most Ecuadorians felt toward a military junta that had been ruling the country for several years into a series of concerted demonstrations. Within a few days, the officers who controlled the country had exiled themselves, and a wealthy businessman from Guayaquil was the new president. But most *Guayaquileños* distrust their own upper class almost as much as they distrust the upper class in the Sierra. As soon as he took power and moved to Quito, they began to regard him as their enemy, too.

The two regions are connected by a single, narrow road, potholed where it is paved, composed of loosely packed dirt for miles at a stretch. A car or bus or truck that swerves off the road in the mountains usually swerves off a high cliff, too. Several times each month the newspapers report that commercial busses carrying dozens of passengers have toppled into the valley far below. There is no way of estimating the accident rate for private vehicles.

The quality of the road is one of the principal reasons that Ecuador's bananas, the country's largest cash crop, are declining in value on the world market, one reason that there isn't enough money in the federal treasury to pay for new public-works projects. You can gain a vivid impression of the country's accelerating economic problems simply by watching the convoys of banana trucks (wood platforms mounted on twenty-year-old truck beds) jostle their way toward Guayaquil. Like the horse-drawn busses that used to carry citizens through Boston in the 1850s, these trucks bear on their sides, in large, crude lettering, the names of heroes, local or international: Velasco Ibarra, Kennedy, Perón, Castro. Guarding the bananas, sitting on splintery benches on the back of the truck or balancing on a fender behind, are small *campesinos* who do not seem entirely aware that the vehicle transporting them is propelled by an engine and not an animal.

By the time the bananas arrive at the port near Guayaquil, they are already badly bruised, poor competition for the Central-American fruits which are loaded and unloaded by machines, not peasants, and carried along superhighways by modern trucks.

Most people who live on Ecuador's Coast are mestizos. In most cases, their ancestry is Spanish as well as Indian. They speak Spanish, wear Western clothes, are not nearly so religious as the inhabitants of the Sierra. But an Indian who wants to live in the city can become a mestizo by cutting his hair, exchanging his poncho for a shirt and a pair of pants, adopting Spanish as his first language. The lines between castes are more cultural than racial, though one often notices a note of condescension when light-skinned *Guayaquileños* talk about Indians or Negroes. The characteristic that seems to define a mestizo is not so much his color, his height, or his accent (people who were born on the Coast hurry their sentences, slur their words, while people who migrated there from the Sierra talk slower, more sibilant Spanish), as the fact that he feels more at home in the urban environment than in any other setting. His life does not seem to be very much influenced by the cultural traditions that govern the lives of the Indians in the Sierra. He knows that he will make his future in the world that the automobile and the transistor radio symbolize.

As I begin to describe Guayaquil, where tens of thousands of mestizos settle each year, I find myself tempted to emphasize its least pleasant features. While we were there, certainly, Rachel and I often succumbed to the prejudices we despised in other people; in fact, Margot used to argue that the only thing that distinguished our small circle of friends from the other volunteers was our willingness to admit our biases openly and try to confront them. After all, we, too, had hired out to alter a reality we couldn't understand, and from the start Guayaquil seemed stubbornly eager to reject our best efforts to affect it. Now, there is a great temptation to explain our own failures—and mock the Peace Corps' programing mistakes—by concentrating on the great difficulties Guayaquil faces as it tries to adapt itself to the modern world: to spotlight its most primitive qualities while I ignore its sophisticated aspects and deny the increasingly complex nature of its social structure.

But by now I carry dozens of conversations with Ecuadorian friends inside my head, and they serve as a kind of internal censor. They remind me that nothing antagonizes all Latins (regardless of their politics) more rapidly than the hated North American assumption (which many of our radicals and conservatives seem to share) that because a country is classified as "underdeveloped" all its people are shackled to primitive tastes and primitive beliefs. Lourdes Vera, Ecuador's first woman architect and Rachel's best friend in Guayaquil, put it this way: "I think that so many of you are cultural imperialists because you learn so little about us in your schools. When you come down here you assume that we will all be Indians who dress ourselves in loincloths and feathers. After a few months you might observe that some of us are at least as cultured as you are, but you never allow that realization to change your basic idea about us."

Peace Corps training reinforced those prejudices. When we arrived in Albuquerque many volunteers didn't know whether they could buy butter in Guayaquil's stores or find flush toilets in its apartments; when we left we worried that every stick of butter might carry bovine tuberculosis, that the deadly *chinchorro* bug might invade any of the city's bathrooms. At one of our orientations in Guayaquil a staff doctor had told us that "there are hundreds of thousands of people in this city who have never known the pleasure of a solid bowel movement." It was a funny line, perhaps an accurate one, but a dangerous way to see a country.

So before I examine the special difficulties that Guayaquil posed for our group of volunteers—and thus focus on its poverty and the inadequacies of its government—I want to describe it in somewhat more general terms, as a visiting journalist might. And I want to offer a guess about an aspect of Ecuadorian development that was totally inconceivable from the information we received during training.

Guayaquil is a place where different levels of civilization have been piled on top of one another, helter-skelter. If hundreds of thousands of Ecuadorians live in terrible poverty, still their lives have been reshaped by the modern technology that brought them to the city in the first place. The technology allows middle-class and wealthy Ecuadorians, and all foreigners, to live in relative comfort in the tropical city. Not only are there dozens of stores where you can buy butter that is perfectly safe and tens of thousands of bathrooms with flush toilets into which the *chinchorro* will never enter; you can also eat good food whenever you want, watch television programs like *Long Hot Summer* or *Peyton Place*, listen to the Rolling Stones on the jukebox, see American movies within a month of their opening in New York. An American never feels far from his own culture.

For one thing, the United States is physically quite close. It takes only four hours to fly from Guayaquil to Miami, and at least one airplane leaves every night. Throughout November and December the airlines take advertisements in the newspapers urging people to "buy your Christmas gifts in Miami," offering special rates to all passengers; not a few Ecuadorians earn themselves a tidy sum of money by selling the clothes they bought in Florida at four times the price when they return to Guayaquil.

If you want to speak to your family in Philadelphia, you can always find an Ecuadorian with a ham radio who will be delighted to run some traffic through; or, if that means of communications is too public, you can make a long-distance phone call to the States within two hours. There are stores and kiosks all over town where you can buy a wide range of English-language paperbacks. *Time* and *Newsweek* arrive only a day late, and the local newspapers daily publish pages of wire-service stories from the United States, translated but never edited. If you want still more information, you can spend an hour at the Phoenix Club (whose membership used to be confined to people from English-speaking countries, but which now has as many Ecuadorians as foreigners on its rolls) and read the *Miami Herald*: the Sunday edition arrives on Tuesday, most daily editions arrive in twenty-four hours.

If you are feeling particularly homesick, you can take the *Time* or *Newsweek* you just bought to drive-in restaurants like the Reyburger or Rosado's Grill or soda fountains like the Melba or the Bongo, where you can order hamburgers and cheeseburgers, chili dogs and chicken-in-the-basket, milkshakes and chocolate sundaes. There are record stores on the city's main street, Nueve de Octubre, where you can find the latest album by Rafael, Latin-America's teen-age idol, or the Beatles. If you are sick, or an insomniac, or experimenting with some kind of drug, you can get virtually any medicine you need—usually without a prescription—at two modern drugstores, one of which is open all night. You can buy marijuana, cheap though illegal, from the dealers at Cerro Santana. If you want paper diapers for your baby, or Gerber's strained vegetables, you can find them at Rosado's Supermarket. Do you want to travel? There are at least two major tourist bureaus in Guayaquil, each of Ecuador's three major airlines has its own large office, or you can buy tickets from large international companies like Braniff, KLM, or Lufthansa. You can find television sets, tape recorders, deep freezes, miniskirts in the stores on Nueve de Octubre.

The sidewalk cafés on the avenue stay open until four a.m. You can usually find someone who wants to discuss movies like *Two for the Road, The Sand Pebble, The Chase, The Professionals,* which had long runs in town; someone who was out at the airport to see the Braniff jet come in can tell you its color, sometimes the object of an informal betting pool; someone who wants to discuss the latest article in *Vistazo,* Guayaquil's leading magazine (the only local publication in Latin America which has a higher circulation than its North American competitors in the country like *Life en Español* or *Selecciones de Reader's Digest*). In 1967, *Vistazo's* star reporter, Alberto Borges, traveled to Vietnam, Israel, and Bolivia (where he interviewed Regis Debray) within the same six months. You can often find him at one of the cafés on Nueve de Octubre, too.

The beer you drink there, Pilsener's, is manufactured in town, and tastes quite good.

The phrase most Ecuadorians use when they want to generalize about their country's biggest city is "*mucho movimiento.*" They say the words admiringly, but to most North Americans who visit the city for the first time the movement seems chaotic. The apparent frenzy on Guayaquil's streets does not seem to bear much relation to the sleek *Playboy* world evoked by the products one sees in the store windows.

The working day does not begin until nine in the morning; it ends at seven; and within those nine hours three are always lost to the siesta. But when Guayaquil is awake and busy the activity there is fantastic. There are always throngs of people in the center of town, and the city's constant heat makes the crowds seem somewhat thicker, very much livelier, than those that walk along New York's Fifth Avenue during the height of the Christmas season. Unlike in the United States, relatively few of the people you see in the city are pedestrians going from one enclosed place of business to the next. A large part of Guayaquil's commercial business, even more than Juárez', takes place in the open air, on the street itself.

Even work that is familiar to visitors from the United States seems somewhat more frantic in Guayaquil. For example, there is a great deal of construction under way now: there has been a boom on ever since the first high-rise building was introduced in the city. Usually the workers use wooden planks, strands of rope— nothing more sturdy—to boost themselves up from one exposed story to the next. The tools and girders must be fairly safe, but one still feels that the workmen who use them are in constant danger.

But it is the vendors who are responsible for most of the noise and most of the activity. The center of Guayaquil is somewhat like the Lower East Side of New York must have been fifty years ago, before its inhabitants' children became lawyers and accountants and moved away from the city. Until noon each day you see dozens of vendors on every block, using their voices as musical instruments to advertise their slightly battered fresh fruits, their sea food, their fresh eggs. Most of them are thin people, no more than five-foot-six, dressed in clothes even more threadbare than those Domingo Guzmán used to wear in Juárez. The fruit salesmen balance huge, heavy trays on their flat palms, displaying at least as much grace as waiters in an expensive restaurant. The sea-food vendors carry their shrimps and crabs dangling by single strings from poles they balance on their shoulders. As they chant the names of their wares, their voices sound almost as melodic as the voices of the Negro peddlers in Baltimore or New Orleans. "Watermelons." "*Chirimoya.*" "Chimneyman." "*Huevos duros.*"

It is the morning of the day *Vistazo* is distributed. Walking down Nueve de Octubre, you must dodge the dozens of boys who rush past the pedestrians, past the fruit and sea-food vendors, crying "*La* Revista Vistazo, *compre la* Revista Vistazo."

Elsewhere there are vendors whose cries are less melodic, much more desperate. You see them all over town, wispy men, old plump women, ragged children standing behind stalls, small home-made stands, carrying wooden display cases: threatening, pleading, crooning; using every inflection known to man to persuade each passer-by that their particular tubes of Colgate toothpaste, packs of Salems, their Bic pens, their ten-cent combs are better than those of their competitors who stand just fifteen feet away, vending with equal energy.

But between five and eight o'clock each evening even the vendors are obscured by hordes of tiny, ragged boys, much younger than the teen-agers who sell *Vistazo*, who run up and down the city's streets begging everyone they see to buy a copy of the town's leading tabloid newspaper, *La Razón*, from their special supply. For those three hours their shrill cries echo back and forth throughout the city, its twilight song.

Listen, now, to some of the sounds the pedestrians make. People in Guayaquil have their own distinct way of attracting each other's attention. If a man is separated from someone he wants to talk to by several paces, or even as much as a block, he will purse his lips together and make them stutter as he releases thin jets of air from under his tongue: so, at certain hours, one can hear low gusts of "pss-pss-pss" almost anywhere. (Once I tried an experiment. I made that noise with ten people I passed and each of them looked in my direction, ready to begin a conversation.) But if the sibilant sound doesn't bring a response, the pedestrian is likely to whistle as loud as he can. Now add to the buzzes and the whistles the constant slurp of wet kisses, the crackling of salacious expressions which come from countless clusters of men who chorus their reactions to any pretty woman who walks by, and the frequent clapping of hands, particularly near the cafés, where impatient customers use that sharp sound to attract the waiters' attention.

But all of those sights and sounds are pleasant compared to the moans and cries of Guayaquil's poorest people: the beggars' dirge. You cannot walk three blocks before one of them stops you. They are as energetic as the vendors, and perhaps even a little more honest about the profession they've chosen (for the vendors do not sell their tubes of toothpaste, they beseech you to buy them). But if you can not harden yourself to their clinging presence, you will not remain sane in Guayaquil. The central city is filled with deformed people. A legless man will drag himself toward you; a man with stumps of flesh instead of arms has pinned some lottery tickets to the numb area where the bones press out against his smooth skin; a skinny, toothless old woman walks hand in hand with her pretty, dirty little grandchild, and the little girl whines at you— "Por favor, señor," "Regáleme," "Una caridad"—until you wonder what kind of beast you've become that you can listen so impassively. You sit down at a sidewalk café, hoping to escape, and an unshaven little man in a torn black suit, shiny with age, stands within six inches of your chair, staring at you with a totally blank expression on his face. You bribe him to leave with a cigarette, which is what he wants, but then you see a boy and girl leading their blind father toward you. A tiny shoeshine boy, sitting at your feet, wails and wails because you have rejected the service he offers. He pleads with you to give him a five-cent handout. Then pity twines with the native American aversion to the dole, and you instruct him to wipe the dust off your feet. That way you will teach him to be a man.

Sometimes, despite myself, the beggars' presence made me feel almost hysterical. It seemed as if Guayaquil had lost a long, bloody war and that there weren't nearly enough hospitals in the city to contain the soldiers and civilians who had been severely wounded.

If an outsider continues to perceive the *"movimiento"* in Guayaquil's streets as an inexplicable sort of frenzy, he will certainly use the word "disorganized" when he describes the city's poor, as our instructors did in training. But the situation can be more accurately summarized by the observation that the mestizos who compose the bulk of Guayaquil's population have at least as much energy and ambition as did the immigrants from Europe to America in the nineteenth century, but not nearly as much focus for their drives. They are not yet comfortable with the modern technology that originally attracted them to the city. They are trying to leap centuries in a single decade, and in a country where even slow upward mobility is still severely restricted.

If one does not judge Ecuadorians by the exact standards one has learned in the United States, it is possible to say that a beggar who works a twelve-hour day in Guayaquil is displaying the same kind of energy and initiative as a hawker in Juárez or an advertising man at the Big Fiesta. A street vendor labors at least as hard as a steelworker in Gary. But their circumstances are entirely different from those of most Americans. As Ecuadorian society is structured at present, it is impossible for them to find genuinely productive labor.

Population figures portray the problem most graphically. Twenty years ago Guayaquil was a city of only fifty thousand people. Then modern technology, the existence of some jobs on the docks, and peasant gossip began to attract *campesinos* to the big city. In 1966, seven hundred thousand people lived there. According to most projections there will be two million *Guayaquileños* in 1980, five million by the year 2000.

Although Guayaquil's development in the past twenty years has been startlingly rapid by the city's previous standards, it still has lagged way behind the population growth. As a result, there are not nearly enough institutions or facilities to provide for the people who live there. There are about fifty thousand productive jobs in the commercial city: perhaps fifteen thousand professional people, white-collar workers, teachers; three thousand factory workers at places like the beer factory and the cement plant; about ten thousand municipal employees like street cleaners, water-truck drivers, garbage collectors; about twenty thousand stevedores. Then, there are about twenty thousand more people who earn adequate livelihoods as cab drivers, bus drivers, carpenters, masons, beauticians. (Exact statistics are very difficult to acquire in Guayaquil: these are based on a list compiled in the mid-1960s by CENDES, an agency for economic development sponsored by the Ecuadorian government and AID, on conversations with businessmen and economists in Guayaquil, and on my own observations.) If the city were about one-third its present population, then few people would be forced to work as beggars or street vendors, or to open their small *tiendas* in the *suburbios*: to hold jobs and live lives that aren't even included in the conception that most middle-class North Americans have of social class and productive work. But now, between four and five hundred thousand of the people living in the city are as poor as the Negroes from Marks, Mississippi, whom Martin Luther King selected as the symbols of the Poor People's Campaign that was supposed to shock the American public.

A survey we made of a hundred seventy-five families in different areas of the *barrios suburbanos* showed that the average monthly income for a family of seven was forty-two dollars. The average amount of money that each person spends on food per day is fifteen cents.

In 1967 there were fifty thousand children who could not attend primary school. There are not enough teachers or enough buildings for most of the shoeshine boys and newspaper boys you see on Nueve de Octubre. Often, in the schools that do exist, the student-teacher ratio is about sixty-five to one.

But Guayaquil's middle class is expanding rather rapidly (by 1980 the city should have facilities enough for five hundred thousand people), and the consequences of that fact will affect the poor as much as their immediate poverty.

During the eighteen months Rachel and I lived in Guayaquil many of the wealthy people who control Ecuador were beginning to invest relatively large sums of money in restaurants, movie theaters, hotels, shopping centers, television stations, advertising campaigns. They seem to have realized that an entirely new clientele has come into existence during the past decade. When we arrived in Guayaquil there was just one television station in town; now there are three. There are three shopping centers in the wealthier suburbs and another will be built soon—in 1966 only part of one had been constructed. There are two new luxury movie theaters, four modern hotels are under construction, and there are seven new drive-in restaurants and soda shops.

But the upper class may not realize that by these investments they are doing more than profiting off the middle class. They are influencing more poor people than a dozen Jorge Rodriguezes could, or five hundred Peace Corps volunteers.

I first realized the explosive effect that the new luxuries could have on the ex-campesinos one day when I was interviewing some people in the dismal barrio Cuba, near the city's fetid stockyards, for a course that Jorge Rodriguez and Rachel and I planned to teach. "Thirty years ago I was a person," said one woman whose house sits right by a canteen that provides cheap liquor and perhaps marijuana to off-duty hog killers. "But you can see what happens here. So many of my children have died. Not one of them has found decent work. My husband has become an alcoholic. We're like animals here."

As I walked back to the church where we were working, across the wooden boards that provided the only pathway above the muck that had been left by last night's rain, I saw a group of the *barrio*'s children walking by me. One of them was wearing one of the Batman T shirts which had become popular as soon as the American program began to appear on Ecuadorian television. That T shirt, I realized, might really be the banner of a revolution.

Certainly it is clear that the new luxuries have made a profound impression on the poor people of Guayaquil and that television has made the profoundest. In 1966, when Rachel and I arrived in the city, the United States Information Service had statistics showing that about thirty thousand people owned sets and that one hundred and forty-seven thousand people watched the city's single channel at least once a week. In the *suburbios,* television sets were beginning to represent capital investments. Entrepreneurs were establishing "Tele-V-Centros" in their own homes and charging their neighbors several cents to watch each show. At that time there was at least one house on every block of the *suburbios* with an antenna above it, and in middle-class neighborhoods most people owned sets.

A year later three channels were functioning. As many as four hundred thousand people must have been watching television regularly. The local programs were usually news, soap operas, or contests. But most Ecuadorians preferred the dubbed, syndicated American programs that were on every night: shows like *Peyton Place, Batman,* and *Combat.* The symbols of those programs were quickly incorporated into the local life, their stars became local heroes. All over town, from the most remote of the *suburbios* to the main shopping streets, you could see little children wearing their Batman T shirts, playing with Batmobiles, or wearing earrings and barrettes shaped like bones with the brand name *Pic-a-Piedra,* in honor of the *Flintstones.*

The stars of the syndicated programs inspired a game called *Cien Amigos* (A Hundred Friends) which turned out to be the most popular contest ever devised in Guayaquil. It was very easy to play. You bought a picture album which contained a hundred empty squares for the hundred trading cards with pictures of television stars which you were supposed to obtain. Vendors gave some of them away, sold others. After a while storeowners and distributors decided to buy into the boom: they purchased the rights to individual cards from the TV announcer who had invented *Cien Amigos* (and made himself a millionaire). So, for example, the Royal Crown distributor had title to the photo of Adam West in *Batman*, and he ruled that people needed twelve bottle caps to acquire the card and thus be a step closer to the first prize, a trip to Miami. The spin-off from the contest was as extraordinary as the game itself. Royal Crown Cola, which no one in Guayaquil had heard of before *Cien Amigos* began, suddenly became one of the most popular beverages in town.

Just as *Cien Amigos* was ending, one of the men who was pictured on a card visited Guayaquil. Some of the most sensitive and intelligent people I knew, like Rachel's friend Lourdes Vera, became quite excited when they learned that they would have a chance to see the actor who plays Dr. Rossi on *Peyton Place*. Hundreds of thousands of people in the tropical Ecuadorian city must have followed the serialized account of life in the superdeveloped New England town as closely as they followed events in their own family. Now they were thrilled that they could see one of the program's heroes. It seemed as if every set in the city was tuned to the brief, flat interview in which he was asked to talk about *Peyton Place* that night.

Now, think of the boy I saw in *barrio* Cuba wearing his Batman T shirt. His parents were probably living in one of the tiny towns in Ecuador's interior as late as 1960, perhaps on the same patch of ground that their ancestors had inhabited since before the Spanish conquest. Virtually no one in the interior attends high school. What did the boy think of his imaginary contemporaries who attended the elaborate Peyton Place High? (Did he realize that they were imaginary? That the huge building in which they spent much of their time was an *escuela*?)

In a sense, of course, the boy is an eavesdropper. The programs he sees were conceived at the Big Fiesta by men who boast of their acquaintance with Norman Mailer and Frank Sinatra, and they were designed for the hipper regions of Nixonia. Often, they seem outrageous to people who live in Vermont or Kansas: they seem to favor male and female promiscuity, they often contain sympathetic portraits of people who will do anything to obtain material goods, sometimes they even seem to favor political revolution. And if shows like *Man from Uncle* and *Peyton Place* shock some older citizens of Nixonia, they have clearly encouraged black people and young people to rebel. The movies and packaged programs that Negroes in Harlem, Watts, Vicksburg have been watching every night since the early 1950s have allowed them to see the more comfortable world that equality would allow them to enter; the newsfilms they have been watching since 1960 have encouraged them to identify with their brothers throughout America who are also struggling to get there. Of course, the mass media have also suggested the content of the hippie movement and provided its weapons. And in the United States, the white middle class, the blacks, and the youth were all somewhat prepared for television when it entered their experience. Both its technology and the substance of its programs bore some relationship to the societies in which they were living.

But the young boy in *barrio* Cuba had no prior knowledge of American or industrial culture, no structure of ideas and assumptions through which the images he sees every night in his cane shack can filter. Values and desires that have always been embargoed from the Ecuadorian poor are smuggled into his mind every day. They must explode in his imagination.

Perhaps, as American radicals tend to argue, the new luxuries like television fill people like the boy in *barrio* Cuba with bloodlust, with an appetite for cheap sex, with a taste for gross, gaudy material goods. I am convinced that if a skilled propagandist, with enough money at his disposal to make sophisticated programs, ever became program director of one of Ecuador's television channels, he could win a demagogue's control over the country within a very few years. Imagine a cross between the Orson Welles who terrified

America with the *War of the Worlds* on CBS radio and the men who created Richard Nixon's image for the 1968 campaign, molding the mind of the boy in *barrio* Cuba.

But the process will be more random and arbitrary than that, and I am less pessimistic about it than most Americans. It seems new luxuries like television tend to liberate poor Ecuadorians from old fears as much as they fill them with new, coarse desires. If the people realize that neither their own upper class nor the North Americans have an exclusive right to the wealth to which they are constantly exposed, then perhaps the unfocused energy which is now so evident on Guayaquil's streets will cohere, and they will fight their way into the modern world their migrant parents were not allowed to enter.

IV

PERHAPS Bill Gshwend had confused Guayaquil with Chicago when he thought about our project. Perhaps he thought that its mayor was a stable force like Richard Daley, that the *municipio* had a power that was equivalent to Daley's City Hall. Whatever the illusion, it was complete. Even though our project in the *municipio* was an undeniable failure long before Gshwend left for Lima, he never seemed able to understand that there were very few *gringos* who could fit into a Latin bureaucracy, or to realize that the *municipio* in Guayaquil was even less powerful than it was stable.

We began to learn that two weeks after we arrived in the city, when Joachim Orrantia, the Mayor with whom Gshwend and Benitez had negotiated the terms of our work, was removed from office. He was succeeded by a man he had appointed Vice-Mayor, Roberto Serrano, Guayaquil's ninth *alcalde* in five years. One of

Serrano's first acts was to fire many of the civil servants who had staffed the municipal offices under Orrantia. Among the departing bureaucrats were some of the men whom Gshwend and Benitez had cultivated most assiduously during those Friday afternoons of gossiping and drinking.

It was never entirely clear why Orrantia had wanted our group in the first place. The most plausible explanation, which I heard from Ecuadorians and North Americans, was that the presence of twenty *gringos* in the *municipio* would help his administration negotiate a large loan from AID. But his replacement once gave me a slightly different explanation. Most municipal officials, Serrano said, had been told that we would perform unpleasant, menial tasks—be file clerks, for example—and I got the impression that they saw us as a source of cheap labor. Because of us, they wouldn't have to provide salaries for twenty Ecuadorian file clerks.

As soon as Orrantia was deposed, most of the people in our group quit working in the *municipio*. They had already become discouraged with their work, and his ouster persuaded them that they weren't wanted at all. Apparently, no one in the City Hall except Jorge Rodriguez and Enrique Huerta, the head of the City Planning Department and a friend of Gshwend's, any longer felt responsibility for the North Americans who roamed through its corridors. Serrano himself was reported to be more anti-*yanqui* than his predecessor. From the day he took office rumors began to circulate in the American community that he wanted to isolate his government from all North American influences, including the influence of our project. (I had quite a few conversations with Serrano, whom Ecuadorians believed to be more interested in graft than in politics, and my impression was that he considered us irrelevant to his plans but not dangerous.)

But even if Orrantia had maintained power, our attempt to "infiltrate" the *municipio* would almost certainly have failed. It took a week, no more, for most of the volunteers to become convinced that few municipal agencies had real work for them. They weren't willing to hang around offices where they weren't really wanted on the off-chance that someday, by attrition, they might gain the degree of influence that was needed to make our infiltration successful.

Sally Wells, who had worked as a secretary in San Francisco, was told during training that she would be assigned to the Department of Personnel. When she arrived in Guayaquil she discovered that there was no such agency, although a woman who worked for AID was trying to persuade the city to create one. Sally spent two weeks filling out pink slips in the Department of Rents and then quit the *municipio* altogether.

At least she was in love with Peter Evans, one of the men in our group, and though they didn't do any work for the next six months they enjoyed themselves courting. But for other volunteers the failure of the *municipio* project created enormous difficulties. For example, when Bert Kalisher's job turned out to be as much of a fraud as Sally's, he began to lose confidence in himself in a way that made one worry that his personality would soon collapse completely.

Bert had spent several summers working in a grocery store in his home town, and for that reason Gshwend assigned him to the Department of Markets. His office was above the sprawling public market, where most of the food was fly-specked and dirty. After he had walked past the crowd of vendors several times he became convinced that no one could persuade the poor people who rented the market's stalls, or the city officials who were supposed to inspect them, to make sure that the rules of hygiene were carefully followed. And if a code of conduct could be enforced (an absurd concept because the city officials were easily bribed), then Guayaquil's precarious economy would suffer—food prices would be driven up so high that slum dwellers would not even be able to afford the bananas and rice on which they usually subsisted. But the only reason Bert had been assigned to the Department of Markets was to persuade the people who worked there to make such changes. What a joke! His *jefe*, who had agreed to accept an outsider only because he owed his job to Mayor Orrantia, was not able to find any work at all for a North American who knew nothing about tropical foods and barely spoke Spanish. Bert felt completely ostracized: even less comfortable than Margot did living in her *barrio*.

And he was a timid person. He was the sort of tall and clumsy man who worries constantly that people will make fun of him. When he spoke he always seemed to be trembling; from his speech rhythms it sounded as if he was always a little short of breath. Often his fears made him seem cruel. In training he picked on Batman to divert attention from himself, in Guayaquil he was meaner to the shoe-shine boys than anyone else in our group. When they laughed at him playfully I'm sure he heard derisive taunts and imagined that they were directed at his ungainly physique and his mediocre Spanish. Sometimes he hit back.

After Bert quit the *municipio* he moved into the *barrio* that Margot had left when she went to live with Nick. He got even more frustrated trying to help the *comité* procure its land fill than she had been and moved on to another *barrio* within a few months. But his failures must have fed each other; he seemed to become increasingly incapable of working with Ecuadorians. "Bert doesn't like us," one of his neighbors told another volunteer. "Either he refuses to speak to us or he calls us names." Soon he moved away from that community, too, into a house which he kept so dismal and bare that the other volunteers began to call it the *casa nada*. He stayed inside it for days at a time. Once, when a friend of his told him that there was a large, comfortable apartment available downtown if he was willing to room with two Ecuadorians, he answered, "I don't want to live in Ekkiesville and speak Spanish with all of those spics."

Clearly, Bert should have gone home, but he couldn't do that either since he had joined the Peace Corps specifically to avoid the draft. The staff didn't care what he did as long as he didn't cause any trouble, so from the day he left his job in the *municipio* until the day his tour of duty ended he remained in Guayaquil, his hide-out.

Nick Zydycrn's response to his own failure in the *municipio* seemed to me particularly appropriate when I thought of Bert.

Gshwend had assigned him to the Department of Public

Works, where he was supposed to be one of the most important people on the project's team, a key to the formation of the "Alinsky-type organization." In the States Nick had spent several summer vacations working as a mechanic, and now that background was supposed to help him make certain that trucks containing land fill arrived in the *barrios* on schedule. If he were clever enough he would be able to tell the volunteers who lived out in the *suburbios* when their communities should petition the city for fill. Perhaps Nick would even be able to devise a way of increasing the flow of dirt into the swampy slums and thus make sure that thousands of people were grateful to the Peace Corps and the inter-*barrio* organization it had created.

But during his first day at work he went down to the garage where the trucks were repaired and noticed that, although the mechanics were short of tools, they had adopted their own system of keeping the vehicles in shape. It was clear that his ideas about maintenance work, based on the presence of equipment, would be irrelevant to them. No one in the shop had been told that Nick planned to work there. Perhaps it was because of their shyness or their lower-class deference, but none of them greeted him or seemed interested in talking with him. And they weren't involved in the sort of informal weekend project during which volunteers sometimes make local friends by offering to help. Nick couldn't step into the midst of a gang that had been working together for months and, broadly smiling, prove that he was a democrat by pitching in.

After he quit that job he expressed his frustrated anger with an observation that would become my own private motto during the year and a half we remained in Guayaquil: "You know, I think the most lucid piece of political theory in the whole twentieth century is '*Yanqui*, go home.'"

After Serrano had been in power for two months, only five of us were working regularly in the *municipio*. Rachel and I were still trying to help Jorge Rodriguez, and three more volunteers, including Bill Dodge, were working in the Department of City Planning.

But Rachel and I stuck to our jobs only because we didn't want to insult Jorge. The idea that Gshwend and Benitez had asserted with such conviction during training—that the city could be affected through its government—seemed to us as inaccurate now that we were living there as the more clearly flawed proposition that the average volunteer could influence the bureaucrats with whom he worked. There was nothing that even a skilled civil servant like Bill Dodge could do there, though Bill, the one person in our group the project's theory suited perfectly, had learned enough about low-cost housing during his years as an examiner for the Bureau of the Budget to assist any municipality that wanted to launch substantial programs.

Neither Gshwend nor Benitez had realized that Guayaquil's city government was almost completely without power. They had never come to terms with the fact that the most powerful men in the country are those whom local people call "*la oligarquía*," and that the oligarchy's interests are fundamentally opposed to substantial municipal reform.

You can tell a great deal about the *municipio* by walking around it, then through it. The lofty, rambling structure, which had been designed by Italian architects at the turn of the century, looked quite impressive from the outside: full of arches and passageways, small, sculpted designs, embossed metal plaques, small entryways protected by soldiers with shining swords on their hips.

But the moment you enter the building you become aware of the poverty which has afflicted each successive city administration, conservative or liberal. On all the *municipio*'s five floors the paint is chipping off the walls and deep gashes show through. Except for the second floor, where the Mayor and city council work (always thronged with petitioners from the *suburbios*), the hallways are barren. Inside the administrative offices there are only as many desks, tables, and chairs as are absolutely necessary, and most of the furniture has been built of wood which is already beginning to decay. Each office has several portable typewriters and a telephone, but practically no other modern equipment. Everywhere there are huge, dusty rooms—the municipal archives, for example, or the athletic association—which look as if they were deserted years ago.

I spent most of my time on the fifth floor of the building, where both Jorge's office and the Department of City Planning were located. Whenever I walked down the hall to talk with Bill Dodge or Enrique Huerta I had the feeling that I was in the midst of a narrow canyon, lost in a land which had been abandoned years before.

When I write that the offices lacked modern equipment, I am talking not only about devices like intercoms, electric typewriters, slide projectors, Xerox machines, dictaphones, which might have made the bureaucracy somewhat more efficient. I am talking about equipment which is absolutely necessary if you want to get a job done. For example, shortly after we began work in the *municipio* the Department of City Planning asked its volunteers to help design a master plan for a town called Duran, across the Guayas River from Guayaquil. But the volunteers realized that the master plan would never amount to more than a pretty pattern mounted on a cardboard sheet when they learned that the department had too little money even to purchase enough pens, pencils, and construction paper for them to work with.

It was the agencies' financial situation that produced the inaction and confusion which Rachel had described shortly after we began working for Jorge. The department chiefs didn't have enough time to plan their projects thoroughly or to follow through on all the necessary details. Their budgets were so low that they couldn't afford to hire Ecuadorian assistants to whom they might have delegated important tasks. But the city's problems were so severe that their offices were always full of poor people demanding services, and their presence made it almost impossible to concentrate on a single sustained piece of work.

The salaries the city government paid Jorge and Huerta were extremely low. Jorge, who had to support a wife and four children, earned about a hundred dollars a month from his job at the *municipio*, though he worked about ten hours a day. To save money he shared a rather small house with his wife's parents, her three sis-

ters, and all of their children. If Jorge was grafting goods and
money from AID, as Gshwend had alleged, it certainly made no
visible difference to his style of life. (What actually happened, I
think, was that Jorge had taken the materials AID offered but rejected the American agency's right to control their use. He redi-
rected them into projects which he thought were relevant.) Enrique Huerta, who also earned about a hundred dollars a month,
was trying to complete a new home which he had designed for his
family several years earlier. But he was often too broke to pay the
construction costs. To earn a little extra money both he and Jorge
taught courses at the university, which paid them about fifty dollars a month, and did whatever free-lance work they could find.
But the average annual income of both men, two of Guayaquil's
leading technicians, was only about three thousand dollars apiece.

It was because of the oligarchy that the conditions inside their
agencies would never improve, that their salaries would never increase. The oligarchy could strangle the municipal government
whenever it pleased. For the *municipio* was actually in hock, partly
mortgaged to a bank owned by Juan X. Marcos, the city's wealth-
iest man. (An anecdote, told to us by an American engineer
whose company was working for Marcos, suggests the sort of financial manipulations that brought the Ecuadorian his millions. He
earned most of his money from a sugar-processing plant, but each
year, we were told, he declared that business bankrupt, so that his
stockholders wouldn't absorb any of his profits, and turned the
bankruptcy over to his bank, which he owned privately.) When
we arrived in Guayaquil the city owed an additional three million
dollars to several other local banks. All of them, of course, were
directed by people whose class interests were the same as Marcos's.
If the city adopted policies they disapproved of, the oligarchs had
the power to foreclose the mortgage on the *municipio* and call in
the debt.

But they had other, more moderate means by which they would
restrain or overthrow a mayor who threatened them. They had
made that clear two years before we came to Guayaquil when they

had been partly responsible for deposing the city's most popular politician, Asad Bucaram (the man who had originally asked AID to send Benitez to make his study).

Bucaram had tried to enforce a policy which the oligarchy disapproved of most strongly. He tried to force them to pay the property taxes they owed the city, amounting to more than twenty million dollars: easily enough to liquidate the mortgage, repay the local banks, launch some programs in the *suburbanos*. The middle class paid taxes on the land it bought, so did foreigners, so did the few poor people who could afford to own property; but not the few hundred families that ruled the country.

The existence of the debt was no secret, nor was the use that most oligarchs made of the funds they saved. I often heard that the upper class sent more money out of the country, into foreign banks, than Ecuador gained from all its foreign loans. Our neighbors in the *barrios* frequently discussed the oligarchy's debt to the *municipio* and to the country. It was one of Jorge's chief complaints, and many of the students we knew cited the problem to prove that Ecuador could never be changed unless there was a revolution. But they were all powerless.

Bucaram, who had the support not only of Guayaquil's poor people but also of its prosperous Lebanese community from which he came (the only substantial immigrant group in the city), had been overthrown during his first term in office, soon after he threatened to expropriate some of Juan Marcos's huge land holdings and made it clear that he intended to collect the rest of the taxes, too.

While we were still in Guayaquil, Bucaram was again elected and became Serrano's legitimate successor, the tenth mayor in five years. But during that term in office he spoke somewhat less frequently and much less specifically about the property taxes. He did not make a serious effort to collect them. For that reason, apparently, he was allowed to remain in office. He tacitly admitted that, like all other politicians, he was powerless before the oligarchy, and in return the oligarchy allowed him to restore a semblance of stability to the *municipio*.

Once I asked a newspaper reporter why his publication didn't print information about the upper class's debts, and his answer left me more impressed than ever with the strength of the forces that were aligned against substantial reform in Guayaquil. He made the gesture of slitting his throat and said, "You don't do that sort of thing in this country." The owner of the newspaper was an oligarch, too, he reminded me, and so were the proprietors of most television stations and magazines and most of the people who bought the advertising that kept them alive. They all owed large debts to the city.

So the decisions that affected Guayaquil's future were made at private homes in the city's two upper-class suburbs, at the tennis club, the country club, the Rotary Club, the Chamber of Commerce, the Union Club—not at the bedraggled old *municipio* which our small band of *gringos* was supposed to infiltrate and transform.

But what I couldn't understand was why Benitez and Gshwend, who had exactly the same information about the *municipio* as we did, should have drawn conclusions that were so different from ours.

Why did they believe that Guayaquil's problems, which were plainly social and economic, could be remedied by the introduction of more modern systems, by personnel who understood the latest administrative techniques, by bureaucrats who liked to talk about their compassion for the poor?

It seemed to me that their commitment to those ideas was very similar to that of the equally well-intentioned Americans who were planning the pacification program in Vietnam. I tried to make a list of some of the assumptions and emotions that lay behind their strategy, so clearly doomed to failure:

1) Although people like Nick and Rachel and Bill Dodge and I, who had to do frustrating jobs in the midst of a society where we were powerless, perceived ourselves as isolated foreigners whose work had to accord with the demands of Ecuadorian culture if it was to succeed at all, Benitez and

Gshwend saw themselves as representatives of large institutions which had a great deal of money, technology, and personnel at their disposal. Therefore, they saw Americans in the foreground, close up, while Ecuadorian society was way in the background, a wide-angle lens shot. Since the North American was the integer of their analysis, then, not the local culture, they could seriously propose that a *gringo* like Nick could influence Guayaquil's Department of Public Works to increase the rate at which fill was sent to the *barrios*.

2) Both of them, but particularly Benitez, believed that Ecuadorians were striving so hard to achieve the things that North Americans had already obtained that to reach their goal they would subordinate themselves to the tutelege of any representative of the United States they happened to meet, even someone like Bert Kalisher.

3) The two men judged Ecuadorian institutions by North American standards. They could never be shaken loose from the impression that, because a building in Guayaquil bore the name MUNICIPIO, it served the same function, had as much power, as a city hall in the United States.

4) Their training and their careers prohibited them from seeing the problem of poverty as a class issue. If a peaceful redistribution of wealth and power, largely based on the existence of an efficient municipal bureaucracy, should prove to be impossible, then they would have to decide whether to support the oligarchy or the poor. If they openly opposed the oligarchy, they would have to oppose Wymberley Coerr, too, and the men who ran the Peace Corps and AID and sat in the Embassy at least once a week for meetings of Coerr's "country team." The actions which their beliefs demanded would soon cost them their jobs.

5) They were both reasonably ambitious, and they knew that promotion within agencies like the Peace Corps and AID generally come to people who can present the most dazzling proposals. Under most circumstances, the men who run foreign-policy organizations do not learn that a project which sounded good on paper has faltered in practice unless, as in the pacification program in Vietnam, the failure has been so disastrous that reporters and politicians begin to discuss it.

6) Gshwend and Benitez felt genuinely guilty, I think, over the fact that when they left Guayaquil they seemed to be abandoning people they had come to love. Our project was a form of conscience money. If it succeeded, then they could feel secure, in their next jobs, that they had not betrayed friends who trusted them.

They suffered from the sort of delusion that makes American colonialism so different from the classic European variety. Many of the men who serve the United States government abroad genuinely believe that they are remolding foreigners for their own good, not for America's profit or protection. They are beguiled by the idealism of their rhetoric, unwilling to look at the reality of the relationships it fails to describe. When Benitez and Gshwend talked about our program in training their tone was always earnest. Sometimes they seemed to have tears in their eyes as they thought of the benefits it would bring to Ecuador. If a French or British colonial administrator in the same position felt obliged to use terms like "infiltration" or "bloodless revolution," his voice would mock his words, his smile would be very cynical.

V

ONE's first impression of Guayaquil's *barrios suburbanos* is always the most shocking. Here is how Rachel described our first trip to the slums:

The first community we visited, located over a salt-water estuary, was the most depressing place I have ever seen.

The people originally moved into a low-lying island in the middle of the estuary and built their houses out over the water. They needed land fill, and when they learned that there would not be enough trucks to bring them dirt for another year they asked the *municipio* to give them garbage. Now they are living in an actual garbage dump. The streets are filled with garbage piled several feet high—mostly trash, but many orange peels, dead cats, dead rats, and old shoes. Flies abound and buzzards wheel overhead and roost on empty house frames, awaiting the arrival of the carrion.

Along one street a small copper-colored boy with long, bushy red-blond hair and a bloated stomach which did not hide his skin-taut ribcage was rolling an old, empty drum through the trash. He was absolutely naked.

An Indian family with eight children lives in one small cane shack in a long row of such shacks built up on stilts. They earn their money by fishing. The father and the two eldest sons were repairing a long pirogue-like boat in which they have to travel a day's distance to fish.

Hank Dawson and Gerald Erlham are both anxious to live in that community, but I really was appalled and very downhearted.

Later we drove out to a huge mud and salt-water swamp into which families are just beginning to move. It is the earliest stage of what will be a prolonged invasion; later on, I am told, hundreds of people will construct houses there overnight. Now pigs have a glorious time in the mud and ducks paddle about in small puddles. The people there are terrifically friendly and they have organized a committee to do something—I think to start a cooperative society to buy wood. They are very anxious to have volunteers work with them.

But the depressing thing is that they want fill for the swamp and they'll probably have to settle for garbage, too.

And more people keep coming in from the country and there is no place for them to go except into the swamps.

Later, you forget about the most dismal parts of the *suburbios* and think of them not as garbage and carrion but as an endless labyrinth of bumpy dirt roads, small gray cane shacks (which make the Guzmáns' house in Juárez seem manorial), sometimes punctuated by a dilapidated old red-brick apartment building, occasionally by a gaudy blue or yellow cement house. You remember the countless little *tiendas*, the thousands of vendors, still poorer than those you see in the center of town, who earn their living by selling each other individual cigarettes, bottles of beer, strands of wire; the municipal water trucks which carry parasites or typhoid directly into the stomachs of the three hundred and fifty thousand people who live in the swampy wasteland; the fifty thousand grubby starch-fat children who will never go to school because a thousand men like Juan X. Marcos don't pay their taxes:

"All representatives of the American government have the same purpose. . . . We have to work with the power structure that exists, and there is not much we can do about inequity there."— Wymberley Coerr.

Bill Gshwend's plan for an "Alinsky-type organization" in the *suburbios* turned out to be about as unrealistic as his hope that we would infiltrate the *municipio*.

He had decided to assign us to our *barrios* according to a pattern he had arranged on a large map of Guayaquil which sat above his desk in the Peace Corps office. Each volunteer was a pin, and the success of the inter-*barrio* organization, he was convinced, largely depended on the symmetrical arrangement of the pins. Volunteers shouldn't bunch up, he counseled, and they should be assigned to places that suited their personalities best. "In this business you have to think strategically all the time."

Off the map, in the real *suburbios*, the distance between each symmetrically arranged volunteer was about one mile. The empty space between each pin represented about twenty thousand people.

But the discovery that surprised us most was that the slum dwellers in Guayaquil were no more disorganized than the poor people we knew in Juárez. The assertions of the returned volunteers in Albuquerque, the assumptions implicit in Gshwend's and Benitez' lectures and plans were as inaccurate in their small way as the intelligence reports that had encouraged John Kennedy to go ahead with the Bay of Pigs invasion.

There were, if anything, too many organizations in the *suburbios*. There were already three separate *barrio*-wide organizations, each the arm of a political party; there were church-sponsored service organizations, self-help organizations that had been created during the land invasions, cooperative societies, school committees, delegations of people who went to the *municipio* each week to negotiate for land fill, women's organizations, associations of students who sought to do everything from teaching literacy to expropriating large areas of the town.

The Peace Corps' *barrio*-wide organization would almost certainly get lost in this sea of groups and never consist of anything more than its own handful of local people, some paper ties to the *municipio*, a few more petitions for overworked department heads to read, a resonant title—and some boastful statements out of the Peace Corps office in Washington. ("They're doing some exciting things down there in Guayaquil.") At best, the Peace Corps would draw about one-tenth as many slum dwellers to its organization as Roberto Serrano would to his, and Serrano wasn't very popular. Asad Bucaram would attract a hundred times as many people as we could.

Very few in the *suburbios* had even heard of the Peace Corps, although it had been working there for more than five years. Even in communities where volunteers had been living people would frequently ask Rachel or me, "*¿Qué es su misión aquí?*" One day I told a woman from the *suburbios* that I worked for the Peace Corps and the conversation that followed was typical:

"Of course, you run those community centers, don't you?" she said. "Yes, why just the other day I saw one of your women driving by in a jeep. Do you mind if I ask you a question? Do you belong to the Evangelist religion?"

"No, I'm Jewish."

"Well, I'm surprised. You see that is the rumor out where I live. All the people there think that your organization has come to Ecuador to spread your religion and make it triumph over Catholicism."

But I am sure that, long after he left Guayaquil, Gshwend remembered that war map in the Peace Corps office nostalgically and continued to believe that he had deployed his troops with great strategic skill. He must have blamed the volunteers for the failure of his battle plan.

In his valedictory speech, the day before he departed for his home leave in Washington, he told us that "at least we can say that the Peace Corps has made the people of the *barrios suburbanos* visible to the rest of Guayaquil."

I had never imagined that I could feel as uncomfortable in a slum community as I did in the *barrios suburbanos*. But after just a few weeks of living there I realized that I was even less equipped to help solve the problems of Guayaquil's poor than to help solve the problems of the Department of Community Development. Though Rachel felt the same way, she was at least able to establish decent human relations with our neighbors. My abiding sense of my own irrelevance left me as depressed and disagreeable as I had ever been.

One special problem that Rachel and I inflicted on ourselves was the size of the house we rented. By the standards of the *suburbios* it was a mansion.

At first we had wanted to settle near the people who were invading the swamp area, but they told us that it would be months before there would be vacant houses. So we decided to commute there from a near-by *barrio*. After a frustrating search we found our home. The house, which rented for thirty dollars a month, was large and yellow, with gardens and trees and vines outside, a sturdy metal gate, a driveway alongside the yard; inside there were five large rooms, including a bathroom with shower, bidet, toilet, and sink. When Rachel and I decided to move into the house we told ourselves that the people in the swamp area would never see it, would never learn enough about us to distrust us for our affluence. Besides, it really was a bargain; much less expensive than the grubbier places where most volunteers lived.

Of course, those reasons were rationalizations. We took the house because we thought it would afford us protection. Its sheer size seemed to insure us privacy. It was the worst decision we made in Ecuador.

We didn't have enough time to act as community organizers for the people in the swamp area. Although Bill Gshwend had assured us in training that we would be able to spend mornings in the *municipio*, afternoons in the *suburbios*, our job in Jorge's office usually kept us busy until suppertime. Though we occasionally attended squatters' meetings at night or on the weekends, it was impossible to get the same sense of their community as we'd had of our neighborhood in Juárez, or to give them any advice about how to function in a city which we barely understood ourselves.

Most organizing we did would have to be in the immediate vicinity of our house. It would be a spare-time job, separate from our own work in the Department of Community Development, since we did not derive nearly enough power from our positions in the *municipio* to justify encouraging slum dwellers to form an "Alinsky-type organization." We would not even be able to devote as much attention to the neighborhood as I had devoted to that block in Chicago where I tried to help build a playground.

The economic and cultural barriers between the *barrio*'s people and ourselves were much higher than the barriers between blacks and white students in the United States, or American Jews and poor Israelis, or between Rachel and me and the people we had known in Juárez. The size of our house aggravated the feeling of isolation from the community that would have disturbed us even if we had moved into a cane shack. It was like living in a fortress: the garden was a moat; the heavy black gate was our outer wall. It was almost as if we were to live in the big house of a plantation and call ourselves civil-rights workers.

But most of the things that made us feel wretched would have been woven into our daily lives in the *barrios* no matter where we had settled. For example, we slept until about eight-thirty every morning, while most of our neighbors woke up at six. Everyone in the *barrios* (which did have electricity) put a nightlight outside his house as protection against burglars. We were convinced that the fact that ours stayed on through so much of the morning provided a constant signal that we were not only wealthy enough to pay high electricity bills but also so lazy that we slept while everyone else worked.

Each morning when Rachel went to the *tienda* she bought four eggs for our breakfast (they cost twenty cents). Most of our neighbors couldn't afford to eat eggs at all. At night I would buy several bottles of beer to drug my persistent insomnia and would frequently forget to return the empty bottles the next morning. By nine o'clock the owner of the *tienda* would have sent his son to our house to collect them. In Guayaquil beer bottles are worth more to impoverished storekeepers than the liquid they contain. Most people bought their cigarettes one at a time, but I could never break the habit of buying by the pack. Once in a while, at night, Rachel or I would throw a cheese rind or some scraps of the rice or potatoes we had eaten for dinner out with the trash. By the time one of us got ready to burn the garbage the next morning every morsel of food a hungry family could possibly eat had disappeared.

We had been careful in New York to buy clothes that seemed both cheap and suited for the tropics, had shopped only in *schlock* shops or army-navy stores for most of the items. I had about six short-sleeved wash-and-wear shirts, a few pairs of khakis, some black chinos, and four pairs of permanent-press pants which I had to wear for work at the *municipio*. Our neighbors always wanted to look at those clothes, feel them, discuss their prices.

From the day we moved into the *barrio* the question we were most frequently asked by the people we were supposed to be organizing was whether we would leave them our clothes when we returned to the States.

Of course we could have changed our sleeping habits, given up eggs for breakfast, burned our trash as soon as we threw it out, learned to return empty bottles promptly. In Juárez, Chicago, and Maryland, and even Mississippi, we had been able to adjust our lives to a neighborhood's poverty without much trouble. But in all of those places we had been buoyed by the people's belief in themselves. In general, they had always been confident that they could win progress through organizations like the Freedom Democratic Party or earn it through individual effort. Our neighbors in the *suburbios,* as organized and hard-working as they could be, were dismally certain that they would never progress. As the Supervolunteer had told us during our first week in the country, they trusted no one: not themselves, not their leaders. Rachel put it this way in a diary passage:

> The main difference I notice between the Mexicans and the Ecuadorians (aside from the fact that the Ecuadorians are physically so much shorter) is that the Mexicans really have a sense of pride which converts itself to individual dignity, whereas the Ecuadorians have a real inferiority complex about their country. I mentioned that to Jorge last night and he agreed with me. He felt that the Mexicans have more self-confidence than the Ecuadorians because they were able to win a revolution.

Because the people with whom we worked in Chicago and in the South, whom we knew in Mexico, had faith in themselves, we were always able to feel that they could make use of our talents. That was true even in Vicksburg, where we had structured the *Citizens' Appeal* in such a way that the white Northerners who worked on the newspaper would be subordinate to the local directors and the black editor whom they selected. It had always seemed as if there was some productive job one could do with black people or Mexicans if one was flexible enough to respond to the nuances of their cultures, self-disciplined enough to recreate one's personality accordingly. The existence of tangible goals which might be achieved sometimes allowed us to submerge the visible differences between ourselves and our hosts, at least for a while, in common plans and shared work.

But none of the activities in which we had been involved in those places, radical or moderate, seemed appropriate to Guayaquil.

Even if it had been possible for us to persuade our neighbors to picket the *municipio,* as Gshwend had urged in training, we would never have made the effort unless we could have joined them. But

Peace Corps officials like Gshwend and Mankiewicz who urged us to agitate among the poor forbade us to share the risks that successful agitation would necessarily involve. If we picketed or sat-in ourselves, our organization might be accused of interfering in host-country politics and expelled from the country.

But Ecuadorians did not need graduates of the civil-rights movement to teach them the tactics of protest. Picket lines and direct confrontations were part of the city's daily routine. There were always teachers or students or municipal workers marching through the city protesting a cut in wages or unacceptable classes or police brutality. And, of course, each day the *municipio* was flooded with the slum dwellers who used every form of argument possible—violent or nonviolent—to try to persuade the Mayor, the City Council members or their assistants to respond to their needs.

Besides, we did not want to do anything that might help increase the existing tension between the residents of the *suburbios* and the *municipio*. It was a conflict that the *oligarquía* wanted very much to sustain. As long as the slum dwellers directed their anger at a powerless Mayor and City Council, the less visible rich people who controlled the city would remain relatively safe.

We had not come to Ecuador to be their tool.

The conventional community-development methods we learned in training were also unsuited to the reality of Guayaquil. In part of a longer letter to her parents Rachel described the kind of conversation that convinced us that the *barrio*'s people were too unsure of themselves, too cynical about their country, to adopt the slow, formal process that the returned volunteers had encouraged us to use:

Last Wednesday was Ecuadorian Independence Day, and we saw the first sign of spirit in the community. A young guy who owns the corner store had organized children's games. In one of them, which looked like the most fun, the kids tried to scramble up a greased pole to reach some prizes at the top. As we stood around watching, we met quite a few people who live here, and we were mobbed by children who seem content to stand near us and stare. The kids here are so different from others I know. Somehow they seem more passive and whiny, although they are pretty independent. Aside from playing soccer in the streets, their favorite game seems to be throwing rocks at each other. Paul got them laughing with his collection of odd noises. But when we stopped playing with them they began to delight in yelling their few English words at us or saying dirty phrases in Spanish.

Later on we got into a long discussion of Ecuadorian politics with one of our neighbors, Pepe. There has been a water strike here, which is causing a great deal of trouble for everyone in the *suburbios*. So he urged Paul and me to go to the Mayor and ask him to tell the city water trucks to make a special trip out to our house. (He thinks that the Mayor will do practically anything that a *gringo* wants.) I told him that the Mayor wouldn't listen to us (which he wouldn't believe) and suggested that an entire delegation from the *barrio* go to the *municipio* and present their demand. He thought that was a good idea, but it wouldn't work in this case because the people are not united, and nobody would care if his neighbor got no water just so long as he himself got some.

Pepe works as a stevedore carrying bunches of bananas onto German ships, and he lives way out here deep in the *barrios*, but still he knows a lot about the corruption that goes on all over Guayaquil. He said (as have so many others, including many of our student friends) that there is nobody in Ecuador who can lead the country, nobody who is honest. Then he followed the statement with a gesture of reaching out to snatch some money and said, "We Latins are that way. Whenever we can make a little profit for ourselves we do."

Paul and I spend an enormous amount of time talking to each other about this, trying to analyze the Peace Corps and to use our experiences here to figure out the role of white Americans in the world. Contrary to the experience of other married volunteers, we find that we are getting to know and love each other more instead of taking out our frustrations on each other.

Paul is now reading a book on immigrant history and he points out that this letter so far shows the kind of ethnic stereotyping that workers at settlement houses directed at the people whom they were trying to help. They, too, were forced to define themselves according to their successes in solving other people's problems. It is true, for we don't know the children here well, and, not being really part of the culture, we tend to see only the outer appearance which is probably misleading. We tend to judge the whole when we see only a small part.

One curious thing is that I am coming to view the Spanish language cynically, since I hear it used mainly in windy speeches and empty promises, and because I don't live in it and feel in it, I don't see its richness and emotion, only its simplicity and pomposity.

This experience is infinitely more complex than anyone was able to suggest to us in training. But there are so many simple-minded volunteers here, and they may return home with the same dull impressions the people we knew in Albuquerque had. Tom Hayden said that they are characterized by a 4-H personality. I think it's more a Boy Scout mentality, only they know about whore houses.

My literary mind might have allowed me to detect the offending stereotype when I leaned over Rachel's shoulder (kissed her neck) and read her letter home, but I could not censor my own emotions about life in the *barrio* as effectively as I could criticize her prose. I could not relate to poor Ecuadorians like our neighbor Pepe as easily as I had related to Don Pedro or the Guzmáns in Juárez. I loved listening to Don Pedro describe his days in the States, his hopes for his *colonia*, or to gossip with Paula Guzmán about her neighbors or with Domingo about the people on his *comité*. But I often began to feel somewhat restless during conversations with Pepe about his years as a *campesino* on a coffee plantation near Guayaquil. The restlessness was largely the result of the guilt I felt at my inability to do anything about his poverty or the pessimism it produced. Sometimes that desperate emotion was a strong, strangling sensation in my throat or in my chest. So I remained somewhat withdrawn from the community, ashamed of

my wealth, my size, my nationality, while Rachel, far more relaxed, entered it rather naturally.

Of course we had many friends in common, and we both knew
that, close up, their lives were not nearly so wretched as the poor,
dusty *barrio* made them appear. Once, for example, we spent a
weekend visiting Pepe and his wife, Evangelina, in their home
town, an eight-hour bus ride up the Pacific Coast from Guayaquil.
Until then I had always been irritated by Evangelina's shrill, rapid
way of speaking Spanish—it woke me up every morning—and I
had always perceived her as a harried, overwrought mother of two
children. But during those two days I realized that in her town's
opinion she was an accomplished, somewhat glamorous woman.
Her family and friends were proud of the fact that she had graduated from high school in the near-by city of Bahia de Caraquez,
that she could read and write quite well, display upper-class manners when the occasion required them, and play a few tunes on
the piano. Since a wide river separated her home town from Bahia
de Caraquez, she had lived away from her family during the years
she had attended school. One morning she guided us along the
smooth beach and up through the broad streets where she had
spent three happy years of her life (where she must have felt her
body come alive). As we sipped coconut milk, she reminisced
about her teachers and her classmates with the same nostalgic enthusiasm as, say, a graduate of Sarah Lawrence might reveal about
her four years in Bronxville. Nor was she an Emma Bovary, confined to the dull *suburbios* of Guayaquil by her husband's me-
diocrity. Pepe, too, was something of a hero in the small town, for
it was an impressive thing to find steady work in the big city.

When Evangelina talked with her old friends about Guayaquil
she seemed much more content with her life there than we had
imagined. For example, one morning she met a woman who had
been riding a donkey to the nearest *tienda*, about five miles from
her home. Evangelina's voice became merry and she began to
boast. "You know, where I live we can buy everything we want on
the street where our house is. Sometimes men even come to the

front door to sell us things. Your life would be easier if you moved to Guayaquil, too."

While Rachel and I were guests in their home town, we both felt close to our neighbors, and Evangelina remained one of Rachel's best friends throughout the months we lived in Guayaquil. But I couldn't sustain a satisfactory relationship with her or with Pepe. I felt like an intruder again and could never forget that I was much more closely connected to Wymberley Coerr's country team than to the community in which we were living. It was not just an idea but a constant, painful physical sensation. I have never felt such acute self-hatred. With part of my mind I began to wish that the Ecuadorians would insist that we give them the food whose remains they stole from our trash each night, that they rip the clothes off my body instead of begging me to leave them a shirt when I returned to the States.

I tried to describe our situation in a letter to my brother, Geoff:

It is another Sunday, warm as usual, loud with children's cries, the cascading complaints of old women, the music of Guayaquil's most popular dance, the *cúmbia*, jangling from half a dozen radios. In Spanish, now, a chorus tells us that nothing does it like Seven-Up. Our neighbor plays a loud game with his two-year-old boy, constantly clanging through our metal gate as noisily as possible. Inside our house, Rachel is mopping the floors. Although the Peace Corps thinks that Sunday is supposed to be the ideal day for community development—the men are home, their families are eager to have a *gringo* sit in their living rooms and tell them what's wrong with their lives—Rachel and I use it for reading, for housework, for writing and reflection.

The distance between our lives and thoughts and our neighbors' might exhaust anyone who really tried to cross it. "I believe that madness would be near the man who could see things through the veils at once of two customs, two educations, two environments," writes T. E. Lawrence. We live in our five-room house with our hot plate, refrigerator, pressure cooker, blender, and hundreds of books; they live in a cane shack and listen to the monotonous *cúmbia* for entertainment, eat corn meal and sugar for a Sunday treat.

Every day we exchange words and sometimes information; occasionally we devote a good deal of time to the effort. But whenever we leave for our mysterious jobs in the City Hall or return, unconscionably late for working people, having been deposited a block away from our house by a taxi that would make the neighbors jealous if they saw it, we find the same uncomprehending smile on the face of Evangelina, who has been waiting up for us. She rarely leaves her cane shack to go to the next block, let alone to the center of town, where we spend so much of our time. And she is so poor. One day she saw Rachel doing a wash in front of our house and asked if she could take over the job each week. It would have been cruel to refuse: the seven and a half dollars we pay her each month provides about a quarter of her family's income. But I can't stand the relationship it suggests (though Rachel is so warm and unself-conscious that the two of them have formed a genuine friendship). To me, it feels as if Fannie Lou Hamer had approached a civil-rights worker in Ruleville, Mississippi, and pleaded to be the project's cook.

One bad day the tension I felt erupted into words which embarrass me as I copy them now:

Twilight, Saturday. A thin breeze has begun to freshen slightly the evening's mugginess. With the breeze, through our dining-room window, comes the smell of dog carcass—a black bitch has been lying outside our house all day: fleshy, decaying. As I sit here typing, I am, as always, awash in the noise of the *barrio*. A metaphor for my feelings, almost exact, is that of a man sitting calmly on the beach where the sand joins the water, too preoccupied to notice the incoming tide. Only he can retreat. When his chest is soaked, his bottom mired in the muddy sand, he can go inland and resume his contemplations. Here there is no escape except time. When the clock finally reaches ten, the *barrio* will begin to sleep. The current of screaming women, crying children, squawking radios will subside for a few sweet hours.

I wrote dozens of pages of notes about our life in the *suburbios,* and most of the passages sound as sad and alienated as those two excerpts from my letters home. Scenes that I would have described with sensual pleasure in my Juárez diary become bitter symbols for the *barrio*'s poverty and my own helplessness. For example, I write about the long, cramped bus ride into the center of town in terms of the physical discomfort it causes me and never draw word sketches of my fellow passengers or record their conversations. When I discuss my neighbors I am much more conscious of the fact that they want me to use my status as a Peace Corps volunteer to help them get a job, a scholarship, a visa to the States than I am of their backgrounds or their relations with each other. When I describe the *barrio*'s noises, which were almost the same as the sounds we heard in the *colonia* in Juárez, I portray them as grating shrieks which threaten my nervous system, not as music that increases my appetite to discover as much as I can about the community.

VI

IF Rachel and Hank Dawson had been typical Peace Corps volunteers, I would have felt the same personal guilt about my reaction to the *suburbios* that Margot described when we arrived in Guayaquil. (By the end of our first summer there, Hank had not only established his *machismo* by proving that he was the best drinker in his *barrio,* but he had also become famous throughout the city as the star of a leading baseball team.) Perhaps I would have explained the unhappiness I felt because I was unable to make friends or organize effective projects in my *barrio* as a case of "culture shock," despite the fact that I had been relatively happy and successful when I lived with poor people in other alien cultures. I might have accepted the Peace Corps' terms, as I had Harvard's and the Big Fiesta's, and focused most of my intellectual energy on criticizing my own personal weaknesses.

But the more I talked to other volunteers who were stationed in Guayaquil, the more convinced I became that Rachel and Hank were rare exceptions. The Peace Corps had assigned about fifty people to the city—community developers, physical education specialists, university teachers, nurses, representatives of the cooperative movement—and most of them were even more frustrated than I was. What was worse, most of them seemed to be paralyzed by their sense of failure. Instead of searching for ways to understand the reasons that their experience in the Peace Corps was so much worse than they had expected, they accepted everything that happened to them as preordained and never tried to question the decisions the organization had made in their behalf.

Many of them began to regard Ecuadorians as barbarians and to dismiss the questions that a few of us were starting to raise about the value of our project as the efforts of "intellectuals" or "activists" to avoid hard work and stir up trouble. That way they could continue to see themselves as representatives of the decent middle-class America whose generous efforts to end human suffering were constantly thwarted by ungrateful poor people and left-wing fanatics.

A few months after we settled in the *barrios* Rachel and I visited two volunteers stationed in a town near Guayaquil, who had been in the country for nearly a year. Soon we realized that they had invited us to stay with them because they wanted to talk to some new people about their frustrations.

One of them told us that his experience in Ecuador had caused him to believe that there really might be such things as superior and inferior races. He had become convinced that birth control was the only salvation for the country, and that laws should be passed making it illegal for women to have more than two children. He had a recurrent fantasy, he told us: "In three or four years I'll be sitting behind one of those big desks in the State Department. Then I'll be able to get back at those little Ekkie bureaucrats who give me such trouble now."

His partner expressed himself even more simply: "I can't wait until the wrong Ecuadorian hits me at the wrong time so that I can beat him up."

Another member of their group had quit his job in a rural school. After traveling all over the country in search of work, he had decided to become a community developer in Guayaquil. But he couldn't find a job in the *suburbios* that satisfied him. Soon he began to stay in his house for days at a stretch. One afternoon a neighbor of his, who thought that he might be lonely, tried to visit him, to show him that he had some friends. "I don't understand that man," she told us later. "He ordered me to get away from his house and to tell everyone else in the *barrio* that he didn't want to be bothered again."

Similar anxieties seemed to be affecting many of my favorite people in our group.

In Albuquerque, Sherwood Parrot had been one of the few trainees who seemed to approve of the fact that Rachel and I had participated in the civil-rights movement. He would have gone to Mississippi himself, he told us once, if he hadn't been forced to get a job that summer so that he could support himself in college.

When Gshwend assigned him to the Department of Community Development, Rachel and I were relieved to learn that we would be working with an ally. But after a few weeks he stopped coming to Jorge's office. He thought it made more sense to work in the *barrios*, he said, and perhaps he was right. But soon we began to hear from the volunteer grapevine (thick with gossip about all of us) that he slept until noon every day.

He lived in one of the few *barrios* in town where there had been Peace Corps volunteers ever since the organization had begun to work in Ecuador, and his neighbors were unusually sophisticated about the work we were supposed to do. After he had stayed away from several *comité* meetings to which he had been specifically invited, his laziness became a local issue. The *comité* talked openly about sending Dan Stringer a petition asking that Sherwood be removed.

By then he was spending most of his time in the Peace Corps

office. Two or three times each week he asked the staff doctor to treat some new ailment. He talked quite openly about the fact that he wanted to be sent home from Ecuador with a medical exemption from the draft. Before his neighbors decided whether or not to circulate their petition, he was in Washington with a case of hepatitis.

Libby White was one of the kindest girls in our group, and easily the most innocent. A graduate of a small woman's college, with a broad, friendly face and a personality to match it, she would have made an excellent grade-school teacher in her small town, or an excellent case worker in a community that didn't threaten her.

But she had been placed in one of the remotest of the *barrios* and advised to board with a couple who had always made a special effort to meet volunteers. A few months after she moved into the house the husband was offering to leave his wife and live with her. There must have been desperate nights when she felt that downtown Guayaquil was as distant from the community where she was living as her home town was from Guayaquil. Soon she began to tell the Peace Corps staff that she was afraid her host would rape her. She had to get out of the *barrio* as quickly as possible.

One day I was in the Peace Corps office when she made an offhand comment which sounded like a perfect distillation of her anger at the Ecuadorians and, perhaps, of her dissatisfaction with herself: "Well, I guess I'll be going back to the *barrios* now. I think I'll take a shower first, though. I don't want to smell like those Ekkies who ride with me on the bus."

Throughout training I had expected that Gerald Erlham would submerge himself completely in Ecuador's culture. "When I get to Guayaquil I'm not going to have anything to do with the volunteers or staff," he would tell us. "I just want it to be me and the people." His experience in Juárez had convinced me that he was prophesying, not boasting. His Spanish was excellent, and he felt even more at home in his *colonia* than we did in ours. For him, too, it had been a happy replay of an earlier experience in the civ-il-rights movement, a summer when he had worked on a voter-reg-istration project in Kansas City.

His idealism had seemed as deep as his personality was flexible. The first time I met him he was talking with Nick about the draft. He opposed the war as strongly as we did, and Nick's de-scription of his months of defiance encouraged Gerald to tell us that he planned to fill out a C.O. form, too. Then he began to talk, very slowly, about his deep belief in pacifism, in the power of love to redeem.

Like most of us, Gerald had assumed that the people in his *barrio* would display the same warm feelings toward him as his neigh-bors in Juárez had. So when he realized that the Ecuadorians could understand his presence only as a sign that they would soon receive material assistance from the United States, he became acutely depressed. The revolution he wanted to make was one in which people would renounce wealth, not beg for it, as the slum dwellers seemed to do when they met him. He tried to explain that he had come to Guayaquil to be their friend, but that simple statement sounded completely implausible to them. Nor could he use the Peace Corps' definition of its work to make himself intelli-gible. How could his neighbors comprehend an American theory called community development which insisted that poor people could improve themselves if they learned to rely on their own re-sources—while the rich continued to rely on theirs?

Since Gerald had not been assigned to any agency in the *muni-cipio*, he could not rely on the excuse that Rachel and I used that we had really come to Guayaquil to serve the city as technicians, an assignment that was formidable enough to give us a little legiti-macy in our *barrio*. His neighbors couldn't figure out what he did with himself every day. When he attended a meeting of the local *comité* one woman stood up and accused him of being a spy. "The CIA sent you out here to discover our plans." He never went to another meeting.

Instead of talking about how eager he was to live in the *subur-*

bios, he began to ask the rest of us how he could avoid the Ecuadorians who invited him to soccer games, to dinner, to their *fiestas.*

In those early months he came over to our house quite frequently, mainly to talk with Rachel. I probably intruded into
those conversations too often, replacing Rachel's gentle manner
with my insistent one, as I tried to force Gerald to see that his unhappiness, like mine, was the result of Peace Corps policies, not
his own deficiencies. By then I resented the organization so deeply
for its sloppy, insensitive planning that I must have sounded like a
fanatic when I discussed it. But I was also trying to understand
the institution's personality in the way a novelist might try to understand the personality of one of his characters, so I usually talked
in analytical terms about its processes and its theories. That way of
thinking must have seemed dull and inhuman to Gerald.

He began to spend much of his time with Hank Dawson, Bert
Kalisher, Sammy Bernstein, and Barney Ableman. I'm sure that he
found their style more soothing than mine, or even Rachel's. They
would play cards all night or go out whoring or get drunk, and
they usually talked to each other in the staccato dialect Hank had
invented where irony and insult were substitutes for thought.

I was thinking of Sherwood and Grant and Libby, and myself,
when I wrote this description of a small party Rachel and I had arranged for some other volunteers:

The evening did not begin very pleasantly. Everyone was depressed, but there wasn't very much we could say. Nick tried
the *Esquire* test on Vietnam and discovered that he was
equipped to discuss the issue. Margot sat in the kitchen helping Rachel soak lettuce in iodine water, the only way we can
be sure that we're not exposed to hepatitis when we eat the
plant. Gerald sat near Rachel, explaining to her his latest unhappy encounter with his neighbors.

"Good food, good grub, go God." So Nick said grace. We
laughed, tried to joke some more, but mainly paraded through
the delicious stew Rachel had cooked in a rather bedraggled
silence.

After dinner someone suggested that we play charades. It was amazing, as we involved ourselves in the game, to see how completely our moods changed. No longer were we adrift in this foreign land, stumped by the assignment that had once seemed such a good way of expressing our ideals, our generosity. Now our lives were back in control, and through our common efforts to illustrate the titles of plays, songs, movies that evoke images from our shared past we found ourselves suddenly knotted into a coherent group. So, I imagine, must other colonialists, other exiles, have sat out their years in bondage.

Bernard Fall writes in one of his books on Vietnam that immediately after World War II the French government sent some of its most idealistic young men, former fighters in the underground, to help administer Indo-China. They were persuaded to go by the hope that they might improve the lives of millions of Asians. But quickly, Fall says, they became absorbed by the colonialist system. By 1947 and 1948, he says (probably in a disguised bit of autobiography), you could see them in the bars and restaurants of Saigon and Hanoi, trying to reconcile their past dreams with their present practices. The passage is a eulogy to a generation that was lost then, is invisible now.

Here, after two months, more than half my fellow volunteers have taken to calling Ecuadorians Ekkies. The term means "You know them, the stupid, smelly people we have to deal with." One rarely hears a kind word about the country, its customs, its people.

VII

Shortly after Bill Gshwend left the country, Jorge Rodriguez offered Rachel and me the opportunity that Bill had instructed us to take by cunning. Jorge had been granted a scholarship to study community development in Italy for three months, and he wanted us to administer his department while he was gone.

Of course we refused. The skills which one needed to survive in that environment were too complex for an outsider to acquire so rapidly. Jorge's genius lay in his ability to prevent serious fights between people in his department and people in the *suburbios*: what Gshwend dismissed as hypocrisy I admired as diplomacy. But it was a talent that depended on an intimate knowledge of the country's customs and sustained personal relationships with thousands of *Guayaquileños*. Those were things that Rachel and I could never fake.

We couldn't work with the man who replaced Jorge. My major dispute with him was over the contents of a page which the city's leading newspaper gave the department each week. I had agreed to take charge of it and was trying to publish photo essays which contained substantial quotes from tape-recorded interviews which Rachel and I were conducting with slum dwellers and *campesinos*. The idea, which we had borrowed from the civil-rights movement, was that if the people we spoke to realized that their words were interesting enough to be published in a newspaper they might develop a new self-confidence.

One day the temporary *jefe* of the department changed my copy so that it showed a *campesino* prefacing an answer to one of my questions with the words "*Ayyy, señor gringo.*" Later in the text he altered another *campesino*'s words so that the man referred to himself as one of the "*gente humilde*" (the term connotes inferiority, not humility). I tried to restore the real quotes, but my *jefe* kept assuring me that "these people talk that way. I know. I worked out there as a school inspector for years."

Although I urged him to listen to our tapes (they hadn't talked that way to Rachel and me), I accepted the changes he made in the text. He had a right to insist that his orders be obeyed since the newspaper page, even my article, would be published under his name. But I decided not to do any more journalism until Jorge returned, and when the new *jefe* seemed somewhat reluctant to find an alternate assignment for me, or any assignment at all for Rachel, we suspended our work in his department altogether.

Now, like most volunteers in our group, we were jobless.

Each morning we would leave our *barrio* by nine-thirty. We wanted our neighbors to continue believing that we had steady work. It was the only way we could remain intelligible to them: we might, just possibly, have taken a house so far from town in order to save money. But once we arrived in the center of the city we had nothing to do. We used to spend hours walking back and forth along Guayaquil's hot streets or drinking beer at the sidewalk cafés. Twice a day, exactly when the mail arrived, we would walk through the commercial section of Nueve de Octubre, through the park where Guayaquil's statue to its war dead is located, past the American Consulate, one of the fanciest buildings in town, and out to the middle-class community where the Peace Corps has its office. We would spend an hour there talking with our fellow *gringos*. At least the mail, which always appeared at the same time, gave a crude structure to our aimless days. It was one of the few pleasures we could always anticipate. Another was the arrival of *Time* and *Newsweek*. On Wednesdays, when those publications were flown into town, we would hurry to the kiosks on Nueve de Octubre and read them as if they were letters from home.

The worst time of the day was the siesta. While the Ecuadorians were in their houses eating lunch, or playing with their children, Rachel and I felt thoroughly lost. The city was completely closed down, but it was impractical to spend forty-five minutes riding all the way out to our house in the *barrios*, fix a quick meal, and ride back to town again promptly enough so that neighbors like Evangelina wouldn't doubt we were gainfully employed. So we usually ate at the Pensión Helbig. The place was always full of volunteers, and after lunch they would remain together for several hours playing gin or poker or pinochle. It was like a tiny, stifling compartment, sealed off from the rest of the country.

Here is a strange episode which came to symbolize those noon hours for Rachel and me:

We had invited our friend Lourdes Vera to eat with us so that we could discuss a student organization with which she was involved. But as soon as we sat down, before we could begin our own conversation, some of the other volunteers started complaining about the fact that the owner of the place, a refugee from Germany, had quit giving them free catsup.

Hank Dawson was especially angry. "The Jew in him is really coming out," he said as soon as he saw me. "How can we organize a boycott against him?" It was the first time Hank had ever seemed interested in my experience in the civil-rights movement.

I didn't know how to respond to his anti-Semitic remark. Months before I had learned that no argument I used could silence him. Besides, as always, he was accompanied by Barney Ableman, who loved to talk about his religion and the origins of his family. Barney never seemed to find Hank's comments insulting.

I asked him why he didn't just talk to the owner of the *pensión*, instead of threatening to boycott the place. It was such a reversal of roles that I would have thought Hank and Barney were putting me on if I hadn't known how much they loved their catsup. Each of them used about half a bottle on every serving of rice and meat.

At first, Hank agreed to join me in negotiating with the owner, but a little later he returned to our table with the report that he was scared to meet the man. "You see, I owe him eight dollars. He'll talk about that instead of the catsup."

My conversation with the owner was quite reasonable. He didn't mind if we used catsup as sauce, he said, just so long as we didn't use it in excess. Then he pointed to Barney. "I saw him pour a whole bottle of it over his rice yesterday. How can I allow them to do things like that and still make a profit?" But it was not hard to reach a compromise. The catsup would be restored to the tables if the volunteers would agree to limit the amount they consumed.

When I reported the results of the negotiation to Hank and Barney and Bert Kalisher and Sammy Bernstein, who were earnestly discussing the most effective means of involving all the volunteers in a boycott, they told me that I had sold them out.

I actually found myself at the point of telling them that I

agreed with the owner about their catsup-eating habits. But then I decided that to discuss the issue at all would be to behave like the rest of them.

As I walked back to my table, I wondered whether there was any way to convey the spirit of this group of North Americans to our friend Lourdes.

Often after lunch at the Helbig Rachel and I would walk over to the Phoenix Club, much quieter, and sit in its deep-brown leather chairs, drinking Seven-Up as we read the *Miami Herald*. It wasn't much of an improvement, though. We were only exchanging the loud, brash neocolonialist Peace Corps environment for the more tranquil setting enjoyed by the Europeans who set out fifty years ago to conquer the continent.

We must have talked about the possibility of leaving Guayaquil every single day during those months. (I was just about to turn twenty-six, so the draft was no longer a problem.) I remember one particularly depressing afternoon in August when Rachel and I sat in the riverfront park near the statue of Bolivar and San Martín, each of us pushing the other toward tears as we dwelled obsessively on our failures and frustrations. (It was the week that Jerry Rubin transformed the House Un-American Activities Committee from a threat into a joke by testifying in a Revolutionary War costume.) We were almost as troubled by the attitude that most volunteers had adopted toward us as by the fact that we had no job. Most people in our group felt that because we lived in a virtual mansion while we criticized the Peace Corps and the work it had assigned us we were hypocrites, unable to live by the standards we had invoked so often in training. Instead of helping the poor, we were demoralizing the other volunteers. One physical-education specialist talked openly about his great desire to "knock Paul Cowan out." Even Bill and Joyce Dodge and Ralph Craft, who agreed with the majority of our criticisms of the Peace Corps, seemed to feel that my intensity was unseemly, perhaps a little crazy, and that Rachel was not the same sweet person she had been just a few months earlier. Nick and Margot were our only real friends.

But we couldn't bring ourselves to quit the Peace Corps, for that act would be an admission of personal failure. In a way, the organization continued to hold the same mythic sway over our minds it had when we'd joined. The more deeply we hated it, the more determined we became to succeed on terms its members could accept.

To a very great extent, our self-respect depended on our ability to find useful work in Guayaquil and to change the Peace Corps so that it would be more responsive to the needs of the Ecuadorians and the feelings of the volunteers.

During the depressing weeks after we left the *municipio* Rachel and I always knew we could find work in Guayaquil to keep us at least as busy as we had been in the Department of Community Development. The fact that we objected to doing it probably strengthened the other volunteers' feeling that we were slackers.

Women's groups were always asking Rachel to teach cooking or sewing or cake decorating in one of the community centers in the *barrios*, but she was convinced that hundreds of Ecuadorian women were at least as equipped to give those courses as she was. By accepting such offers, as girls in the Peace Corps often did, she would be depriving a poor *Guayaquileña* of a decent week's wage.

There was no exact male equivalent to those jobs, but I could have involved myself in small projects like showing United States Information Service movies in the *barrios*, or obtaining uniforms for soccer teams, or organizing Boy Scout troops. Those were the kinds of roles Bill Gshwend had urged us to fill, for they would cover us as we agitated for peaceful revolution. And I think that if I had joined the Peace Corps before I went to Mississippi, when I was twenty-three instead of twenty-five, I would not only have done that sort of work diligently but been very harsh in my appraisals of volunteers like my present self who seemed to scorn small jobs because they were grubby. But now it all seemed like waste motion. It made no sense for *gringos* to work alone in Guayaquil. The only way to succeed on the city's terms was to co-ordinate one's activities with Ecuadorians like Jorge, whose programs had some chance of taking root in the local culture. But now Jorge was gone, and it was extremely difficult to find professional people or students who trusted us enough to work with us.

At a party one night we met the president of the Guayaquil Broadcasters Association. When he told us that he owned a radio station and said that he wanted to explore the possibility of inaugurating a series of educational radio and television programs, we volunteered to help him. He sounded as interested in us as we were in him, so we sent him a letter confirming our conversation and suggesting a time when we might meet again. No answer. Another letter from us. No answer from him. We went to his office to find him. His secretary said he wasn't there. We returned the next day. He had just gone out. Finally, after several weeks, we gave up.

At first we wondered whether we had offended him in some way. Then, to reassure ourselves that we weren't such clumsy diplomats, we decided that his behavior was a reflection of his—and his country's—erratic personality. But later Lourdes Vera provided a more plausible explanation for the episode. "He needs skilled people to do that work," she said, "and he must have realized that you are called volunteers. In this country that means that you are unskilled. If you had been able to present yourselves as technicians who know as much about the profession as he does, you would have heard from him the next day."

At about the same time we met some members of DUC (*Desarollo Universitario Comunal*), a group of university students which had been formed to work in the *suburbios*, and we asked them if we could coordinate our activity with theirs. Hector Montoya, the organization's president, became a good friend of ours, and he and some other students helped us plan and conduct a survey of the *barrios*. Sometimes at night we would go to the movies with them or invite them to our house for dinner or drink with them at one of the sidewalk cafés. My birthday and the *santo* of Teresa Vera, Lourdes's sister, fell in the same week, so we organized a very pleasant party at the Veras' house for about fifty Ecuadorian students and Peace Corps volunteers.

But when Hector Montoya told Rachel and me that we could participate in a three-day retreat in the *campo* where DUC would discuss its future plans, we became an issue that threatened to tear the organization apart. At least half its executive board insisted that no North American should be alowed to learn DUC's inner secrets. By agreeing to let us come to the conference, Hector had betrayed the Ecuadorians' interests.

As soon as we heard about the fight we told Hector that we would be glad to stay in Guayaquil that weekend. But to demonstrate his loyalty to us, and to maintain his power in DUC, he insisted that the organization had to abide by his original decision.

The night before the conference he told us that we needn't bother to wait at the DUC office. Instead, we should be at the Peace Corps office at one o'clock the next afternoon, when their bus would pass by to pick us up. When it had not arrived by three, I decided that my Spanish had undergone another of its periodic collapses the night before and caused me to misunderstand Hector's instructions. I telephoned his office to doublecheck our arrangements. A janitor relayed the message he had left me:

At the last minute, there had been an unexpectedly large turnout of Ecuadorian students, Hector had written. There was no room on the bus for Rachel or me.

That night Rachel described our reaction in a letter home:

At first we were a little annoyed because we had been kept waiting, but later got very depressed by the futility of working in a city where we cannot communicate with the students because they are so suspicious of the Peace Corps and so prejudiced against Americans. If the Peace Corps had begun to live up to its claim that it was completely free from U.S. political interests, by now it would have persuaded some students that it is not to be feared. But the majority of them think that we are all CIA agents, and our reputation for doing good community-development work is so limited that they have no incentive to ignore their suspicions and come to us to learn from our mistakes, let alone our successes.

After DUC's conference, Lourdes, who had attended it, told Rachel that there had been about five empty seats on the bus. But Hector had been afraid that he would be fired as president of DUC if he had allowed us to fill two of them.

VIII

BILL DODGE found an appropriate metaphor to describe the organizational process that had left Libby White, Gerald Erlham, and Sherwood Parrot stranded and miserable in the *suburbios*, given us our impossible assignment in the *municipio*, made it so difficult for us to win the trust of DUC and of the head of the Guayaquil Broadcasters Association. "The Peace Corps," Bill said, "is like a lower order of animal. It never learns from one generation to the next."

I used the word "autistic" to describe our discovery that although there had been volunteers and staff members in Guayaquil for more than five years, none of them had ever been able to accumulate information about the world around them.

As we searched through the Peace Corps' records to discover the empirical information that had been used to justify our project we found that all programing and evaluation was done in terms of the Peace Corps itself, not of the Ecuadorians. In the regional office, where the representative and his secretary spent most of their time, there were drawers full of memos from Sargent Shriver and Jack Hood Vaughn to their employees around the world, or of psychiatrists' reports on hundreds of volunteers or personal correspondence between staff members. But there was not a single manila envelope that contained information about Guayaquil.

We couldn't even find a record of the agencies with which the volunteers had worked in the past or of the Ecuadorians whom they had assisted.

Nor were there documents that recorded the commitments the Peace Corps had made. Often *Guayaquileños* would complain to Rachel or me about a promise which a volunteer or staff member had broken—to establish a cooperative society in one *barrio,* to teach at a school for the blind, even to give English classes. But by now the rep or volunteer who had guaranteed his assistance was back in the States. He had left no record at all of the discussions that had been held or the agreements that had been reached. So the Ecuadorians were at the mercy of the Peace Corps' most recent arrivals, and often, to assert their independence, new volunteers and new reps broke off all relations with the people who had been closest to their predecessors. Thus, many Ecuadorians who had based months of planning on assurances they had received from Bill Gshwend found themselves systematically ignored by Dan Stringer, who felt that his reputation within the Peace Corps hierarchy depended on his ability to establish his own programs with his own local people.

I received my clearest impession of the Peace Corps' autistic nature when I persuaded Dan Stringer's secretary to let me read some files, technically classified from volunteers, which contained discussions of the problems the organization had faced during its first years in Guayaquil. The authors of some of the memoranda were members of the Washington staff, so I assumed that their observations about the Peace Corps' difficulties in Ecuador were consistent with their ideas about how the organization could work successfully throughout the world.

The document that interested me most was a report which Richard Ottinger, then Peace Corps Director for the West Coast of Latin America, now a Congressman from Westchester County, New York, had sent to Jack Hood Vaughn, then Director of the Latin-American region, after returning from a visit to Guayaquil:

The morale of the volunteers was terrible. I made it clear that those who were unwilling to do a constructive job would be sent home. To those who are moaning about a lack of equipment as an excuse for lack of accomplishment I tried to explain the necessity of making do with the resources already in the center. [Most of the volunteers had been assigned to work in Jorge Rodriguez' community centers.] *Indeed, these barrios are so deprived that it takes no imagination whatsoever to find things that anyone can do, even the most skilless person—which is a fair description of most of our volunteers on this project* [My italics.]

Ottinger's assumption seemed to be that you did not have to give any thought to methods of working with poor people. "These *barrios* are so deprived that it takes no imagination whatsoever to find things that anyone can do." Just put a volunteer like Bert Kalisher or Libby White or Gerald Erlham down next to a slum dweller like my neighbor Pepe and the relationship would always be symbiotic: the volunteer stayed sane, the Ecuadorian (or Thai or Ghanaian—deprived slums were interchangeable) always benefited.

About three months after we settled in Guayaquil we witnessed a replay of the process by which our disastrous project had evolved. Shortly after Erich Hofmann returned from his vacation the entire country staff gathered in Quito to write a five-year plan that would be sent to Washington. No volunteers were present, nor any Ecuadorians except two whom the Peace Corps employed: no political figures, representatives of service organizations, students, or poor people. We knew from talking to volunteers in other parts of the country that the vacuum of information we had discovered in Guayaquil existed everywhere. So the five-year plan would be an exact reflection of the impressionistic view that men like Caleb Roehrig (whose defense of the marriage rule was so adamant) had of Ecuador.

I could imagine Bill Gshwend sitting in a similar meeting, weaving his conversations with Benitez, Orrantia, and some *barrio* leaders into a carefully embroidered proposal. He must have impressed the rest of the staff as a man who was very close to

Guayaquil's leading figures: perhaps he gave the impression (and believed himself) that each discussion had been an act of genuine statesmanship. So they listened to his daydream, called it a plan, and told Mankiewicz's office in Washington that they were about to foment a peaceful revolution.

IX

THIS much was clear: in many cases the Peace Corps as an institution, with its close ties to conservatives in the State Department, its insensitivity to the local culture and the careless planning that insensitivity produced, subverted the idealism that some of the volunteers had brought to training and transformed the vague xenophobic instincts most of them had acquired in Nixonia into active prejudices against host-country nationals. That was especially true in Ecuador (and, it followed, in other semifeudal societies where the Peace Corps worked), whose oligarchy didn't want social change, whose poor people didn't believe it could come.

Thus, the volunteers were all trapped by two political systems that had no use for them except as displays. To the State Department they were cheap advertising for the American way of life; to Ecuadorian oligarchs like Joachim Orrantia, the Mayor with whom Benitez and Gshwend had negotiated, they were mannequins whose presence in the *municipio* might induce AID to negotiate a loan. Erich Hofmann once described the initial dealings between the Peace Corps and the Ecuadorian government to several of us in Guayaquil. At the beginning of the Kennedy Administration, Carlos Julio Arosemena, a left-winger, was President of Ecuador. (Late in 1965 Arosemena's cousin Otto, much more conservative, would accede to power.) The Peace Corps sent two of its cleverest staff members to negotiate with him. At first he refused to have anything to do with the *yanqui* organization. But the Americans, who knew that Arosemena liked his liquor (his nickname was *el borracho*, the drunk), had brought along several bottles of Scotch. They talked through most of the night, according to Hofmann. By the time they left the bottles were empty and the Ecuadorian President had agreed to make a formal request for a Peace Corps project.

As Jorge Rodriquez had complained, Libby and Gerald and Sherwood had no skills to offer the Ecuadorians, but even if they'd been trained nurses, electricians, or agronomists they might not have found jobs. The Peace Corps had sent several dozen specialists to Ecuador and most of them were unemployed, too. If one added up all the technical agencies and all the small towns in the *campo* that really wanted volunteers and would make use of them, one saw that there was work enough for about thirty of the three hundred people who had been assigned to the country. Few enough people, in other words, to be administered by an agency that was much more modest—in its scope and its claims—than the Peace Corps, whose name, size, and public image allowed most Americans to believe that there was a benevolent side to our foreign policy during the years that we were escalating the war in Vietnam.

Gerald and Sherwood and Libby had joined the Peace Corps to help other people, not to spend two years smiling as brightly as the girl in the Ultra Brite toothpaste commercial in order to win friends for the United States. During training they had accepted the glamorous metaphors Gshwend and Benitez used to describe our assignments in Guayaquil. Now they knew that the metaphors had been misleading. In reality, they were irrelevant to Ecuador's development, virtually unable to do anything about its terrible poverty. So their idealism, which had never before been tested, quickly gave way to self-hatred and a loathing for the slum dwellers whose plight made them feel so inadequate. Like so many Americans, they began to console themselves with the belief that poverty is really the fault of the poor.

Apparently, volunteers throughout Latin America shared many

of the same fears and prejudices. That summer Harold Ickes traveled through the Dominican Republic, Ecuador, Peru, and Chile, where his girl friend was serving in a rural community-development project, and when he stayed with us in Guayaquil on his way home he said that our stories matched his own observations about the Peace Corps. Volunteers who had gone to other countries on vacations, or who were visiting Ecuador from other parts of the continent, often told tales that agreed with Harold's. Often the *Volunteer* magazine published letters, or even articles, by people who sounded as unhappy as we were.

Nevertheless, to share my gloomy analysis with other members of our group I would have to persuade them to confront emotions in themselves that they desperately wanted to ignore. I'd been trying to do that in meeting after meeting for several months and had managed only to deepen the volunteers' dislike of me. What if a situation could be created in which they were forced to see themselves from as many points of view as possible—in which they would have to come to terms with other people's opinions of them? What if we invited students, professionals, and volunteers from as many Latin-American cities as possible to the conference that all Peace Corps groups are supposed to have after they've been in the field for six months, and turned the occasion into the sort of "University in Dispersion" that Harris Wofford had talked about, where "dialogue between the other volunteers and host-country friends would be open, expansive, and long into the night?"

It would be like a giant teach-in. Caleb Roehrig said that he found the idea interesting and asked me to turn it into a formal proposal which I would mail to Erich Hofmann in Quito. Because I was still somewhat intimidated by the Director I tried to word my statement as moderately as possible. Rachel and I took an embarrassingly long time to decide that the best way to sustain an acceptable relationship with him was by beginning the accompanying letter with "Dear Erich" instead of "Dear Mr. Hofmann."

Several weeks earlier, soon after he returned from his vacation, Hofmann had visited our project. His service in the Luftwaffe, the tone of the rules we received when we arrived in the country, the descriptions of his brusque, insensitive behavior which I'd heard from staff members and veteran volunteers prepared me to meet a man whose authoritarian personality would force me to confront him at once, though I was rather frightened of his disposition and his office. Shortly after he arrived in our office he had a brief private conversation with Sid Raschi which fortified that impression. At the end of training, when Sid was sworn into the Peace Corps, he had told Gerald Erlham that "it sure felt good to stick that old right hand in the air and say the words to that oath," but now he was as ill-at-ease in the *barrios* as the rest of us. When he complained about his work in the *suburbios* Hofmann told him that like so many volunteers all over the world he was suffering from culture shock and refused to discuss the matter further. Within a few hours all the volunteers had heard Sid's story. At a Peace Corps party that night they treated the Director in somewhat the same way children treat the old lady down the street who is said to live in a haunted house. They would approach him timidly, defy him with a mild taunt (about the fact that the beer he was drinking had been brewed in Ecuador, not Germany, for example), and then hide behind their embarrassed laughter.

When Erich and I were introduced that evening they gathered around us like kids about to watch a brawl between two champion street fighters. Physically, we were about evenly matched: both of us were taller and sturdier than the other volunteers and reps. But, surprisingly, the brief conversation we had then, and a longer one the next day, proved to be more agreeable than most of my talks with his subordinates.

He had appeared anxious to help me overcome my dissatisfaction with the Peace Corps. "Frankly, I'm very worried about the attitude you express toward us," he had said. "I have the feeling that you are so bitter toward us that if it weren't for other considerations"—the draft and the war—"you'd quit, and better today than tomorrow." Then, instead of treating me like a heretic, he had begun to suggest jobs I might enjoy.

He seemed considerably less sympathetic at a formal meeting with our entire group in which he refused to let us see the five-year plan which the staff had drafted in Quito ("We wouldn't want the Ecuadorians to read it," he said), and then offered the same rationale for the Peace Corps' work in Guayaquil that had produced our project. "All of us, from Jack Hood Vaughn on down, are out to produce a revolution in Latin America. But we want it to be slow, controlled, bloodless."

Nevertheless, some remarks Erich made about his youth in Nazi Germany, and the unusual sympathy he had shown toward my problems in Guayaquil, allowed me to believe that I might be able to work with him. I was quite relieved.

When he was a teen-ager he had been arrested for circulating petitions against Germany's role in the war and had remained in prison overnight, terrifying his parents. After a few years in boarding school he enlisted in the Luftwaffe, but only because he was certain to be drafted by the SS in the winter of 1943, when he passed his eighteenth birthday. He would have been a conscientious objector if that had been possible. As I listened to him talk, it seemed to me that he would have been very grateful to be able to join something like the Peace Corps when he was a young man, and that he felt pride in the fact that his adopted country had been able to create such a generous, humane institution. If that pride accounted for the unconscious arrogance of his comment on revolution, the rest of his story suggested that there might be an unusually brave person hidden behind the brusque manner that intimidated so many volunteers and staff members. The act of circulating those petitions was certainly more courageous than anything I had ever done to oppose the war in Vietnam.

And, in the back of my mind I was also convinced, though I would never admit it, that the fact that Hofmann was German and I was Jewish would help me communicate with him. He would make a special effort to understand what I was trying to say, and even accede to some of my requests, in order to make a personal apology for his people.

"I wish I were an Art Buchwald to reply adequately to your paper," his response to my proposal for the international conference began. "Since I am not, my response will be less humorous." First he spent a page reminding me that volunteer conferences were usually quite limited in their scope and complaining that my scheme would cost the organization about ten thousand dollars. (Less than it costs to keep one volunteer in the field for two years.)

Then his criticism became more personal:

Paul, I wish you'd realize by now what the role of a Peace Corps Volunteer is. Clearly you are off on a wild tangent or somewhere on cloud nine. Why don't you spend some of the time and energy that seems to go into such papers on some concrete projects . . . ?

Please accept the fact that you are a Peace Corps Volunteer and not a Conference Coordinator appointed by Jack Hood Vaughn to plan a major conference.

. . . Frankly, I am still worried about some of your group members' attitude, concept of your job, and the direction in which you seem to be moving. Urban Community Development is unglamorous, tough, slow, frustrating, and frequently dirty work, and the sooner you realize this, as well as the fact that you will not be able to have an impact beyond a very narrow area (physically as well as psychologically), the better it will be for your future in the Peace Corps as well as what comes beyond.

Margot, who had known Hofmann for nearly a year by then, was not at all surprised by his letter. "He was nice to you when he was in Guayaquil in order to shut you up and keep you in the country. He didn't want you to leave early any more than he wants you to keep dissenting, because when volunteers quit the Peace Corps' image suffers. When you were polite to him he must have thought that he'd found a way to handle you. You have to understand that Erich is even more worried about our making trouble than the other staff members are. He's just getting his American citizenship this year and he probably thinks that he won't get another good job if the Peace Corps gives him a bad recommendation. So he hoped that you would keep quiet for two years and pretend to work, like the other volunteers, and guarantee yourself two years' safety from the army and maybe a staff job when you terminate. I guess he saw your proposal as a sign that you plan to keep asking questions in public. Nobody here has ever done that before. He got mad because he's decided that you really are a serious threat to his authority."

Freddy Marsdon, our group's outstanding con man, added some proof to Margot's assertion. When the Peace Corps changed offices, the month after we arrived in Guayaquil, Freddy had told Dan Stringer that he was an expert carpenter and volunteered to build all the new doors and walls free of charge. Soon he had keys to every lock in the building, including the lock to the files. He had been a pretty good friend of mine since training and he offered to help me get hold of the classified documents. At first I refused—it was a form of dishonesty I'd been trained to abhor. Then Freddy walked over to the cabinet and pulled out a letter which, he said, he had seen on Dan Stringer's desk the day before. It was addressed to Dan, signed by Erich, and it read, simply: "Please send me anything Paul Cowan writes (if you can call it that)." Of course I had no objection to Erich's reading my proposals or polemics, but I did resent the fact that he'd sent a confidential letter deputizing Dan Stringer to serve, in effect, as his spy. From then on I followed Freddy's lead and rifled the files at least once a month. (Later I found a letter in which Stringer apologized to Hofmann because he hadn't yet found any papers by Paul Cowan to send on.)

The Peace Corps evaluator who had been assigned to report on our project told me that Hofmann was convinced that I wanted to get him fired as Country Director. Nevertheless, I am certain that Erich felt guilty about his behavior toward me. "I wouldn't be surprised if Paul Cowan thinks I'm Adolf Eichmann," he told a mutual friend at dinner one night.

X

THERE is a way in which Hofmann's background and personality distort the situation I am trying to describe, for the fact that he served in the German air force during World War II may make him sound exceptional, when the truth is that he was typical of the American officials I knew in Ecuador, better than many of them.

So now I want to provide more of a perspective for him by compiling a brief compendium of quotations from some of the representatives of the Peace Corps, AID, the USIS, and the State Department who also played on Wymberley Coerr's "country team."

Art Nayer was in charge of the United States Information Service in Guayaquil. Once he refused a request of ours to let a visiting American band play at an open-air theater to which the slum dwellers who lived near Nick and Margot had access. His explanation was that USIS directs its programs at only the middle and upper middle class. "You don't know these people yet. They aren't able to appreciate the things we do for them. The poor people here are like animals. They should never have been allowed to come to the city. The government should have a policy making it illegal for them to migrate."

"Then you'd put them in strategic hamlets, as we're doing in Vietnam?" I asked.

"That would be one idea."

"Or out on some island, as William Buckley suggested for welfare cases in New York?"

"I'm not so sure about New York, but that would be a good idea for these people."

Later, Nick and Margot and Rachel and I used all the pressure at our disposal to force him to let us arrange a concert at the theater. But it was the sort of hollow victory we often won. By the time The All American Teen-age Honor Band got to its featured number, "Ode to a Sonic Boom," the stands, which had been full when the program began, were nearly empty. The Ecuadorians were bored by the music.

Another time Art saw me leaving the Consulate with my mail, which included an issue of the *Village Voice*. "You know, USIS isn't allowed to distribute the *Voice* or *Ramparts* any more," he said.

"Then take my copy as a bootleg edition."

"I might get in trouble if anyone sees me reading it. But I'm not afraid." He put the newspaper under his jacket, mocking himself as he did so, and returned to his office.

Harlan Hobgood, an AID technician, was making a new study of Guayaquil's *municipio*, similar to Benitez'. He wanted us to help him investigate the systems by which taxes were administered and collected in all the city's agencies so that AID could devise more efficient collection methods and classify them on IBM cards.

Then we would all participate in what he called a "bureaucratic scorched-earth policy." His goal was to destroy all the Ecuadorian records and replace them with his own computerized system. "We'll march through there just like Sherman's army."

He was genuinely surprised when Serrano expelled him from the *municipio*.

Harlan remained in Ecuador for less than a year, and had one outstanding success. When a theater group composed of Americans put on a production of the *Music Man* he was brilliant in the title role.

Once I asked Mark McGrath, a Ph.D. in social planning from Brandeis who was the Peace Corps' programing director in Ecuador, to join us in protesting the fact that all American agencies excluded local people from the policy-making meetings.

Mark looked at me as if he finally understood why I was such a troublemaker. "Now I know your problem, Paul. You care more about justice than you do about the Peace Corps."

Rachel began to work with a birth-control clinic in Guayaquil, and one of the Americans she dealt with most frequently was Arthur Angel, Population Officer of AID. One day she told him that she thought it was unethical and coercive to have birth-control programs without equally intensive sex-education programs at the same time.

"Oh, I couldn't agree more, Rachel. We'd be making the same mistake as we did in the States when we gave the niggers the right to vote and didn't teach them how to use it."

Joyce Dodge wanted to do some research into the dietary habits of the people who lived in the *suburbios,* and find out what foods they would like to eat, so that she could incorporate the information into a home-economics program she was trying to start.

When she described the plan to Dan Stringer, he derided it. "What do you need that information for anyway? All you people do is research, you never work. They all love rice. That's all you need to know."

Ever since we arrived in Guayaquil we had been hearing complaints that the American Embassy had encouraged a Catholic relief organization named Caritas to distribute a shipment of Food for Peace in the *suburbios* on the same day that Ecuador's most popular politician, Dr. José Velasco Ibarra, returned to the country after a long exile. (Dr. Velasco had been Ecuador's President three times and would be elected again after we left.) Apparently the State Department wanted to prevent poor people from gathering in the center of town where they might riot against the current government on Dr. Velasco's behalf. If the story was true, it was an explicit violation of the Food for Peace legislation. It was true, according to Jesus Ramirez, an ex-Peace Corps volunteer who now worked for Caritas. "The Ambassador wanted us to help prevent 'chaos.' That's the word he used. But there won't be any repercussions in the States. No Congressman would attack a program that's giving food to starving people. But I wish you wouldn't sound so holier-than-thou when you talk to me. Don't you realize that the Peace Corps is used the same way?"

I had thought that we might be able to communicate our discoveries about community development in Guayaquil to Kirby Jones, the Ecuador desk officer in the Peace Corps' Washington office, a protégé of Mankiewicz's and Wofford's.

Kirby had been in Santo Domingo when the American troops invaded the Dominican Republic and had traveled back and forth across enemy lines with the kind of courage that had led my radical friend in Chicago to tell me that he considered Peace Corps people his representatives abroad.

But the first time I talked to Kirby he told me a story which showed that his political response to the invasion had been much less courageous. His group of volunteers had terminated while American troops were still on the island, he said, and at their final conference they had spent a great deal of time discussing ways to influence American public opinion. They wrote a petition to be mailed to the newspapers, but first they decided to show it to Frank Mankiewicz. After a conversation with Bill Moyers, who had worked for the Peace Corps before he joined Lyndon Johnson's staff, Mankiewicz decided that if the petition were published the Peace Corps' image would suffer. Besides, the President would be annoyed. So he urged the volunteers to withdraw their statement, according to Kirby. They accepted his advice. Shortly afterward, Kirby joined the Peace Corps staff and soon was classed, with Bill Gshwend, as an expert on community development.

I told him that most of our work in Guayaquil seemed senseless, citing as an example of absurdity one volunteer who had spent several months helping his town build a statue to motherhood. Then he exposed us to his view of the community-development process which he, like Mankiewicz, asserted might bring about peaceful revolution. It was essentially the same as the one we had learned in training—organize people around small objectives and someday they will have enough power to change their lives—but Kirby added a new wrinkle: "If there had been a Peace Corps in Russia before 1917, letting people act out their desire to build statues to motherhood, then there would have been no need for a violent revolution."

PART SEVEN

I

WHEN we told Hofmann about the survey of the *barrios* that Hector Montoya and the other members of DUC, were helping us to prepare, he responded, characteristically, with a demand. "I don't want you to write semimasters theses that go on for six pages. You must remember that the other volunteers won't read anything that long. Make your reports short, hard-hitting, to the point. I don't want to see them be longer than one page."

Well, it takes more than one page—and fewer than six—to show how the survey added substance to the impression Rachel and I had gained from talking to our neighbor Pepe: that even the conservative theory of community development we had learned in training, which was implicit in Hofmann's letter to me, was too progressive to be applied to the *barrios suburbanos* of Guayaquil. The theory was designed for capitalist communities, like lower-middle-class neighborhoods in the United States, where people had steady jobs and, more important, a chance of owning their own homes; it was irrelevant to a feudalist country like Ecuador. Even the term "community development" was a misnomer. Although some of the slum neighborhoods in Guayaquil had been given names, although maps of the city showed that certain blocks were supposed to serve as boundaries between them, in fact, with very few exceptions, they would never be cohesive communities.

Not, at least, until a substantial number of slum dwellers were able to gain title to their land, and under present circumstances that was virtually impossible in Guayaquil. For the oligarchy had even more control over the *suburbios* than it did over the *municipio*: the few hundred families, like Juan Marcos's, who controlled the country had title to most of the swampy land, and they were not about to relinquish territory that might one day prove to be valuable. Only fifteen per cent of the one hundred and seventy-five poor families we interviewed possessed a deed to the few feet of property surrounding their small houses, and only a few of the rest knew how to acquire such a document. So about eighty-five per cent of the people the volunteers had been assigned to work with lived in constant fear that the oligarchs on whose land they had squatted would begin to charge them rents which they were too poor to pay (they had fled from the center of town because cane apartments there cost them fifteen dollars a month). Evidently that fear materialized rather frequently. Only about thirty-five per cent of the people we talked to had lived in the same neighborhood for longer than four years.

So, for real or psychological reasons, most of those who came from the *campo* to Guayaquil insured themselves a nomad's life, wandering from *barrio* to *barrio* with little chance of finding a real home. Some of their children were among the fifty thousand in the city who weren't being educated at all; others moved from one crowded school to another every year, or even every term. As a result, the adults rarely made friends in the neighborhoods where they perched, and the children had trouble sustaining stable relationships. Nor did the ex-*campesinos* often find people to whom they could look for leadership. In that sense, they had undergone considerable psychological change since migrating from the villages their families had inhabited for hundreds of years. Ecuadorians who lived in the rural areas always knew many of their townsmen intimately, and there were always several *campesinos* who had gained the respect of the entire community. But in Guayaquil the exact opposite situation existed: one hundred and sixty-five of the one hundred and seventy-five families interviewed told us that there was no one in their neighborhood they could trust.

If the neighborhoods were not communities, then, even the simplest community-development projects were apt to fail, as had the health center which the Supervolunteer had described to us when we first arrived in Guayaquil. Sid Raschi, the member of our group who replaced him, never spent much time in the *suburbios,* and after six months he moved to an apartment in the central city and began to give English lessons. Six months later he was stationed in Quito, also teaching English. Soon the delicate coalition that the Supervolunteer had sustained by his persistence and the strength of his personality began to collapse. The doctors quit coming to the neighborhood, and the *comité* was so distracted by its internal tensions that it could not manage to plan work on the health center. By the time AID got around to donating the roof—in a ceremony which took place a year after the Supervolunteer left—most of the people in the *barrio* had completely lost interest in the project. Perhaps they realized that the Supervolunteer, whose presence must have seemed to promise so many changes, had organized just one simple project, and that would begin to operate efficiently only long after most of them had moved to another part of Guayaquil, if ever.

On the other hand, our interviews convinced us that the slum dwellers did not need us to organize them around the problems that were important, like land fill. For example, the people who had invaded the swampy land where Rachel and I had planned to live needed fill so badly that they transcended the spiderweb of distrust that would have prevented them from building a health center or a community center. As soon as the land invasion gained momentum, they told us, they formed a *comité* which journeyed to the *municipio* several times each week in order to meet with the Mayor and his assistants. They were among the clusters of petitioners Rachel and I used to see every time we went down to the second floor of the *municipio.* So far as I could tell, even the

Peace Corps' belief that the presence of a volunteer would give them added clout with the city officials was false. Though Margot spent several months of her life "batting my big blues," as she put it, at a procession of enchanted civil servants, still the trucks full of dirt began to come out to the *barrios* only when a right-wing political leader decided to use the Civic Action Program, sponsored partly by the American army, to build up his strength in the slum neighborhoods. Similarly, though Hank Dawson spent much of his time trying to figure out the intricate internal politics of his *barrio's comité* which wanted to get dirt instead of garbage for fill, the neighborhood became livable only after the President of Ecuador had decided to win the support of the *barrio's* people with a gimmicky fund-raising televised marathon (like the old Martin and Lewis telethons for muscular dystrophy) called "Operation: Rescue the *Barrios Suburbanos.*"

If volunteers were irrelevant to the transient *comités* which the poor people felt forced to form, they were specifically forbidden to work with the permanent city-wide organizations like the Civil Action Program or Asad Bucaram's political party, Concentración de Fuerzas Populares (CFP), which could occasionally help the slum dwellers and which certainly enlisted their deepest loyalties. For the Congressional legislation that had created the Peace Corps demanded that the organization remain outside politics. Though that restriction seemed sensible to most volunteers, myself included, it also spotlighted the difficulty of our role in the *barrios*. For the political parties were the only institutions in town which could obtain even a few of the objectives that Gshwend had defined for our "Alinsky-type" organization. The Ecuadorians who wandered from slum to slum made it clear to us that long-established organizations like Bucaram's CFP, which had some patronage and some resources at its disposal, which had branches all over the city, were the only institutions to which they could remain faithful wherever they happened to settle. Most of the people we talked to were ardent supporters of Don Buca, as they called the ex-Mayor. Indeed, long after Bucaram had become sufficiently moderate to placate the upper class and therefore survive his second term in office, many poor people continued to believe that his administration would introduce some stability into their lives by seizing the *suburbios* from the oligarchs and reselling the land at a dollar-fifty per meter instead of its current price of ten dollars.

Of course that would never happen.

The problem that made poor people unable to form the sort of organization that community developers sought to inspire would not be solved by Peace Corps volunteers or by the political process. To become loyal to their communities they would have to be convinced that they had a chance to own some property. But they would never be able to acquire much land in the *suburbios* until the oligarchy was forced to renounce its class interests.

Forced! no one was going to persuade a man like Juan Marcos to surrender his wealth voluntarily.

The data from our survey showed me, then, that the Peace Corps was in an even more contradictory position than I had understood. When I received Hofmann's letter directing me to concentrate my "time and energy" on some "concrete project," I had regarded the tasks he had in mind as dull and somewhat insulting to my Ecuadorian neighbors. Now I realized that they were virtually impossible. Very few effective health centers would be built, very few community centers would form, until there was a substantial redistribution of land in Guayaquil.

Even on its own terms, by its own definition of community development, the Peace Corps would not succeed until Ecuador underwent a real (that is to say, violent) revolution.

PART EIGHT

I

I HAD never forgotten one casual, terrifying remark General Hershey had made when I interviewed him for the *Voice*. He prefaced a complaint about the few people who were already trying to bust the draft in November 1965 with these words: "I believe that they can think whatever they want. I'm proud that we have that kind of liberty in America." It sounded as if he was accustomed to talking with people who disagreed; who argued that free thought was a threat to the American way of life, nearly as dangerous as free speech or the freedom to act on your ideas. He seemed to think that the concession would persuade me that he was a liberal.

Still, for a while, back in New York, I was able to dismiss Hershey's comment as the opinion of a slightly senile old codger who held his substantial power almost by accident. There was certainly plenty of freedom at the Big Fiesta, and no writer or editor or agent seemed even slightly worried that it would be restricted. I felt a little paranoid whenever I told people there about the fear Hershey's words had planted in me. But in Guayaquil I became convinced that Hershey spoke for millions of Americans: no more than a few of the volunteers and staff members I knew were perceptibly more libertarian than the General, not when it came to criticism of their institution.

A typical remark came from Dave Carrasco, head of the Peace Corps' physical education program in Ecuador, and a good friend of Hofmann's: "Can't you settle down, Paul? Can't you stop thinking and writing, and just teach people?" (Dave was later named Special Assistant at the American Embassy in Mexico City in time for the 1968 Olympics. How must he have dealt with black militants like John Carlos and Tommy Smith, the sprinters who raised their fists in black-power salutes during the victory ceremonies?)

It was an attitude that intimidated Rachel and me more than most Peace Corps people realized. For we were not strong enough to reject entirely the definitions of our personalities that their unyielding opinons implied. Were we drawing-room radicals who couldn't make it in the *barrios*, as Hank Dawson and his friends thought? Were we abrasive agitators whose arrogance made it impossible for us to accept the good advice of our elders? Was it possible that we were still suffering from culture shock, that our dissent was a neurotic response: a way of clinging to America by wrestling against its representatives abroad? In the staff's terms, freethinkers like us were lazy, evil, or insane, and it was impossible for Rachel and me not to wonder if they were right.

Hofmann might have said the same thing to me, more forcefully if less crudely than Carrasco—so might Kirby Jones or Dan Stringer or Caleb Roehrig. Although they wanted us to stay at the jobs we'd been assigned in the *barrios*, they didn't particularly care if dissatisfied volunteers moved to Quito or the *campo*, just so long as they remained silent. But they regarded our questions about the Peace Corps' role in Ecuador, and our insistence that the organization heed the results of research, like our survey of the *barrios*, as a form of treason.

It was also impossible to ignore the fact that if the staff did not change its attitude toward us, we would soon be fired. That threat had been slightly veiled in Hofmann's letter to me and his note to Dan Stringer; later on, Dan made it explicit when he warned Nick and me that Hofmann was looking for a reason to order our expulsion. According to both Hofmann and Stringer, a man who is expelled from the Peace Corps will never be hired by another government agency. "Their personnel people will look at your records and decide that you have an unstable personality," Dan told us. That prospect alone was enough to keep most people in our group from dissenting.

Though I didn't care much about my future in the civil service, I was nevertheless almost as scared of expulsion as most other volunteers. That was partly the result of my years at Choate, where I was always afraid of a hidden force which would suddenly discover that I had violated some rule and send me home, in shame. But it was even more closely linked to the belief that still guided me that protest should be constructive. I had always channeled my anger into activities like the chapel speech that won such a favorable response from the Choate faculty, like the civil-rights movement and the Peace Corps, which were considered praiseworthy by most of the Americans I knew. I still wanted that approval very much.

II

LATE in October 1966, nearly five months after we settled in Guayaquil, Nick and Margot and Rachel and I decided to give a party especially designed to acquaint some of the other volunteers with as wide a range of Ecuadorians as possible: poor people, students, and professionals we had been meeting as we searched for useful work. In a way, the party was an organizer's device. If some volunteers formed warm friendships with relatively progressive *Guayaquileños* outside their *barrios*, then they would soon begin to share our generalized disgust at the disregard the Peace

Corps and the rest of the "country team" constantly displayed toward the feelings of local people. So we invited only volunteers who we thought might be able to relate to our new Ecuadorian friends.

Before I describe the party I want to introduce some of Guayaquil's students and professional people who were present.

Of course Lourdes Vera was there, with several of her sisters. The Veras were now among our closest Ecuadorian friends.

There were eleven in the family, ten children and a widowed mother, and their small house in one of Guayaquil's middle-class suburbs (a few blocks away from the Peace Corps office) was always filled with an assortment of spouses, cousins, grandchildren, fiancés, friends: eating, talking, playing cards or Monopoly, mooning over tonight's episode of *Peyton Place*. Rachel and I must have visited the Veras fifty times while we were in Guayaquil, and there couldn't have been more than five occasions when we knew everybody in the house. We loved that hectic atmosphere.

They were several social levels below the oligarchy, though Señora Vera's parents had been wealthy cocoa growers until a plant disease ravaged their *hacienda*, destroying all the crops. She still liked to gossip about the rich people she once knew, to recall the luxuries she had enjoyed as a girl. But now the family was forced to maintain itself on the small inheritance it had received from Dr. Vera, who had been a fairly successful general practitioner, on a small pension they got from the state, and on the combined income of the children who were old enough to work.

Antulo, at thirty-two the oldest brother, was still famous as the first man in Guayaquil's history ever to pitch a no-hit baseball game. After he graduated from the University of Guayaquil he joined the Ecuadorian air force and was sent to Lackland Air Force base in San Antonio, Texas, where he received most of his training. We could see how very Americanized he'd become there when we visited the house where he lived with his wife and daughter. The living-room walls were covered with pennants from Texas colleges: it was a little like entering the bedroom of an American high-school kid. Off the living room was a small, *Playboy*-style bar room Antulo had built for himself, complete with some gross trinkets he'd acquired in the States—an ashtray which gave the finger, a tumbler shaped like a penis. When we drove up to his house he was dressed in blue jeans and a checked shirt, squatting in front of the white picket fence that surrounded his yard, repainting it. "Just like Picasso," he said in English when he saw us. "We'll have an old-fashioned cookout this weekend," he added a moment later. That night I heard him whistling "Stars and Stripes Forever" and "Yankee Doodle Dandy" to his little daughter to lull her to sleep.

But if Antulo was Americanized, he was not particularly pro-American. He opposed the war in Vietnam and the invasion of the Dominican Republic, he told me that weekend. "We all do here," he said. But that was not true. I knew dozens of conservative Ecuadorians, in and out of the military, whose justification for American policy seemed to me just as jingoist as anything one reads in the *Chicago Tribune*. The "we" who opposed America's adventures must have been Antulo's friends in the air force.

If he had been born in the States, he would have been a campus sports hero and then, perhaps, a successful politician. He was a vigorous, strapping, charming man, with lively black eyes and curly black hair, witty and always ready to smile. I imagined that he would become one of the leaders of a band of progressive soldiers like his friends in the air force, or even a radical hero like Francisco Camaaño Dena, Juan Bosch's ally in the Dominican Republic. Of all those I knew in Ecuador, Antulo seemed one of the very few who might become actively, dangerously involved in a movement that had some chance of seizing power from the oligarchy. But Antulo was killed in an airplane crash in November 1968.

Lourdes, twenty-eight, is determined to succeed in a city whose professional world has until very recently excluded women completely. And her intelligence is so disciplined that she will certainly make herself into a first-rate architect, just as, several years ago, she made herself into one of Guayaquil's most attractive women by dieting for six months and losing fifty pounds.

A few years ago she was deeply religious, but now constant, almost obsessive, thought has turned her into an agnostic. She devotes even more attention to Guayaquil's social problems, to which her work constantly exposes her, than to her private crisis of faith. The word she uses to characterize the city is "selfish." Its professions, she says, are dominated not only by men, but by old, complacent men who will not make room for people like her to explore their modern ideas. She is searching for a way to make Guayaquil more open. But politics, which she sometimes thinks she should enter, means small quarrels and trivial conversations, and she is reluctant to dull her mind and sharpen her temper in that fetid atmosphere.

Sometimes she agrees with her brother Edmundo, five years younger and then a student in the Faculty of Psychology at the University of Guayaquil, who argues that a revolution is the only solution for Ecuador. Many people, conservatives included, seem to feel that the country is psychologically ready for a guerrilla movement, but there is no group to lead it. At least not in Guayaquil. So, for the moment, Lourdes is concentrating her searching intelligence on the narrower question of how to survive and create in a city that is not really ready for people like her.

At the time we arranged the party, Hector Montoya was visibly, dramatically, in love with Lourdes, and Lourdes was trying to figure out a polite way of rejecting him.

For one thing, their personal styles were entirely different. Hector, who came from an extremely rich family, had been living in Buenos Aires for the past several years, studying medicine and writing plays. If the experience had encouraged him to develop political attitudes that angered his parents to the point where they expelled him from their house, it also filled him with social attitudes that were much more permissive than any that could be found in Ecuador. He believed that if you were in love with a woman you not only slept with her, you lived with her, too, but most middle-class Ecuadorian women were shocked by the idea of premarital sex. In Argentina he had constant access to drugs, both through school and through the artists he knew, and he tripped out with many of his friends; but most Ecuadorians, even intellectuals who regarded themselves as liberated from their parents' conservative traditions, consider marijuana the source of lower-class crime. Indeed, the word *"marijuanero"* means "delinquent" to virtually all *Guayaquileños.* So Hector could not even talk to Lourdes about pot or acid. He could take dope only with the Peace Corps volunteers, many of whom were willing to ignore Ecuadorian customs, too, and use it quite heavily.

But Hector would have been an unusually intense person even if he had never left Guayaquil, and it was the almost frantic side of his personality that bothered Lourdes most. He was never without a cigarette and a cup of coffee. Though he was only twenty-six, his fingers were already yellowed with tobacco stains and his hands trembled when he talked. And he talked constantly. He used to keep Lourdes up until six each morning with monologues about Himself, Herself, Their Relationship.

Hector was brilliant, too. During the few months we knew him in Guayaquil he learned to speak fluent English by reading novels (Poe was his favorite writer) and insisting that we converse with him in our language. After he had spent just a few days in the *suburbios*, interviewing the poor people who lived there, he understood aspects of their problems that it had taken Rachel and me months to perceive. Once he gave me a short story he had written in Buenos Aires, and, though my Spanish wasn't good enough for me to judge his style, I found it interesting.

He had so much intelligence and charm that his plan to use DUC as a springboard to real power in Ecuador sounded entirely plausible when he confided it to me one night during dinner at the Veras'. He seemed to have plotted his career as carefully as he plotted his stories. He was able to describe the personalities he would have to influence as he rose to power, to show me how he would gain their respect. "You watch, Paul. In ten years I'll be the Ecuadorian John F. Kennedy." I had the meddlesome outsider's elated reaction to his boast—it gave me a chance to play Pygmalion for an hour—and I promised to get him a Spanish-language copy of *The Making of the President,* 1960, from Art Nayer at

USIS. At some buried level of my mind I was back five years at Harvard, forward ten years as a Latin-American adviser to a new Kennedy Administration, subtly boasting about my good friend Hector, the most progressive president in Ecuador's history.

He left before we did that night, and I asked Señora Vera about his family. Now that he was out of the room, I thought of how much trouble I was having losing my upper-middle-class reflexes even though I accepted most of the left-wing's principles, and I began to wonder whether an Ecuadorian could transform himself from an oligarch to a radical as easily as Hector expected to. So did Señora Vera.

Though the family history she described seemed to me unusually full of scandal and cruelty, she claimed that it was typical of an entire class. Hector's father had married several times and always kept women on the side; one uncle was a homosexual; one of his stepmothers was known throughout the city for her promiscuity. And it sounded as if Hector's father was even more brutal to his workers than careless with his women. He owned a large *hacienda* in the *campo* where, according to Señora Vera, he frequently punished *campesinos* by hanging them by their thumbs for hours at a time.

It turned out that Hector's boasts were founded in illusions. He was, finally, more trapped by his own class background than most Peace Corps volunteers, much more trapped than the Veras. We saw that clearly one night, about a month after our party, when we went to his sister's luxurious house for dinner. She had been married to a man whose sugar plantation was nearly as lucrative as Juan Marcos's and had been spending most of her time in Miami since her divorce. The only reason she had returned to Guayaquil was to visit Hector. The butler, who lived alone in the house throughout most of the year, served us our dinner. "He's a very smart boy," she told us at one point (he was about thirty). "Sometimes too smart," she continued, chuckling. "My husband and I started to teach him English when he was first with us. We thought it would be a good way to amuse ourselves. But we had to quit because he was beginning to understand when we talked to each other in the language."

Later on, while Hector was telling his sister about the horrible conditions in the *suburbios*, he clapped his hands once, sharply, and, using the *tú* form of the verb, ordered the butler to bring him a pack of cigarettes from a near-by table. He continued to treat the man that way throughout the night.

It was almost the last time we saw Hector. A few weeks later, after Lourdes had finally persuaded him that she would never marry him, he turned DUC over to some students who were more stable—and much less interesting—and left Ecuador to stay with his sister in Miami. We never heard from him again.

Javier Espinoza, a thirty-two-year-old professor of sociology at the University of Guayaquil, a good friend of the Veras' and of Hector's, seemed to be one of the most conventional people we knew in the city. He was at least as connected to the oligarchy as Hector (his grandfather had been President of Ecuador). He is rather conservative politically, and a very devout Catholic. Javier is a short man who always looks as if he has just showered and shaved: his expensive clothes are always immaculate, his manner of speech so slow and precise that I was able to understand him perfectly from the day I met him. The same fastidiousness characterizes his social views. For example, when Bergman's movie *The Silence* was shown in Guayaquil, with the scenes of women masturbating uncensored, his strongest reaction was to fear the effect the movie would have on the masses. Similarly, he was very cautious about the use of contraceptive devices. Once he told a class which he was teaching with Jorge, Rachel, and me that population control was genocidal in the same way that concentration camps had been. On a more personal level, he argued that as soon as the poor women in the *suburbios* begin to use diaphragms or intrauterine devices their men will take advantage of the fact that sex is now safe and treat them like animals.

But Javier's carefully controlled personality hid a continuing struggle within him. He has spent years of his life outside Ecuador, studying in Rome and Brazil, traveling in Europe, Latin America, and the United States. Javier has traveled and read widely enough to realize that if his class is to survive, if his country is to develop without a revolution, his contemporaries must act upon ideas that are several generations more advanced than those of their parents. One of the things that he talked about most frequently was the tension between generations. Though he lived at home, I had the feeling that he must have quarreled often with his father, who had studied in Switzerland. Once he told me that the educational development that made him most optimistic about Latin America's future was that most of his contemporaries throughout the continent have studied in the United States instead of Europe, where most men of his father's generation had been trained. Only at schools like Berkeley, Harvard, Michigan, he thinks, can one acquire ideas that are applicable to a country like Ecuador. Soon he hopes to spend several years at a North American university.

Though he has a degree in law, he is committed to using the sociology which he studied abroad to make himself a career. It isn't easy. There isn't much demand yet for sociologists in Ecuador. But whenever he considers adopting the safer legal profession, in which some of his family's friends would quickly become his clients, he reminds himself that his goal in life is not to earn money but to discover the causes of his country's problems and try to evolve some solutions.

But his background has a pronounced effect on the sort of solutions he will accept. When I told him that I planned to talk to the class we were teaching about my analysis of the land problem in the *suburbios*, he got angrier than I had ever seen him and accused me of spreading the kind of ideas that would lead to revolution. But he did not like to discover such reactionary emotions in himself, I'm sure. For he frequently asked me whether I thought that his mind was so filled with inherited attitudes and academic theory that he couldn't get a clear view of the world in which he lived.

Javier is an anguished man. And isolated, too. Many of his parents' friends regard him as a radical, while many of his contemporaries consider him too conservative. More than anyone else I knew in Guayaquil, Javier saw life "through the veil of two customs." He loved the past, whose traditions he was trying to escape, while he must have realized that he would never be able to accept the ideas that history had forced him to acquire.

Jaime Diaz, in his mid-thirties, the grandson of Chinese immigrants to Ecuador, has benefited greatly from the currents of history that have cast Javier adrift.

Now he is a reporter on Guayaquil's leading newspaper, *El Universo*, but just twenty years ago he would have had a great deal of trouble pursuing a profession which took him so far outside his own community. For in Ecuador the Chinese are the objects of the same prejudices that are directed against the Jews in America. The verb *"chinear"* ("to Chinese"), which is still used in the newspapers, means "to cheat a man," "to jew him down."

Not that Jaime has really succeeded yet. He lives in a somewhat ramshackle house between the city and the *suburbios* in which there is not nearly enough space for his wife, his mother-in-law, and his six children. The purchase of a record player and a television set, I'm certain, represented major investments. The large family still doesn't have a car.

But Jaime's reputation in Guayaquil was spreading rapidly. He was frequently recognized on the street, his name was mentioned at parties, and we were looked at with increased respect when we said that Jaime was a friend of ours. His assignments became increasingly interesting, too. Shortly after we left Ecuador he wrote a series of articles, clearly inspired by Jim Bishop, called "A Day in the Life of President Arosemena," which increased his reputation throughout the country.

You can tell that Jaime enjoys his life greatly. He feels the newspaperman's special, intimate love for the place in which he works. He knows Guayaquil's midnights and its dawns. The city's rhythms are his own.

III

Nɪᴄᴋ and Margot and Rachel and I had worked especially hard to make the party enjoyable. As we were planning it we kept looking for ways to make conversations between Ecuadorians and North Americans flow as smoothly as possible. We arranged the furniture so that people could sit in small groups, talking with each other (often at parties in Guayaquil the guests sat in long rows, waiting to dance), and we tried to make the light in the room dim enough so that relative strangers could feel some intimacy, though not so dark that Javier's Catholic conscience would insist that he flee before he became involved in a Greenwich Village orgy. All four of us were most uncomfortable at *fiestas* in Guayaquil where there often seemed to be nothing to do but drink and dance the *cúmbia,* record player blaring, so we decided to practice a little cultural imperialism and mix some Johnny Cash, Ray Charles, and Bob Dylan in with the Latin music. We turned the volume on the phonograph low enough so that people who wanted to talk could hear each other.

For most of the evening the experiment worked quite well. Most conversations were in Spanish—which was not altogether common at binational parties, where North Americans often gathered in one part of the room, Ecuadorians in another—and the volunteers and Ecuadorians seemed quite relaxed. Our most interesting discovery was that many of the *Guayaquileños* we had invited scarcely knew one another, or about each other's activities, though some of them had a great deal in common. For example, Hector had never met Pepe Martinez, a playwright whose dramas were already appearing on Ecuadorian television, and as soon as they were introduced they began a long, intricate discussion of

Spanish theater (until Hector suddenly bolted over to Lourdes to kneel on the floor and tell her how much he loved her).

The only thing that troubled the four of us was that Gerald Erlham hadn't shown up yet. We were worried that we might have offended him because we had deliberately refrained from inviting Hank Dawson.

Hank was not only the most popular volunteer in our group; he was also, ironically, our Supervolunteer whose ability to outdrink, outcurse, outfuck the men in his *barrio* made him seem heroic to his friends. Though I hated to admit it, it was clear to me that Hank felt much more at home with his neighbors than I did with mine. Months later, when Jorge Rodriguez praised him with the remark that "Hank is completely at home here—he isn't a citizen of Ecuador, or even Guayaquil, but of his block in the *barrio*," I would have to agree.

But the prejudices which had revealed themselves in Hank's remarks about Jews and political activists were apparent when he talked about Ecuadorians, too. Though he spoke of the residents of his *barrio* with affection, they were always "little people" who "run around" and "yell and scream" at meetings. And if his attitude toward Guayaquil's poor was somewhat patronizing, he had an abiding contempt for its middle class, for most of the people we had invited to our party. "They don't care about their own people nearly as much as we do," he claimed when I argued that volunteers should be responsible to Ecuadorian administrators like Jorge, not to Erich Hofmann or Dan Stringer. But his contempt for Guayaquil's middle class would never make him into a radical. Hank was the only visceral anti-Communist in our group (the only volunteer who was still supporting the war in Vietnam at the time of the Pentagon march), and he disliked the city's students and professional people who generalized from their compassion for the slum dwellers to become revolutionaries even more than he disliked those whom he considered apathetic. Like us, they were "activists."

So far as I was concerned, Hank embodied the best and the worst of the Peace Corps ideal as it worked out in practice. He was a populist-imperialist who felt considerable sympathy for the poor, but a much deeper commitment to the belief that he and his fellow North Americans could determine their future much better than any Latin.

Still, I was now rather disturbed that we hadn't invited Hank to the party (it seemed somewhat spiteful), so I was pleased when he and Gerald arrived at midnight with two students from Guayaquil's School of Agronomy. But they all greeted us rather curtly, and instead of mixing with the other guests, they formed their own little circle in one corner of the living room, where they commenced to tell dirty jokes and pass around bottle after bottle of Pilsener beer.

Just as Javier, who had a car, was preparing to take the Veras and Hector home, Hank and Gerald and the agronomy students began to scream at each other. "*Chinga tu madre.*" "*Hijo de puta.*" "*Pendejo.*" "Fuck your mother." "You son of a whore." "You pubic hair." But none of them was angry. Hank and Gerald were swearing in the same heavily ironic tone they used when they talked their jargon in English.

Our Ecuadorian friends must have noticed the clamor, but they were too polite to say anything. They told us how much they had enjoyed the *fiesta* and left—rather hurriedly, I thought. For months thereafter Javier frequently told Rachel and me that we should warn our superiors in the Peace Corps that many volunteers seemed unable to adapt themselves to Guayaquil, though he was never bold enough to make specific mention of the incident at the party.

After all our Ecuadorian guests had gone, Margot commanded Hank and Gerald to leave her apartment. They refused and kept drinking. Hank, still sober, insisted that the agronomy students match him glass for glass, though one of them was so drunk that his head was nodding. "At least you guys can help us clean this place up," Nick suggested. Gerald, who must have felt a little guilty, began to gather a few glasses, but Hank remained in his chair. Margot began to yell at him—she's a terror when she's angry —but just then one of the Ecuadorians bolted for the bathroom.

He puked and pissed, and missed the toilet with both liquids. Apparently, the urine seeped through a crack in the floor. A minute later the downstairs neighbor was pounding on the ceiling, yelling that his bed was getting wet. We all left immediately.

The next day I saw Gerald at one of the sidewalk cafés on Nueve de Octubre and began to tell him how angry the episode had made me. He seemed surprisingly willing to discuss his behavior rationally, even earnestly.

"It wasn't an accident, Paul, as you might think. We didn't throw that show because we got carried away. No, we've been up for something like that for months now. It was a way of getting revenge for all the times the Ecuadorians have gotten us drunk in the *barrios*."

Revenge! When slum dwellers invited us to their parties they usually plied us with beer, or sometimes with *puro*, to show us that we were special guests and make us comfortable. They were so polite to us that they often seemed obsequious, and there was nothing about my role as a volunteer I hated so much as the feeling that people who (however mistakenly) thought I might be able to help them were Uncle Tomming me. If, like Hank Dawson, one wanted to turn such gestures of friendship into tests of *machismo*, one's hosts were more than willing to accede. But it was far from a requisite part of their code.

They desperately wanted to please us, strangers whose customs they barely understood, whose presence might miraculously release them from their poverty. As a result, they were sometimes insulted when we refrained from drinking their beverages or eating their foods, for they interpreted such refusals as signs that we were rejecting them as people. That could create situations that were extremely awkward. Once, Rachel and I were interviewing *campesinos* for one of our newspaper articles, and they offered us water from a pond in which we'd seen pigs bathing. Though we were obviously very thirsty, we were even more worried about germs, and we asked them to boil it. We told them that hot water is a special luxury in our country, but I think they were still insulted. Another time, when we went to a *fiesta* in the *campo* with our neighbors Pepe and Evangelina, I had to make several trips outdoors to force myself to vomit the beer that my hosts kept giving me so that I could guzzle all night without getting drunk. But it would have been mad to blame the Ecuadorians for causing such discomforts.

Gerald Erlham still planned to file for conscientious-objector status when he returned to the United States. He said that he believed more deeply than ever in the redemptive power of love and was reading whatever books on Buddhism he could find in order to learn how to purify himself. But after six months as a Peace Corps volunteer in Guayaquil, neither pacifism nor spiritualism was enough to prevent him from spending weeks planning to get revenge on the people he had been so eager to serve while we were still in training, whose attempts to be courteous seemed like malice to him now.

But it seemed to me useless to remain angry at Gerald for his behavior at the party. He was as much a victim as the students he had victimized that night.

As I thought about him, about all of us, I realized it is almost an axiom that as long as institutions make it virtually impossible to help people in slum neighborhoods—as long as it is politically impossible for the poor to make substantial progress—then, with the exception of a few Supervolunteers, any outsider who tries to bring measured reforms to the ghettos of the United States or the *barrios* of Latin America will feel like something of an alien and probably experience as much irritation with the oppressed as hatred for the oppressor. That is particularly true when one has a large peer group to share one's irritation with, as Gerald had in Guayaquil, as I had in Vicksburg.

Thus, Stokely Carmichael, after condemning the Summer Project at great length, had accompanied the expulsion of white people from the civil-rights movement with the cryptic message that they should "organize in their own communities." The slogan seemed to me even more applicable to the Peace Corps in Ecuador. In my terms, it meant: leave the *barrios* and begin to devote more energy to confronting the institutions that are oppressing poor people than to helping individual black people or mestizos try to achieve successes that are nearly impossible.

Of course Rachel and I had been edging toward that conclusion for months, but it had been extremely difficult to make the decision actually to pack our bags and books and leave. Were we abandoning the commitment each of us had made when we first decided to go south, to fight injustice even if the battle brought us great discomfort or even death? We went over the arguments time and again. It always seemed more sensible to depart than to remain, but we were nevertheless stopped by the feeling that we would betray our neighbors if we moved away. That was particularly true of Rachel, whose decision to become a social worker had been premised on the belief that, with enough skill and sensitivity, she could help anyone. And I was worried about the reaction of the rest of our group. "The Cowans couldn't take it in the *barrios*, even in that big house." "Rachel was doing very well, but you know Paul. He talks a lot, but he doesn't really like poor people." Or maybe it wasn't the other volunteers my imagination heard, but my own conscience.

But Gerald's and Hank's behavior toward the Ecuadorian students, and Gerald's later explanation of it, illustrated the reason that we decided we had to move downtown after we had been living in the *barrios* for five months. Partly it was their act itself; to a greater extent it was our discovery that the act hadn't really surprised us. Many of the volunteers we knew would have been just as vicious. If some were not so crude as Gerald and Hank, still all of us, Nick and Margot and Rachel and me included, were allowing ourselves to give active support to the United States' foreign policies that the four of us, at least, regarded as inhuman and even criminal. We were not opposing the war in Vietnam by our efforts in Guayaquil; we were strengthening the government that waged that war. And not strengthening it in some distant Asian country either; we were helping Wymberley Coerr's country team develop cold-war tactics in Ecuador. Those were not innocent little gatherings that Erich Hofmann attended at the Embassy every week. They usually included representatives of the CIA and of the United States' military mission. What use did those men make of the information Erich must have contributed? We had been told that at least ten per cent of all the AID workers in Ecuador reported to the CIA. How did they use the facts and impressions that earnest volunteers like Bill Dodge or the Supervolunteer divulged, as they argued for technical assistance and money for their work in the *barrios*? How did the United States government use the energies of the slum dwellers and civil servants whose loyalties effective volunteers won as they sought to find and train local leaders? Frequently, AID or the State Department sent such people off to special training programs in Puerto Rico, Mexico, or the United States, and then tantalized them with tempting work when they returned: turned some of them into mini-North Americans whose livelihood depended on their capacity to please our government; or, perhaps, into conscious agents whose role was to furnish the kind of data that would make United States programs more effective.

And even when the State Department did not employ the volunteers' information or contacts for specific ends, it sought to use us as a propaganda device: to put an angel's face on the devil's policies. According to Dan Stringer, James Raaf, the manager of Grace Lines in Ecuador (the most powerful United States company in the country), once remarked that the Peace Corps makes Grace Lines' work much easier. He meant that effective volunteers persuade some Ecuadorians that North Americans can be trusted after all.

So the Peace Corps, supposedly the best of America, turned decent people like Gerald Erlham into vengeful brutes, at least for a time, and made everyone who sought to strengthen the organization (even through proposals like mine for an international conference) into servants of a dishonest and often brutal foreign policy.

The same emotional logic that had once sent us south now said that we had to combat the Peace Corps openly, not use our talents to burnish its image. We could be more useful to Pepe,

Evangelina, and their friends if we left the *barrios* and concentrated on ways to confront the American country team—and confront Ecuador's oligarchy, too, if that possibility was available to a foreigner—than if we remained in our large house next to their shacks, while I nearly strangled in self-hatred as we tried unsuccessfully to organize the community centers and health centers that would be of real use only after a revolution.

At least that was what we told each other. But neither of us would quite trust our ability to act on that decision (to fight the Peace Corps and not just live in more enjoyable surroundings downtown) until we had been tested. There was nothing in our experience to give us confidence that we could defy an entire organization, and a much broader mystique, when the time came.

IV

WE found a fifth-floor walk-up in downtown Guayaquil, a wood and plasterboard apartment which had been erected on the roof of a cement building near Nueve de Octubre. We were a block away from Rosado's Supermarket, from one of the biggest movie theaters in town, and just a little farther from the Flamingo and La Balama, the two most popular sidewalk cafés.

Eighty-five steps up to our front door—I had given up smoking the week before we moved, and the climb was a constant incentive to keep my lungs clean. (I haven't had a cigarette since.)

The place cost us fifty dollars a month, twenty dollars more than our mansion in the *barrio*. It was a kind of graduate-student pad. There were two big rooms in front and they gave off on a narrow terrace, where we ate most of our meals. Rachel grew avocados there, and ferns, and a rubber plant. Later, the terrace became a bedroom for a turtle named Maurice and a cat named Che.

There was a flush toilet in our bathroom, and cold water was pumped up (usually in trickles) throughout most of the day. For several months we slept in a rickety maid's room which seemed to have been fastened to the roof behind the kitchen as a sort of afterthought. In February and March, Guayaquil's hottest months, the sun seared through the tin roof, roasting us. Finally, luckily, our bed broke, and we decided to sprawl our thin, broad mattress on the floor of one of the cooler front rooms.

As soon as we moved into town, we felt like human beings again, not creatures set down in the midst of a planet whose people couldn't comprehend them. There had been some Italian engineers in our apartment before we moved in; an immigrant from Switzerland and an Ecuadorian mechanic who had just returned from the States lived downstairs. All of our neighbors seemed to accept our presence as a natural part of life in a cosmopolitan city.

During siestas we could prepare our own meals—hamburgers or cold cuts, which we bought at Rosado's—and read or talk with friends, or sleep. That, more than anything else, finally gave us the feeling that we had gained some control over our own lives.

At night, if we didn't have guests, we could go to the movies without worrying about the crowded, bumpy bus ride back to our *barrio*. There were about twenty theaters in Guayaquil, the most expensive of them costs only fifty cents, and there was a city ordinance that every show had to be a double feature. Often two theaters would have to share copies of the same film, and they would hire boys to bicycle the print back and forth, reel by reel. During the year we lived in our new apartment Rachel and I became movie addicts. I began to see some Hollywood heroes as spiritual allies. In our fight against the Peace Corps I was Burt Lancaster in *The Professionals*, Steve McQueen in *The Sand Pebbles*, Paul Newman in *Cool Hand Luke*: any hero who kept his sense of humor while he grew tougher resisting authority. It is a measure of America's attitude toward women that, though we saw more than a hundred movies that year, there wasn't a single actress with whom Rachel could feel the same kind of identification.

But the most important thing about our new apartment was

that it allowed us to develop increasingly intimate relations with Jaime and Javier, the Veras, and, when he returned, Jorge. As long as we lived in the *suburbios*, we never felt comfortable about asking people with homes in town to come all the way out there for a visit, especially for dinner. Erich Hofmann had once told us that "if you get two Ecuadorian students to dirty their shoes in the mud of the *barrios* then your stay here will have been a success, because they might be future leaders." We were absurdly proud about having exceeded his quota by several dozen. Nevertheless, the half-hour bus ride seemed too much to ask of people who had been working all day. We almost always treated those who made it as special guests and turned what should have been casual, pleasant visits into formal occasions.

Rachel had become quite expert at cooking on our one-burner hot plate, and now that we were living downtown, the only barrier between our Ecuadorian and North American friends and her repertoire of shrimp curry, hamburger stroganoff, beef stew, creamed tuna fish, pork chops and cabbage, veal parmigiana and spaghetti were those eighty-five steps. It was usually surmounted.

V

JORGE RODRIGUEZ returned from his seminar in Rome in mid-November, just a few days after we had moved into our new apartment—twenty-four hours after his leave of absence ended. The Mayor used his tardiness as a pretext to fire him.

Evidently, Serrano had been planning to get rid of Jorge ever since he took office. If Rachel and I had continued to work in the Community Development Department while Rodriguez was in Italy, the Mayor and the temporary *jefe* might have tried to manipulate us into accomplishing the same objective that Gshwend had proposed during training.

One reason for Jorge's firing, Serrano claimed, was that his political ideas were too "pro-*yanqui*" (Gshwend, it will be remembered, had wanted him deposed because he might be a Communist). But Victor Hugo Silva, a reporter for *Vistazo*, gave us a different explanation. The two men had been fighting over a building and some land in the *barrios*. Jorge wanted to operate a community center there while a friend of the Mayor's wanted title to the property so that he could open a factory some day. The Mayor was afraid, Silva said, that Jorge would organize followers in the neighborhood and seize the building.

Jorge had a very different interpretation of Serrano's act. It was entirely political, he said. The Mayor wanted to take credit for all the projects the Community Development Department had initiated so that he could inherit Jorge's constituency in time to defeat Bucaram in the next election. (Actually, in the middle of the campaign, Serrano decided that he couldn't win and withdrew his name.)

When we went to Jorge's house the night after his return from Italy, both he and his wife seemed nearly in shock. The three-month seminar had been a great triumph for him, he said. He had won a prize as the best student in an international class of thirty. After graduation he had been offered several attractive jobs (including the chance to be director of all community-development projects in Cameroon) but had turned them down to return to Guayaquil. As he talked, his wife Emelina, who had accompanied him on the trip, was crying. His personal success, the pleasures they had shared in Europe were still lively memories, conflicting incomprehensibly with the news they had received as soon as they returned home. Jorge kept interrupting the conversation about Serrano's behavior to show slides he had acquired in Europe. "Oh, look at the Sistine Chapel, Pablo, isn't it beautiful?" "How can they fire me like that, Raquelita? Where will I get another job? How can I fight back?"

But Jorge's misfortune turned out to be a piece of good luck for him and for Rachel and me. An American minister who ran an Episcopalian community center offered us a chance to give any kind of course to any group of students we could find. Father John Roen, who quickly became one of the few *gringos* Rachel and I trusted in Guayaquil, promised us that Jorge would have complete control of the course and that it would have nothing to do with the church's missionary work. So we agreed that Jorge would lecture for an hour a day on community development, that Rachel and I would organize the students to do a survey of *barrio* Cuba, similar to the one we had made with DUC, and that I would lead class discussions on subjects like the distribution of land in Guayaquil. We would use radio and television to recruit people from the *barrios* and the university and try to get time on news and discussion programs to describe our projects and our findings.

We assured Jorge that we would begin to help him plan the course when we returned from our Christmas vacation in Mexico.

VI

WE had been in the Peace Corps for only nine months, in Guayaquil for six, but I already felt as if I had dropped off the plane of reality that contained Harvard, New York, and the movement, off and into Nixonia.

Instead of worrying where my next article would be published, or how the next antiwar demonstration would be orchestrated, or debating whether Tom Hayden and Staughton Lynd should have gone to Bobby Kennedy's apartment to talk about the war in Vietnam, we had been trying to push our way past the Peace Corps' definition of our role in the *barrios* and maneuver ourselves into working relations with Ecuadorians who seemed relatively progressive. Rachel and I had grown much closer to each other in the process and learned a frightening amount about America. In many ways, the battles we were fighting seemed to us much more important than the battles people waged in the sectarian left and at the Big Fiesta. Nevertheless, we had been arguing with Peace Corps people for so long that we had begun to accept their terms, their definitions of flexibility, of democracy, of reasonable dissent. We could see past Erich Hofmann but no longer as far as Bob Moses. I could insist to Caleb Roehrig that the Peace Corps' marriage rule was a form of *apartheid*, but I could not quite believe my own memory when it said that Rachel and I had once belonged to a group of people who had risked their lives to combat that sort of thing in Mississippi.

Then we went to Mexico City to spend Christmas with Rachel's family and my brother.

We arrived there at two o'clock one morning, several days before we were to meet our relatives. Neither Rachel nor I can ever sleep in a new city until we spend several hours exploring, so we left our hotel for a long walk. We were so much smaller than the buildings that surrounded us! It was a sensation we had nearly forgotten in Guayaquil. Soon we saw an Americanized drugstore, Sanborn's, that was open all night. The previous morning's *New York Times* was on sale inside (it wouldn't arrive in Guayaquil for three more weeks). (The big story was William Manchester's fight with the Kennedys.) There were copies of *Harper's, Esquire,* the *Saturday Evening Post,* which had come out two months later than those displayed on the kiosks in Guayaquil. The waitress brought us cheeseburgers with onions which tasted like the food I thought I remembered buying in midtown Manhattan, altogether different from the looser, blander sandwiches that are advertised by the same name in the Reyburger and the Melba in Guayaquil.

To Sanborn's we came, burning in the night. And we ate and we drank and we read our way back toward the world we had left nine months before.

Later, when we began to talk with our families, we discovered that they were amazed, then outraged, at our stories about the Peace Corps, and their reactions convinced us that we were right to be dissenting. In fact, as Rachel's sisters Connie and Peggy and my brother, Geoff, told us about the United States we began to feel that we had been much too timid. For they talked about an America we scarcely knew, where the impudent, angry speeches in the play *MacBird* reflected emotions that millions of people felt toward their government, where students at Harvard and Berkeley and Amherst stayed up all night seriously wondering whether it would be moral to bomb buildings and assassinate politicians if the immoral war continued, where Lyndon Johnson's mad foreign policy had done what no group of organizers ever could, created a radical movement far larger and, for all its talk of destruction, far more creative than anyone could have imagined when we left the country.

We talked to our families almost incessantly, but we relaxed, too. Certainly we were lucky to be in Mexico City . . . to walk through its festive parks, to eat its rich foods, to explore its fascinating ruins. But we would have laughed together and loved each other wherever we had been. For the first time since training began, Rachel and I were completely free of the definitions which the Peace Corps had imposed on our personalities. We didn't fear that our integrity depended on our willingness to fight the bigotry of our peers, and that feeling persuaded us at last that we were not fanatics or outcasts or fools but ordinary human beings, born into a crippled time, who were honestly seeking a way to do nothing more complex than build a productive, loving life for ourselves and our friends.

VII

WE had hoped to take that attitude back to Guayaquil with us and preserve it while we prepared our course with Jorge and turned our apartment into a place where an increasing number of Ecuadorians and North Americans would feel free to mingle. In Mexico, Rachel had persuaded me that our rage at the Peace Corps had made us more intolerant than we had realized. It was easy to agree. As we talked about our experiences to our families, we both constantly wondered whether our stories described real incidents or whether they were products of our own paranoia. "When you're in the rest of America, Mississippi seems unreal," Bob Moses once said (no more). We knew that eventually we'd have to fight Hofmann, at least, and we wanted to tussle with Wymberley Coerr, but while we were still outside of Guayaquil we thought that it would be possible to choose the time and the terms of our battle.

It wasn't. As soon as we arrived in Ecuador we found ourselves involved in the most confusing, most dismal fight yet. The vacation had dulled our reflexes and blurred our perceptions. We were genuinely shocked to hear Nick and Margot describe the methods Hofmann had used to expel three volunteers—Freddy Marsdon, Sammy Bernstein, and Bobby Jefferson—for smoking marijuana, to learn how Hofmann had inflated a trivial rumor into the pot crisis, which began three days before our return.

In January 1967 there were about fifty volunteers working in community development and physical education, as advisers to cooperative projects and as university teachers, and, by our count, twenty-six of them had smoked marijuana at least once. (When we first arrived in Ecuador Rachel and I turned on occasionally, but when we discovered that Hofmann was seeking reasons to expel us we decided to quit. When our bust came we wanted it to be for politics, not for pot. We probably would have abstained anyway, or at least been extremely discreet—as Nick and Margot were—when we realized how deeply our Ecuadorian friends disliked marijuana.) Although most of the real heads seemed to use drugs as they would have used liquor a few years earlier—to escape experience, not enhance it—Freddy Marsdon was an exception. He used pot to practice therapy.

I had found Freddy's bold style appealing when he taught me

how to rifle the Peace Corps' files, but when he dealt with people rather than institutions the style turned into a rather frightening confidence in his ability to save his friends by subordinating them to his liberated will. In training he had made himself quite unpopular by assuring timid members of our group that he would "bring them out" as soon as they began to trust him.

Marijuana, which he began to use heavily after he arrived in Guayaquil, seemed to fortify his certainty that he knew where to build walls and where to open doors in other people's minds. (Who knows what secrets he wanted to find?) He often smoked with the same two volunteers, and when they were stoned he played God while the others acted as his acolytes. One of them always called him *"Dioscito,"* high or not.

From the stories I heard about Sammy Bernstein and Bobby Jefferson, I gathered that they used marijuana to comfort themselves, not to manipulate other people. Bobby, a physical-education volunteer who was an expert on the trampoline, began to smoke pot only when an Ecuadorian he was teaching took an incorrect fall and broke his neck. He was too depressed to work, too paralyzed by his depression to help the injured man. He should have gone back to the States, but he knew he'd be drafted. So he spent most of his time inside his house, usually stoned.

Sammy had been close to SDS before he joined the Peace Corps and still considered himself a true radical. From his point of view, Rachel and I seemed to be imposters. He was convinced that for all our talk about the civil-rights movement, we had revealed our true bourgeois natures when we moved out of the *barrio*. Like most volunteers, he seemed to idolize Hank Dawson, despite Hank's epithets like "silly little yid." And he was at least as diligent as Hank about his work in the *barrios*. Though he frequently complained about his neighbors and spoke Spanish so badly that I felt fluent by comparison, he still spent most of his time helping the people on his block obtain the services they needed from the *municipio*.

But he seemed to be under a great deal of psychological pressure. Ever since we had been told about "culture shock" in training, Sammy's conversation had been filled with references to the ailment. Even when he used the term jokingly, it was clear that he needed to release some sort of tension. And he used liquor and drugs much more regularly than words to treat the problems that afflicted him.

In Albuquerque, at the bar where we all hung out, he would drink himself into a stupor at least once a week. Soon after we arrived in Guayaquil we were all invited to a Fourth of July picnic sponsored by the American Consulate, and as it ended, Sammy, each of his pockets filled with a bottle of free beer, was so drunk that he literally toppled onto his back in front of a dozen Ecuadorians and U.S. diplomats. ("He's one of my boys," Dan Stringer said proudly that day, "the sort of volunteer who can drink with the men in the *barrios*.") Later, he switched from alcohol to drugs. I heard that he was stoned nearly every night and that he was always experimenting with nutmeg, with pills, with whatever new stimulant he heard about. Once he told Margot that he had gotten high by eating four crabs on an empty stomach.

Sammy's instability was one of the subjects the volunteers in Guayaquil discussed most frequently. In a way, it was comforting, because his behavior gave other frightened people the sense that they were relatively strong and secure. But even the members of our group who were genuinely worried about him realized that they lacked the power to do anything.

It was from the staff doctors, Ronald Peterson and David Foote, that we learned the details of the Peace Corps response to the pot crisis. They seemed to feel guilty enough about their role in it to discuss the episode quite freely with any volunteers who were interested. I spent a lot of time with Dr. Peterson, who was stationed in Guayaquil during that period, and I sometimes felt as if he was asking me to exonerate him on behalf of Sammy and Bobby and Freddy. (Like most staff physicians, he was in his twenties and was serving a two-year stint in the Peace Corps via a Public Health Service program that affords doctors an alternative to the army.) But I couldn't do it; something inside me had hardened. Although

I listened to him carefully and tried to help him make sense out of information that was internally inconsistent, I did not want to show him the kind of sympathy that would allow him to feel that Stringer and Hofmann were to blame for the episode, while he and Foote were entirely innocent. The doctors could have done something to stall the process, if only they had been willing to take significant risks.

The decision to terminate the volunteers, as we would later discover, had been preceded by a weird variation of the children's game of telephone, but played in this instance by bureaucrats earning between fifteen and twenty thousand dollars a year, with their careers perhaps at stake. It was chilling to think of how many government decisions, major and minor, are made on the strength of similar information, for similar reasons.

It began innocently enough when Kip Warren, Bobby Jefferson's roommate, happened to ask an Ecuadorian whose brother worked for the police department, whether he could get into trouble because his roommate used marijuana regularly. The Ecuadorian answered that the police sometimes put known drug users under surveillance. That night Kip, who had been in Guayaquil only a few months, ran into Freddy Marsdon at one of the sidewalk cafés on Nueve de Octubre and decided to ask him whether it would be advisable to move out of Jefferson's apartment.

If Kip had talked to any volunteer but Freddy, the incident would have ended right there. But Freddy decided to assume his identity as *Dioscito*, and tell Dr. Peterson about Bobby Jefferson's chronic depression, his method of escape, before Bobby went insane. But there was always some ulterior motive for any action Freddy took. In this case, he knew that Dr. Peterson had already caught him in one lie: found out that Freddy had borrowed the doctor's Peace Corps jeep for the weekend on the pretext that he would take it to a garage for repairs and then used it for his own purposes. Now, Freddy was probably using Bobby Jefferson's problem as a ruse, Dr. Peterson realized later: perhaps the doctor would forget his anger as they discussed an interesting psychological problem.

Whether Freddy was an altruist or a con man that day, he could not have realized that he was exposing Bobby, and himself, to serious trouble. For the Peace Corps promises its volunteers that anything they tell its doctors will be held in the strictest confidence.

But the word "police" bothered Dr. Peterson, who was new to the Peace Corps himself, so he decided to telephone his superior in Quito, David Foote, to ask his advice. That noon, when he decided to call, Dr. Joseph Little, the head of the Peace Corps' medical staff for Latin America who was then visiting Ecuador for a few days, had just arrived at Dr. Foote's house for lunch. During the course of the telephone conversation, in which Dr. Foote suggested that the whole issue be approached very slowly, treated very calmly, the word "marijuana" was used, and Dr. Little overheard it. Alarm bells must have jangled in his brain. He insisted that Erich Hofmann be telephoned at once and informed that volunteers were breaking a Peace Corps rule. But that act would be a violation of sacred confidence, Foote argued. A rule's a rule, his superior replied. Soon the call was made.

By the time Kip Warren's story reached Hofmann's ears, a casual conversation about possible police surveillance had become an urgent warning about an imminent police raid. Dr. Peterson and Dr. Foote both told us later that they had telephoned reports of the same story that Kip had originally told Freddy. But it is easy to guess how the words "marijuana" and "police" must have sounded to Hofmann. "I never thought that any of you would stoop so low as to smoke marijuana," he told Nick the next day. "The red press would love to get its hands on a story like this one." "The what?" Nick asked. "The red press. You know, it operates out of Cairo."

Soon after Hofmann received Dr. Foote's phone call, he apparently decided to hurry to Guayaquil and root out the guilty volunteer himself. (A few hours later he learned that it was the guilty volunteers, when several members of the physical-education group decided to avenge their friend Bobby Jefferson by divulging Freddy's name to another staff member in Quito. One of them also mentioned Sammy Bernstein, to show that Bobby wasn't the only heavy user in the country.) But according to the doctors' account of the incident, Hofmann had to figure out a way to obscure the fact that he had learned of the volunteers' offense through a violation of medical confidence, and explain why he had been given the Ambassador's special plane to fly to Guayaquil. So, though all the evidence suggests that Hofmann called Wymberley Coerr because he wanted to share his uneasiness, the Director told us that Coerr had called him as soon as Dr. Foote hung up to say that he had learned from independent sources that Bobby Jefferson was smoking marijuana and that his house would be raided the next day. But the coincidence was too great. It was difficult to believe that the Ambassador could have heard the same story that Freddy Marsdon told Dr. Peterson, with the threat of a raid that had materialized during the telephone game, at exactly the same time as Freddy's information was being circulated.

When we asked Dan Stringer who Coerr's sources were he told us about a small platoon of Ecuadorian "consultants" who spend their time at bars and whore houses where gringos hang out, keeping tabs on the Americans who work in Guayaquil. Perhaps Stringer had blurted out a disturbing truth to protect Hofmann, but it was hard to believe that any of the "consultants" had produced evidence about this case. Why couldn't they name more of the twenty-six volunteers who smoked marijuana than merely the one whose identity had been divulged? And there was no way the "consultants" could have known about the raid, since it had never been planned. Through Supercop, the Peace Corps had excellent sources at the police department, and the next morning, while Hofmann was in Guayaquil waiting for Bobby Jefferson's dope to be seized, members of the police force told both Supercop and Dan Stringer that no law enforcement official in the city even knew that Jefferson, Bernstein, and their friends used marijuana.

As soon as Hofmann arrived in Guayaquil he went over to the Peace Corps office where, by coincidence, Sammy Bernstein was checking his mail for the last time before he began a vacation. He had no idea of what had happened the day before, no idea that his name had become a weapon in a battle that should never have begun. So when Dr. Peterson, who was with Hofmann, asked to talk to him privately, he agreed, a little puzzled. Then the doctor asked Sam if he used marijuana. An outright admission, he implied, would keep the volunteer out of trouble. So Sam confessed, assuming that the conversation was confidential. Dr. Peterson reported the confession to Hofmann immediately. Bernstein was terminated that morning.

Erich would continue to deny the version of the story that I have reported here, would always insist that the Ambassador telephoned him first. The doctors would never be as specific about the process by which Sammy Bernstein had been led to confess as about less compromising details of the case, though several volunteers had been told the story by Sammy himself. For a time, Erich's account would seem credible to people like Ed Fagerlund and Bill and Joyce Dodge, who shared a general feeling that Peace Corpsmen shouldn't smoke marijuana but felt no need to pay close attention to the details of the episode as it unfolded. But it was impossible for most volunteers who had been intimately involved in the pot crisis to trust Erich or the doctors, then or ever again, though many would remain intimidated by their authority.

VIII

WHILE Freddy Marsdon was telling Dr. Peterson about Bobby Jefferson, Rachel and I were in Panama City on our way back from Mexico. We were spending several days interviewing volunteers there, trying to find out whether they were more satisfied than the volunteers in our group. They weren't. Their complaints were the same as ours. I felt as if I might be listening to an excerpt from my own diary as I sat in a tiny one-room apartment in the worst slum in town listening to a girl, whose dedication I instinctively admired, explain, "It's not that I'm failing to make a dent here in Panama. I expected that when I joined the Peace Corps, I think. But the real problem is that I don't feel as if I'm a part of anything bigger than myself, anything I really believe in."

By the time we arrived in Guayaquil the three volunteers were already expelled, though they hadn't gone home yet. Margot told us that they were supposed to be present at a final meeting with Hofmann, to be held in a few hours. As she described the past few days to us, she looked even paler, angrier than she had after the party in her apartment. But much more controlled. "This time we're not the only people who are fighting," she said. "All the volunteers are mad. You know, Sammy is their friend. And Nick's been great as their spokesman. He hasn't let Hofmann give him any shit at all."

She and Nick had worked out a tentative strategy, and they thought it might engage the rest of the group. Nick would try to involve Hofmann in a long, personal discussion of the difficulties we were having on the project, to create an atmosphere in the room where everybody felt free to talk about himself. Then, he hoped, most of the volunteers who had smoked marijuana would tell Hofmann that they turned on, too.

As I listened to Margot, I realized that the issue wasn't the right to smoke pot but the right to a fair trial. It sounded as if the words "police" and "marijuana" had made Hofmann so fearful for the Peace Corps reputation that he had obtained a confession from Sammy Bernstein on a pretext and relied on hearsay evidence as the substance of his case against the other volunteers. It was the clearest expression yet of an infuriating paradox. Volunteers went abroad as representatives of American democracy, but they had no civil rights within their own organization.

If Nick's strategy worked it could produce the kind of revealing discussion that forces people to confront themselves and to change. For we would have to explore the reasons that so many volunteers were as oblivious to the problems of using marijuana indiscriminately in a culture where it was despised as they were to the effect of acts like locking Ecuadorians out of their houses in the *barrios*, or swearing at them and getting them drunk at parties, or constantly breaking promises to complete specific jobs. Most Ecuadorians—indeed, most Latins—consider *marijuaneros* delinquents, and have no comprehension of the opinion that is increasingly popular in the United States, that people who turn on are often intellectuals or sensitive drop-outs or unhappy G.I.s, in search of greater freedom. I believed that we had to respect their feelings, just as civil-rights workers in Mississippi had to respect the rather conservative habits of Mississippi blacks (just as North American radicals who travel to revolutionary countries like Cuba and North Vietnam must respect their somewhat puritanical norms). But it was common knowledge that volunteers would talk freely with Ecuadorians about their drug experiences, or discuss them loudly with one another at restaurants and bars; that volunteers would walk through the streets of Cerro Santana, asking any passer-by where they could purchase marijuana; that they turned on freely at binational parties, once when Mayor Serrano's niece was a guest. Someday, perhaps, the disaster that Hofmann had feared during the pot crisis would materialize. So from his point of view, as well as from ours, it could have made sense to explore the reasons for the volunteers' alienation from Ecuadorian culture, their indifference to Ecuadorians' attitudes, at the same time as we discussed the reasons for the staff's indifference to volunteers' rights, or to the emotional problems that often produced their objectionable behavior.

Hofmann usually prefaced meetings with stock speeches. This time he began by telling us he had to catch a plane to Quito in two hours. "There isn't time for any of your fruitless dialogues today," he said, looking directly at Nick.

He seemed to embody great authority. His somewhat rigid manner seemed a sign of unshakable self-confidence. His German accent, which was soft, almost Scots in relaxed conversation, now sounded clipped and forbidding.

Looking at Nick, he said, "If anyone wants to stand up right now and admit that he smokes marijuana, he will be sent home tonight. There can be no discussion about that." Then he paused for a moment to see if anyone would confess. There was silence. He turned to the other volunteers and added, in a somewhat friendlier voice, "We're not as rigid as you might think, though. If any of you has a drug problem and he wants to discuss it with one of the doctors, then of course the conversation is privileged." He emphasized that he wasn't out to get any of us and reminded us (his voice was a wink) that if we broke laws so discreetly that the staff didn't hear about our transgressions, then of course nothing could be done. But surely we could sympathize with the fact that his job required him to punish anyone whose actions might endanger the Peace Corps' work in Ecuador.

He tried to make the danger more tangible by putting it into a broader context. January is always a volatile month in Guayaquil, he said, because of the anniversary of the Rio Protocols, in which Franklin Roosevelt's government had sided with Peru over Ecuador in a border dispute. Local people resented the United States for that stand. "This year January is 'get America month,'" he told us. "We have information that certain organizations are going to make things especially difficult for the United States during the next four weeks. So we have to act with great caution." (There was no visible increase in anti-American sentiment that month nor had a single North American or Ecuadorian heard of the campaign whose specter Hofmann had evoked.)

Erich had made Nick's strategy unworkable. He had managed to bribe the other volunteers, as well as frighten them, and had provided a plausible political explanation for his actions.

Still, Nick tried to reach him with words. "Listen, Erich, I don't think you understand a thing we've been saying. You talk about a 'drug problem' and say that anyone who takes drugs should see a doctor. But that's your hang-up, Erich. I think that pot is a hell of a lot better than the alcohol your generation uses, but that's not what I'm trying to talk about. And I don't want to hide from the truth behind word games or little bargains or threats either. I want to talk about the way we're living in Guayaquil now, what's happening to us. Why can't you do that?"

"I heard enough about the so-called generation gap from you yesterday, Nick. There is no generation gap in this organization. In the Peace Corps there are only talkers and workers. Anyone who feels that he has to keep talking about how much he dislikes the way we do things might as well get out."

The rest of the volunteers seemed paralyzed: unable to respond to the fact that rules had been manipulated to preserve an organization's image and to pacify possible dissenters; unable to see that Hofmann, Dan Stringer, and the three Peace Corps doctors were all willing to risk inflicting damage on Bobby, Sammy, and Freddy in order to avoid a scandal (which most likely would not have occurred) and thus be sure that their careers were protected. Unable, even, to realize that Hofmann had just told Nick, in effect, that free speech was forbidden in the Peace Corps. To volunteers and staff alike, it seemed, due process, human sensitivity, and free speech were small things next to personal security, a permanent place in the sterile paradise.

I could imagine Hofmann using the same words as General Hershey, turning from Nick and assuring the other volunteers that "you still have the right to think what you want. And if you speak freely, discreetly, where none of the staff can hear you, well there's nothing I can do about that. We're not as rigid as you might think," he continued in my fantasy. "I'm certainly not out to get any of you. But you have to understand that we have to punish anyone whose criticism of the Peace Corps might endanger the important work we are all doing here."

And I was sure that if he had made that incredible speech Hank and Gerald and Barney and Bert would have decided that they agreed with him.

So then I blurted out the sort of argument that I had expected to nurture for several months. I was trying to support Nick, trying to move toward a discussion of fears and frustrations and the attitude toward the Ecuadorians they produced, but my anger curdled my words, made them unpalatable to almost everyone in the room. I told Hofmann that there was a sickness in Guayaquil and it was far more serious than the way that some volunteers smoked some pot. "The word I would use is 'racism.' Or what else would you call it when some of the volunteers hit shoeshine boys on the street, and most of them call Ecuadorians . . ."

"Just a minute, Paul. You always talk during these meetings, and you always say the same things. I've written some things down here that are on my mind, and I'd like to say them to Mr. Hofmann now."

It was Sammy Bernstein. He seemed to rock from nervousness as he talked, and his voice never stopped trembling. He spoke very slowly, as if he was having difficulty developing any single idea, finding words that began to suggest the jumble of emotions he felt. But he was more lucid than ever before.

He had not joined the Peace Corps to work under people like Hofmann, he said, and he resented very much the fact that "you are our *jefe* and not our friend." He had come to Guayaquil to work with poor people. "I know that my neighbors don't want me to be kicked out for this. I've talked with many of them since yesterday morning, and they've told me that they are eager to sign a petition requesting that you let me stay in the country. I have always believed that things like those that have happened to me in the last day could only happen" (he paused) "in Russia or Communist China, not in America."

Margot and I both thought that we saw Hofmann smile uneasily while Sammy was speaking. He was paying great attention to his watch and his metal pipe cleaner.

As soon as Sammy finished, Hofmann began to speak in his briskest voice. "Thank you very much, Sam. Now that we've heard what you want to say I think it's time to adjourn." I suppose, in his clumsy way, he was trying to prove that free speech still did exist in the Peace Corps. We were supposed to appreciate the fact that he had allowed Sammy an opportunity to express his opinion.

Most of the volunteers seemed eager to leave, too. But Sammy's words had moved me so much that I couldn't let them. I might have felt differently if he hadn't sounded so fucking idealistic and patriotic. But by the time he finished talking, I was afraid that I saw the future of America in that room.

So I stood up and faced the other volunteers. "You've all let yourselves be castrated. Every single one of you complains behind Erich's back, but when he's here not one of you has the courage to speak out." I was pointing at them, and I must have been shouting. "That sort of thing has happened in . . . other countries, too." (I couldn't say Nazi Germany, either.) "I'm ashamed to be in the same organization with you. With all of you."

In a crazy way, it was more of a benediction than a denunciation. I seemed to have provided the volunteers with a ritualistic symbol to exit on. Not that they were walking out on me—I hadn't made them angry enough for that. No, they had grown bored with all the talk, and now they wanted to go back to the Pensión Helbig and get some lunch.

Hofmann had failed to stop the volunteers from smoking marijuana, though. Increasing numbers of them would turn on during the next months, as carelessly as ever. The next summer three members of the physical-education group were expelled for smoking grass, but that didn't deter the rest of the volunteers any more than the pot crisis had. A friend of mine, whose tour of duty in Ecuador ended in May 1969, estimated that about ninety per cent of the volunteers who were in the country when he left had used marijuana.

IX

HOFMANN THOUGHT that one of the Peace Corps doctors should accompany the three volunteers back to Washington, in case they experienced "withdrawal symptoms." Dr. Peterson told me that it took a good deal of time to persuade the Director that his fears had no medical foundation.

As soon as Sammy Bernstein left Ecuador, the staff that had expelled him began to use his name to symbolize the kind of unflagging devotion to the poor that Nick and I were supposed to lack. Later that week Dan Stringer began a meeting of our group that Rachel had urged him to call, to discuss new ways of working in Guayaquil, with a twenty-minute sermon in praise of the community-development methods we had learned about in training, using Sammy's last words as his text. Rachel, who still thought that I was too intolerant of the other volunteers, was particularly eager to describe the "team approach" we had learned about in Panama, where Peace Corps people and host-country nationals from a variety of professions concentrate their skills on a single community. Instead, Dan urged us to quit experimenting with so many ideas and begin to work in the *barrios* as the lately martyred Saint Samuel would have done.

"He told me right before he left that what this city needs is a thousand more volunteers," Dan said, "and I think he's right. Of course they'd have to come in phases. I couldn't request more than fifty at first." Then he began to outline a scheme he and Sammy had worked out. The Peace Corps office would be moved out to the *barrios* near a large meeting hall. The new wave of volunteers would be assigned to live two blocks away from one another. Each would organize a *comité* in his tiny area, and every week the local leaders would meet to discuss their problems. That way the Peace Corps could finally create the city-wide organization that had been Gshwend's dream.

"Of course none of that could happen right now," Dan continued, "so here's what I'm going to do from today on. I'm going to follow Sammy's example and stay away from this office as much as I can. Starting tomorrow I'm going to put on my hip boots and drive out to the *suburbios* early every day so that I can work side by side with you volunteers."

When his monologue was over, Rachel asked the volunteers to discuss the projects they had been working on for the past few months. Only Peter Evans, who rarely talked at meetings, spoke up. A month earlier he had married Sally Wells, the girl he'd been courting ever since training, and now he wanted to make a confession. "I guess I really have been working only about three hours a week teaching English at the Lion's Club. I feel pretty guilty about that. We've tried hard to find things to do in the *barrios* but nothing ever works out right. Anyway, Sally and I are happier just being together in our apartment than we could be doing anything else. We don't seem to have any other needs. I suppose we'll find a job soon, but I don't want to be part of any team. I value my freedom too much for that."

But Rachel kept trying to interest the other volunteers in her idea. She was still convinced that the best way to help the volunteers was to encourage them to find satisfying work, that angry denunciations like mine at the meeting with Hofmann only made their problems more severe. To set an example, she described the birth-control program she was working on and suggested ways it might be coordinated with nutrition programs, health programs, credit cooperative programs.

But Dan interrupted her before she could finish. "I don't want to see these groups meeting too often. Sammy Bernstein told me before he left that meetings only confused him and made him feel that he was wasting time which belonged to the people in the *barrios*."

Most of the volunteers seemed to agree. Most of them were as wary of the team approach as Peter Evans. "You have to realize that the Peace Corps is an organization of rugged individualists," Dan told Rachel as the meeting ended. Even my gentle wife was becoming convinced that she couldn't work with the volunteers or the staff.

Two weeks after he was sent home, Sammy Bernstein returned to Ecuador. Though Freddy and Bobby were terminated immediately, he had not been expelled.

Apparently, he had impressed the staff psychiatrists and the administrators in the Latin-American division with his great commitment to Guayaquil's poor. Dan (who still spent most of his time in the Peace Corps office) told us that Sammy had showed them an eight-millimeter film of life in the *barrios* and accompanied it with a stirring narrative. Sammy claimed, and Dan agreed, that he had persuaded members of the Washington staff that his new plan for saturating the *suburbios* with volunteers was at least interesting and possibly plausible.

(Perhaps the mystique of the Peace Corps was so powerful that its directors could get away with sending fifty more Bert Kalishers, Hank Dawsons, and Gerald Erlhams to the *barrios* of Guayaquil. But I was sure that any new community-development project would suffer the same frustrations as our group had and that volunteers would develop similar prejudices against Ecuadorians which might, with so many *gringos* living in close proximity, erupt into outright violence.)

Hofmann refused to let Sammy move back into his *barrio*, or even live in Guayaquil, for fear that he would begin taking drugs again.

So Sammy was forced to wander around the country, feeling increasingly aimless as he searched for work. He spent about a month at a summer camp the Peace Corps organized for some of the children of the *suburbios*. He tried to start some community-development projects in Duran, a ten-minute ferry-boat ride from Guayaquil. Then he drifted down to a much smaller village on the Pacific coast, where a staff member wanted a cooperative organized. When that job didn't work out either, he journeyed to Quito, where he was supposed to become a sort of big brother in an orphanage.

The pointlessness of his new life in Ecuador encouraged him to drink and use drugs more extensively than ever. In June he asked to be sent back to the States.

X

I HAD been certain that the volunteers would be unwilling to adopt the team approach. Before that meeting, as I listened to Rachel and Bill Dodge tell Dan Stringer about the new forms of work they thought might save the project, I had found myself experiencing the sort of weariness and frustration that must have suffused Bob Moses when he heard me talk enthusiastically about our elaborate plans for the people of Vicksburg instead of admitting that the tension between Papa Doc and me was a reflection of a problem that the Summer Project had only aggravated.

I felt unusually isolated from Rachel. I began to realize that those years at Choate when I was tormented by bigots had left me with an instinctive, defensive insight into racism, a lastingly angry commitment to its destruction, that Rachel never had to develop during her adolescence in Wellesley.

But if I talked at all it was only to add a detail or two to her description of the team approach. Then, just as the meeting was about to end, Dan Stringer's self-satisfied comment about the volunteers' rugged individualism infuriated me so much that I had to speak. It was such a crazy perversion of the American past in which I had once believed. Whose myths I still loved.

It seemed obvious to me that the word to describe Peter Evans' reluctance to work on the team Rachel talked about was "selfish," not "individualistic." He didn't want to discipline himself to do a complex job. People who were "ruggedly individualistic" were supposed to be "self-reliant," too, but I was certain that the attitude which kept them from responding to Rachel's request was a fear that made them mutually dependent. That was why they were so reluctant to admit new ideas or unusual people into their clique.

How could Gerald, Bert, or Peter Evans become "individual-istic" or "self-reliant" in a society whose wealth and talent were geared to an unceasing effort to make them conform to the demands of authority so that they could advance themselves and obtain the kinds of possessions they read about in *Playboy?* Their cravings had destroyed their characters: they were part of a nation of addicts. The real frontiersman in Nixonia is the Marlboro man, slumping in his saddle from the pain in his chest while he reaches into the saddle bag for a new cigarette. He can't break the habit, though he knows he has cancer.

It seemed to me that as long as the volunteers remained in Guaya-quil their personalities, supposedly marvelous advertisements for the American way of life, would continue to decompose. Already most of them had quit hoping that they would find satisfying ways to help Ecuador's people. Though Hank Dawson remained active in the *barrios*, Ralph Craft and Gerald were planning to move downtown, and Gerald had begun to summarize his aspirations in the Peace Corps with the sentence, "I just want to talk to *Guaya-quileños* about my mother and let them talk to me about theirs." Bert Kalisher spent most of his time in his *casa nada*, refrained from picking up his mail for weeks at a stretch, and often failed to open the letters he received. Sid Raschi had transferred to Quito (he would not find work he enjoyed there, either, and would move on to Loja, a town near the Peruvian border). Libby White, who would settle in Quito, too, had begun a rather depressing relation-ship with a married Ecuadorian (in some ways it seemed to parallel the relationship she had fled in the *suburbios*) which, to judge from her conversations, consumed most of her attention during the rest of the time she was in the country. Barney Ableman, who had worked in the Mayor's office and then in a library in the *bar-rios*, was now in love with a volunteer from Margot's group, and gave the affair as the reason he couldn't complete his share of the *municipio* study that Harlan Hobgood had requested. He spent a few hours each week in the library, and did nothing else. That June he left the Peace Corps, and he and his girl friend got mar-ried in the States. Though Bill Dodge and Bill Hennemuth, one of the architects with whom he had worked in the *municipio*, were now earnestly trying to launch a low-cost housing project in the *suburbios* (without much support from the Ecuadorians), the other architect had transferred to Quito after Dr. Peterson had warned him that he might suffer a nervous breakdown if he remained in Guayaquil. Sherwood Parrot was still angling for his medical discharge.

I still believed that one could release some of them from their mood of apathy and anguish if one could find words that would encourage them to confront the brutality and fear it produced. When I talked my tone was alternately harsh and pleading: "The only reason to discuss abstract concepts like a 'team approach' is to find a way of telling each other that we are all frustrated and lonely down here and need each other's help very badly. Can't we talk about the things we feel instead of living the lie that we're the cheerful productive volunteers the people in America want to believe in? Why do we see the Ecuadorians as 'Ekkies' and 'spics' instead of human beings and hit shoeshine boys on Nueve de Octubre? Let's admit that we're becoming a bunch of racists."

But Margot was the only other person in the room who seemed willing to support me. Even Nick and Rachel looked embarrassed. "I thought it was an exaggeration to call them racists," Rachel said later. "Besides, that business about hitting shoeshine boys just isn't true. Bert Kalisher's the only one who does that." Then she paused. "But I guess I also stayed quiet because I was afraid to have them so angry at me."

The rest of the volunteers were outraged. What did I mean with all this talk about our project's being sick? Didn't I realize that when I'd used that word in front of Erich Hofmann I had given him another reason to believe we were crazy?

Why didn't I ever show more loyalty to my group?

Finally, Dan Stringer turned to the only black man in the room (just five of the three hundred volunteers in Ecuador were black), a schoolteacher who worked in the *campo* and happened to be visiting Guayaquil for the day. "Tell me, Eddie, do you think the Peace Corps is racist?"

"No, Dan, I don't."

Stringer looked at me triumphantly. "See, Paul, even he disagrees with you."

After the meeting Peter and Sally Evans started a conversation with me. "I don't get too angry when you talk about racism and immorality, Paul," Sally began. "Maybe that's because I've known you since training. You're not like that Margot. I don't know how she can talk about morality when she's been living in sin with Nick for so long."

Maybe we should have talked then about their attitude toward sex, but the subject seemed too delicate. I wanted to threaten them as little as possible, so I tried to show what I meant about racism by making an example out of my own problems in the *barrios*. Peter's response was very honest. "You have to understand that there's a big difference between us, Paul. You want more out of life than we do, and you're probably talented enough to get it. When you get back to the States you'll be a writer or go into politics or something. All I'll ever be is a schoolteacher who makes enough money to keep Sally and our children happy. It's the same thing down here. You and Rachel keep trying to do big things. But we just want to show the Ecuadorians that there are Americans who are willing to spend two years living in the same houses as they do, eating the same foods, riding the same buses. That's enough."

It was impossible to show Peter that his attitude would have sounded extremely condescending to any Ecuadorian with pride. "We just want to show the Negroes in Mississippi that there are white people who are willing to spend two years living in the same houses as they do, eating the same foods, riding the same buses." But he would have seen nothing wrong with that statement either.

Later that week Rachel and I saw *The Chase*, in which a townful of white Americans beat up Marlon Brando, the chief of police who is trying to prevent them from lynching an escaped convict, set fire to the junkyard to which the convict had fled, then murder him on the steps of the courthouse. We were both Brando, the other volunteers were the townspeople, drinking, shouting, laughing as they destroyed in the name of justice. I'm sure that if the director had chosen to tell the story differently we would have seen equivalents of Erich Hofmann, Dan Stringer, Hank Dawson, Gerald Erlham, Bert Kalisher in the crowd, each with private problems and private justifications that made his behavior understandable. If a reporter had done interviews in town the next day he would have found the streets full of people like Peter and Sally Evans, eager to tell him that they were basically decent folk, that their town was a pleasant place to live.

"The movie made me realize that I think I'm living in hell here," Rachel said as we were walking home. "There are the same lies, the same viciousness. But everybody thinks he is doing such good."

PART NINE

I

During February and March 1967, I played the Rolling Stones' new album *Aftermath* so often that soon the record became a source of tension between Rachel and me. She hated harsh songs like "Going Home" and "Look at That Stupid Girl," felt more comfortable in the sweeter world that the Beatles and the Lovin' Spoonful evoked in "Yellow Submarine" and "Summer in the City."

But the United States' Yellow Submarine was a Polaris so far as most of the world was concerned; summer in the city was Newark or Watts. The Stones' hard, angry beat expressed my increasing disillusionment with America just as clearly as Pete Seeger's open, optimistic voice had expressed the faith I felt in the country when the decade began. Since John Kennedy's assassination the image of a gunman crouched to kill had never left my brain. I grieved for the land I had wanted to help build then. I still felt much more compassion than hatred for its people. But now I knew that I could never live in the sterile paradise which most white Americans saw as their home.

Those months were the worst in Guayaquil, the muggiest part of the rainy season. "Sweat creeps out of my skin and just seems to hover over it so that I feel I will soon begin to grow a mold crust," Rachel wrote to her sister. During that time she and I devoted most of our energy to the course we were teaching with Jorge, spent a great deal of time with our Ecuadorian friends, read enormously, and tried to keep careful notes on everything we were learning about Guayaquil. We rarely talked to any volunteers except for Nick and Margot, Ralph Craft (who had decided that he preferred working with us to living in the *barrios*, and was helping with the course), and the Dodges. We never went to the Peace Corps office. But I realized that our influence in the organization must be more subtly extensive than I had understood after the depressing open confrontations that had marked the pot crisis.

The other volunteers had begun to criticize the staff more openly, and after we taught them the lessons we'd learned from Freddy Marsdon, many of them began to raid the files. The marriage rule had been modified, though it was still a kind of segregation. (Now Hofmann would permit volunteers to marry Ecuadorians if he approved of the match.) A visitor from Washington told us that the training center at the University of New Mexico had been closed down, partly as a result of our complaints. All the volunteers except Hank Dawson and the Evanses had moved in from the *barrios*.

The *Volunteer* magazine had surprised me by accepting and printing an article I wrote which described the failure of our project. At the end of the piece I asked, "Is the same thing happening all over the Peace Corps world?" and the response to that question amazed me. Forty-four people sent letters either to me or to the *Volunteer*, and all but one of them agreed with my argument:

. . . after being in Iran for eight months, most of us in this program realize how absurdly conceived, poorly trained, and ill-informed we were as to the actual work situation (i.e., lack of work situation) we were to face.

[Paul Cowan] sounded as if he could be quoting us. As registered nurses, we came to Afghanistan to teach nursing skills, only to find out that there were not enough teaching positions available for us. Often feeling very unwanted, many of us have been placed in hospitals to work as cheap labor [and are] unable to make any changes or improvements in nursing care.

To [Paul Cowan's] question in the last paragraph of his article, I can only argue that certainly the same failures he speaks of are happening here in India. Not only in urban projects like his but in rural ones like India XX, of which I am a member. In India we are being told that these failures are, after all, unimportant because the Peace Corps is an educational endeavor. This has the effect of inviting the volunteer to forget that he has a job to do, to not try to come to grips with the reason for his failure if the job is not being done, and to treat his time in India as if it were part of the junior-year-abroad program of some American university.

[From a volunteer in Quito whom I had never met]: Peace Corps has consistently taken a very simplistic attitude toward community development: to take B.A. generalists fresh out of college and call them community developers after three months of training is so pretentious that one cannot help but think that the Peace Corps can afford this attitude only because volunteers are relatively inexpensive (in terms of hard cash).

My depression lingered after the pot crisis. But I didn't feel beaten. Rachel and I kept saving each other from despair. We were able to share everything, to learn from our differences in background and temperament, not worry about them. We kept discovering each other.

Besides, we were finally involved in work that occupied and interested us.

About forty people had enrolled for the course we were teaching with Jorge. They were *barrio* leaders, university students and social workers, doctors and lawyers. I had to teach every day, and the fact that I held the students' interest gave me a self-confidence that I'd been lacking. Though I usually led discussions instead of lecturing, still I had to perform in Spanish for an hour at a time, and that was more than I had believed I could do. I realized that one reason Rachel had related to people so much more easily than I had while we were living in the *suburbios* was that she never doubted her command of the language (she was virtually fluent after she'd studied it for three months), while my Spanish, which was adequate, sounded coarse to me, especially when I compared it to hers. But now I was more concerned about communicating with the students than I was about my immigrant's accent, my terrible grammar.

To prepare for my lectures and the survey (patterned on the one we made with DUC) I was organizing, I talked with dozens of people in the impoverished *barrio* Cuba, and discovered that the problem of land distribution was more acute there than in virtually any other part of the city. What made the situation particularly infuriating was that the entire *barrio* belonged to one of Guayaquil's leading Communists, Antonio Parra Velasco, a former rector at the Central University, an eloquent foe of *yanqui* imperialism. Although the families who lived there were even poorer than most of the squatters in the *suburbios* (on the other side of town from *barrio* Cuba), Parra Velasco charged them between two and eight dollars rent each month. It was a fixed cost. None of them could afford to pay their Communist landlord ten dollars per square meter for land.

One man in the *barrio* told me that a few years earlier he had been a member of a *comité* which persuaded the *municipio* to install water pipes. But Parra Velasco had responded by raising the rents and land costs. "Now most people here are afraid to ask for things that will bring progress. They think that improvements will do them harm." Many of the people I met didn't want the city to provide them with a decent sewage system for fear that Parra Velasco would increase land costs another five dollars per square meter.

Most of our students, I discovered, didn't know about the situation in *barrio* Cuba when the course began. I spoke about it frequently in class and devised survey questions that would encourage the slum dwellers to talk about Parra Velasco (whom many of the students respected as a dedicated radical), and the effects of his greed. But that response still seemed inadequate: there must be some way to create a situation that would inspire the students and slum dwellers to form an overt alliance. So I did what I was always telling other volunteers not to do: tried to create an institution based on North American analogies. I used the American radio program *Town Meeting of the Air* and the confrontations that were always taking place between poor people and War on Poverty officials as my models for something called *Pregunte a Sus Candidatos* (Question Your Candidates), a series that was supposed to run through the mayoralty campaign. My idea was that the five candidates for office would come to the community center where the class met, where they would have to answer difficult questions about their platforms in front of Jaime Diaz, who promised to cover the meetings, and at least one radio microphone. Hundreds of students and slum dwellers would attend the meetings, I thought, and it would soon become clear to them that even Bucaram couldn't do anything to solve *barrio* Cuba's problems. Then, the two groups might feel enough commitment to one another to discuss ways of attacking Parra Velasco, their real enemy.

The best I can say about *Pregunte a Sus Candidatos* is that it didn't hurt anybody. Serrano, who needed votes desperately, gave a long, rather interesting speech about the city's budgetary problems to about fifty students and poor people, which Jaime turned into an article. The only other candidate who was less popular than the Mayor, José Hanna, came to speak twice, but both times there were only about ten people present to hear him, so he left, increasingly insulted. (Bucaram, who hated Hanna, later gave him his major campaign issue when he said that Hanna had emerged from a "rotten uterus.") Neither Bucaram nor Pedro Menendez, his closest opponent, even bothered to talk with us.

I would probably have given up on *Pregunte a Sus Candidatos*, even if it hadn't been for the bizarre episode which grew out of our attempt to talk with Enrique Baquerizo, the fifth candidate for Mayor, and made me unwilling to pursue the contact.

We had to arrange to meet Baquerizo through Hugo Torres, a

twenty-two-year-old prodigy who was regarded as one of the leaders of Guayaquil's Conservative Party. Hugo was famous throughout the city for his girth: he is five-eight, and weighs close to three hundred fifty pounds.

When we talked to him about *Pregunte a Sus Candidatos* he seemed to offer us a sort of *quid pro quo.* Of course he'd introduce us to Baquerizo, but he'd be very much obliged if Rachel would help him do a study of the women of Guayaquil which would be made available to "interested parties" throughout the world.

A few days later we returned to his office with Margot, who was looking for some short job she could do in the few months before her tour of duty ended. She was wearing a dress with a diamond-shaped cutout in the bodice and the curve of her breast was visible. It seemed to me that Hugo addressed most of his remarks to her naked flesh.

He told us that his project had grown out of a discussion he'd had with a UNESCO official, a member of the Commission for the Equilibrium of the Races. It was still confidential—even classi-fied—from most members of the government, so we shouldn't dis-cuss it with anyone. The study was supposed to concentrate on the sex life of Guayaquil's women.

Hugo had already sent some postcards to a group whose names were selected at random, he said. Each card contained a different question. "One might ask, 'How many times do you make love each week?'" he explained. "A second might ask whether the woman was a virgin before she got married. A third might ask whether the woman has any special sexual problems. At the bot-tom of every card I tell the woman to come to my office for an in-terview."

"Do they talk to you?" Margot wondered aloud. "When I lived in the *barrios* I found out that women were shy about discussing their sex lives even with me."

"That," Hugo answered, "is probably because you were too care-ful when you talked with them. You were probably searching for the right way to gain their sympathy. My technique is different. I sit them down in a chair in my office and shoot questions at them.

Crude! Brutal! I mean crudely, brutally. They are so startled that they answer."

Somewhat incredulous, I asked him to explain the point of the survey.

He wanted to make Ecuador resemble the Scandinavian countries, he said, so that it can develop as rapidly as they have. "We have to become more like the Nordic peoples. But most of our women, especially our poor women, are nervous about sex. Perhaps it is the influence of the Catholic Church, but they are as frigid as the Swedes and Danes are free. When Ecuadorian men come home at night and want to make love they are always refused. So they are tired and irritable at work the next day. If our sex habits don't change, our people will never become more efficient."

But Hugo did not really believe that a more libertarian Ecuador would change very much either.

"To be honest, what we need here is some Nordic blood. The Latins are too romantic. They will never develop the country alone. Of course the Indians are an inferior race. But there are already hundreds of people who want to come here because they are tired of Europe. We must teach our people to appeal to them sexually, to adopt their customs, so that we can attract more and they will all breed with us."

Then he told us about a group of Jewish businessmen he claimed to have spoken with who were in the business of selling Nordic sperm. He seemed to think he could import that, if he couldn't attract Nordic people, and use it to impregnate Ecuadorian women.

Rachel wanted to know whether UNESCO felt much sympathy with his strategy to improve the race.

"What I am describing is the job of the UNESCO Commission on the Equilibrium of the Races," he said.

At the beginning of the conversation Margot had volunteered to help Hugo design a questionnaire for *barrio* women. Now he asked Rachel and me to leave the room so that he could talk to her alone for five minutes. She seemed willing to stay. Maybe she could learn more about the schemer, or his scheme.

They seemed friendly enough when they rejoined us twenty minutes later. But as soon as Hugo had stuffed himself into his Volkswagen to drive home, Margot began to describe the discussion: "One thing about Hugo I can tell you right now. He doesn't lie about his technique." He wanted to know how frequently Margot had intercourse, with whom, when she had lost her virginity. Then he began to read her a letter from a woman who had always found sex painful because her husband liked to make love while sitting on hard chairs. When Margot said she didn't understand why he was reading her the letter, Hugo walked toward her, carrying a ruler in one of his pudgy hands. "He acted as if he could solve the lady's problems if he measured the distance between my knees.

"Until then I'd been playing him along, trying to find out what this is all about. But that was too much. I suddenly realized that Hugo is so fat he probably has to make love sitting on hard chairs. So I told him that the two of you were outside and we had to get to an important meeting." The next day we checked, and of course learned that there is nothing like a UNESCO Commission on the Equilibrium of the Races.

II

AFTER the failure of *Pregunte a Sus Candidatos*, I realized that I couldn't do much with my class except raise some issues and hope that the students would respond to them. From then on Rachel and I began to pay more attention to the complicated relationship that she and I were developing with Jorge Rodriguez than to any other aspect of the course. Though we always argued that Ecuadorians like Jorge had to devise their own solutions to their country's problems, that outsiders might be able to serve as their subordinates but never as their surrogates, it was not always easy for Rachel and me to put the principle into practice. We felt somewhat uncomfortable as Jorge's subordinates.

Though we liked him very much, and admired him still more, there were still some deep tensions between him and us that were both personal and cultural. For example, he is as fastidious as I am impatient. To assure himself that the course was entirely under control he often found it necessary to discuss the most minute details of academic or organizational procedure for hours at a stretch. If he had been a North American, I would have argued with him that many of the questions he considered important were quite irrelevant, or at least tried to make jokes that would liven discussions like the ones we had every afternoon for a week about the kind of symbols students should use when they mapped the economic resources of *barrio* Cuba. But I was afraid that such responses would insult Jorge. The only way I could survive the dullest of those daily meetings was to invent telephone calls I had to make, questions I had to discuss with Father Roen, and remain in retreat for long periods of time. Even when I was present, I often took advantage of Rachel's fluent Spanish and her astonishing patience, and left her to sustain the conversations (which she found as dull as I did) while I escaped into daydreams about our future in the United States.

Perhaps Jorge paid more attention to details than to substantial programs because somewhere inside himself he realized that nothing he did could really succeed. It was a way to keep a screen between himself and that dismal reality. Certainly his sense of powerlessness forced him to enter into sycophantic relationships with the North Americans Rachel and I were struggling with. Because he had no independent resources with which he could support his projects, he had developed some of the qualities one associates with presidents of Negro colleges: to survive he was forced to make favorable impressions on visitors he must have despised. I suppose that is what Gshwend meant when he complained that Jorge was a hypocrite. I often felt betrayed by his feeling that he had to treat Hofmann and Kirby Jones like visiting dignitaries—and rather embarrassed for Jorge, too. For he knew as well as I did that they would use the brief, ritualistic visits they paid to community-development projects in Guayaquil as evidence of their expertise when they met with their superiors in the States. They would generalize from hasty conversations with Jorge, and much longer conversations with Americans like Gshwend and Dan Stringer about Jorge's work, to suggest policies that would affect him for years.

But nothing was harder for Rachel and me to accept than the fact that Jorge's precarious position forced him to adopt strategies for working in Guayaquil that were considerably more moderate than his own analysis of the situation should have decreed. The programs he wanted us to help organize should have appealed to the Americans who still followed the Peace Corps' line more than they appealed to Rachel and me. The goal of our course was "the preparation of personnel," he often said, and while that phrase had a dozen potential meanings I knew that he had brought it back to Guayaquil from the class in community development (sponsored by Shell Oil) which he had attended in Rome. He wanted our graduates to fan out into the *suburbios,* founding new community centers which offered courses in literacy and accounting, sewing and typing, cake decorating and hair dressing. He wanted to "prepare personnel" to train poor people to find work within the oligarchic structure that ruled Ecuador, not rebel against it.

I don't want to suggest that we possessed any special information that Jorge lacked—or that we had reached any general conclusions with which he disagreed—when I write that it was not even possible for all of the students in our course to find work in Ecuador. Jorge had been the first person to tell us about the two hundred thousand Ecuadorian nationals, many of them high-school and college graduates, who had gone abroad to earn their livings. He had shown us the astonishingly high percentage of university graduates still living in Guayaquil who were forced to work as messenger boys or postal clerks or stevedores. Nothing angered him more than the spectacle of his country's wasting most of its people.

Through many conversations with him and with our other middle-class friends, we had begun to understand why the Latin educational system seemed volatile to us, and why some of the brightest people who attended universities in Ecuador spend more time trying to disrupt their institutions than they do studying. Since they know that there will be little demand for their services when they graduate, they feel that their years at school are nothing but a meaningless ritual. Thus, they rage against the fact that their class has no future.

The University of Guayaquil is public and has far more students from the middle class and lower middle class than from the oligarchy, which usually sends its children to the smaller, private Catholic University or to college in the United States. Edmundo Vera, who had run for vice-president of its student body as a candidate of the most radical party, often sounded like an irrational militant (even to me) when he boasted of a strike he had led which closed the Department of Psychology for six months. But the issue around which he had organized the boycott made as much sense as any issue in a North American labor strike. He and the other students wanted their faculty to help them work out an agreement with high schools in Guayaquil to insure that graduates of the department could find employment as guidance counselors. Eventually they won, and Edmundo (who might otherwise have joined his younger brother Pancho as a clerk in the post office) began to work with students at a vocational school. He discussed the problems and rewards of that job with as much interest as he had once discussed the problems and rewards of closing down his department. But he was luckier than most Ecuadorian college graduates. The University of Guayaquil has about the same relation to education as the *municipio* has to public administration. Only a tiny proportion of its faculty members are full-time professors. The rest, like Jorge, work eight hours a day at other jobs and teach only to earn some extra money. It was said that the older teachers read the same lectures year after year, decade after decade, despite the great changes that were constantly taking place in the institutions and professions they were supposed to describe. The buildings and classrooms in which they taught were in such disrepair that you knew that no one with real power in Ecuador even cared enough about education to create the impression that the country's second largest university was functioning efficiently. There were no adequate textbooks for students who wanted to read beyond the banal lectures they were receiving. Besides, books cost more than most of them could afford to spend.

Even when an exceptionally diligent person like Lourdes Vera managed to extract a good education from the university, there was no way she could put it to use. Architecture, like most professions, was dominated by old men who were terrified of new methods. The few young people they accepted as colleagues were usually the offspring of the elite, even more conservative than Javier, who had returned from the United States with specific ideas about how to keep the oligarchy in power. The men who controlled feudal Ecuador would do everything they could to prevent people like Lourdes and Edmundo, Javier and Jorge from developing into a self-conscious "new class" of technicians and professionals which might become sophisticated enough to replace the class that Juan Marcos represented. The society, as an organism, wanted to reject its newly educated young. Thus, the universities decayed and the students demonstrated. They caused trouble because, as a class, they realized (as their contemporaries in Europe and the United States were realizing, too) that they would be thwarted whenever they tried to channel their energy into constructive action.

Jorge encouraged us to discuss such things in the course, to show how the oligarchy was hoarding space in the professions that should have belonged to younger members of the middle class, just as it was hoarding land in the *suburbios* that should have belonged to poor people. But he did not feel that he could construct a program out of such radical perceptions. His instinct, instead, was to train a new, more sophisticated generation of social workers.

Nor did we try to pressure him to change his mind. Rachel was instinctively too tactful to do more than express her disagreements gently, and I was determined not to say anything that might threaten Jorge. I was always worried that a fight with him would be a re-enactment of my fight with Papa Doc, even though the political contexts were altogether different. For the cultural contexts were very similar. Besides, neither Rachel nor I, even privately, believed that we were equipped to devise any sort of clear alternatives to Jorge's approach. How could our students bring about the transfer of land in *barrio* Cuba from Antonio Parra Velasco to the poor people who lived there? The only possible answer: by making a revolution. Logically, then, we should try to mold our students into the nucleus of an SDS type of movement whose purpose was to expose and destroy Ecuadorian oligarchs and American imperialists. But that strategy, which would have seemed tempting back in the States, sounded as absurd in Guayaquil as the Peace Corps' idea that volunteers could influence people who lived in the *suburbios* to resemble middle-class Americans. The failure of *Pregunte a Sus Candidatos* was one small example of the distance between my assumptions and the Ecuadorians'. The failure of Gshwend's plan to establish an "Alinsky-type organization" provided us with a constant reminder that foreigners who insist they can bridge the psychological distance with political programs, reformist or revolutionary, quickly become arrogant and imperialistic, unable to respond to the nuances of reality.

So we adopted the sort of attitude toward Jorge that Erich Hofmann wanted us to adopt toward the Peace Corps. Instead of quitting our job with him or trying to force him to change, we concentrated on the many qualities about him we liked and tried to ignore his tendency to make compromises we regarded as unnecessary. We resolved to set forth our own opinions and analyses in our lectures and our talks with the students but to integrate our ideas and enthusiasms with Jorge's decisions on general policy.

In return, he always consulted us and was entirely willing to let me experiment with *Pregunte a Sus Candidatos*, though he and Rachel had both doubted it would succeed. The longer the three of us worked together, the more deeply we came to trust each other, the more frequently we found ourselves agreeing. Our respect for Jorge's tact, diligence, and understanding of Guayaquil continued to grow, and I think that we impressed him enough with our ideas, and our willingness to express them under relatively dangerous circumstances, to make him somewhat more radical and outspoken.

But in order to maintain our working relationship, Rachel and I consciously narrowed our personalities and softened our opinions whenever we were with him. If we had been his subordinates inside an American bureaucracy, our fellow workers might have called us clever office politicians. If we had been members of the Foreign Service who modified our personalities in order to communicate with Jorge because he was the head of a great nation, we would have been regarded as skilled diplomats. If we had been blacks who flattered him because he was our white boss, we would have been criticized as Uncle Toms. But there is no word of praise or blame that provides an accurate characterization of the relationship which we felt we should establish with Ecuadorians like Jorge.

No satisfactory word exists to characterize the relationship that tens of thousands of white Americans in the civil-rights movement, VISTA, and the Peace Corps have said they wanted to establish with the people whose cultures they enter.

PART TEN

I

In grade school, when we were given those psychological tests in which you are supposed to draw your family, your home, yourself, I would always picture myself as a boy with an outsized head and an undersized body. I was told that meant, among many other things, that from my family, and from teachers at Dalton, I had acquired a profound belief in reason, a fear of irrational conflict, a feeling that violence was always immoral.

I remember hurrying home from school every afternoon to watch the Army-McCarthy hearings on television. My parents, their friends, and my teachers all despised McCarthy, and I knew people whose lives he and his fellow witchhunters had ruined. One school friend of mine had an uncle who had been driven to suicide by the Red scare, another's parents had exiled themselves from the United States, several others had fathers who had been driven out of their professions. So I hated Joseph McCarthy with a young boy's passion.

When I was about thirteen I developed a fantasy that one day I would be called upon to testify in front of the House Un-American Activities Committee and that the speech I would give in defense of my beliefs would be the most dramatic act of my life. The fantasy persisted for years. At Harvard I discovered that other liberals with childhoods similar to mine shared it. But now I realize that the testimony I was always editing and rewriting in my brain was extremely defensive. It was an apology for the fact that my experience in America had made me into a dissenter; I was a good boy, not a subversive, who had become involved in the peace and civil-rights movements only because he wanted to improve the country they controlled. I had already accepted HUAC's terms.

I began to lose my faith in America's capacity to act rationally when the "liberals" escalated the war in Vietnam and began their harsh attacks on the civil-rights movement. The feeling became more specific and more frightening during my months at the Big Fiesta, when I saw that for the most part those who controlled the mass media and the performers they hired to be writers or broadcasters tailored contemporary reality to fit New York's assumptions about the nation's taste; and that many of the intellectuals who were always pleading for balanced thought, who claimed to despise the concessions one had to make in order to reach a mass audience nevertheless used their considerable intelligences to construct arguments that had far more to do with self-interest than with reason. Indeed, the fact that they inhabited a small, self-enclosed world allowed them to be irrationally angry at the new political and cultural ideas (symbolized by the New Left and the hippies) for which some employees of *Life*, *Esquire*, CBS must have the kind of sympathy and understanding that makes exploitation possible.

But everything I felt at the Big Fiesta was tempered by my own self-doubts. I thought that my criticisms of the New York literary world might reflect nothing more substantial than my desire to console my impatient self because I had failed to achieve quick success there. So I became convinced that my instincts about the United States' irrationality were more right than wrong only after my friends and I had spent nearly two years trying to persuade the wide range of Americans we met in the Peace Corps of a few principles that seemed moderate and virtually self-evident: that cross-cultural work is so complicated that it must be discussed and evaluated constantly by people who feel free to represent all of the constituencies involved; that it is made impossible if you are administratively responsible to one society while your job is to serve another society; that the strain the situation produces is more than most of the inexperienced young people who undergo it can bear.

Of course we could marshal a great deal of evidence to support those generalizations, but few people we met in the Peace Corps could listen dispassionately enough to talk instead of argue. There were staff members and volunteers who agreed with us, but most of them lacked the courage to fight their superiors over practices they knew were wrong. The agency, supposedly the most progressive in the United States government, had such a grip on its employees' ambitions and emotions that they could not respond to reason. And I am talking not only about frightened, narrow-minded, middle-level bureaucrats like Hofmann and Dan Stringer and Caleb Roehrig and Gshwend, the Peace Corps' common denominator. It seems to me that the charge applies in nearly the same measure to Frank Mankiewicz and Harris Wofford, supposedly the two most progressive men in the organization. They were so beguiled by their own metaphors like "world-wide sit-in" and "Socratic seminar writ large," so committed to their belief that progressive, humane programs could be administered through United States government agencies (the belief that was the moral justification for their careers) that they made no serious effort to find out whether their optimistic, lyrical language conformed to reality. Then, less than a year after their phrases had brought hundreds of people like Nick and Margot and Rachel and me into the Peace Corps and had put us in a position where we were always battling our superiors to preserve the spirit that Wofford and Mankiewicz had seemed to represent, they were out of the organization altogether. There were justifications, of course. They told people privately that they felt less comfortable working under Jack Hood Vaughn than they had under Sargent Shriver, and sometimes added that they were adhering to a rule which prohibited all Peace Corps staff members from remaining in the organization for more than five years. (The rule didn't really apply to people who, like them, had been there at the start. Hofmann, for example, ignored it.) Besides, each of them had been offered new jobs which seemed at least as useful as the work they were doing at the Peace Corps. So they left their memoranda behind them and got out. (Mankiewicz became Bobby Kennedy's press secretary; Wofford became president of a branch of the State University of New York.)

Wofford was considerably more responsible to his past promises than was Mankiewicz. He was always trying to incorporate ex-volunteers into his projects at the new experimental state university at Old Westbury, New York. He tried to establish the kinds of programs at his university that he had talked about in the Peace Corps, and was willing to take a public stand when the Peace Corps tried to prevent volunteers from criticizing United States foreign policy. (But several years later Wofford would leave Old Westbury, which he had described in the glowing terms he once reserved for the Peace Corps, to become president of Bryn Mawr College.)

Nevertheless, neither Wofford nor Mankiewicz seemed willing to devote another year or two to waging bureaucratic battles over "The Revolutionary Force" or "The University in Dispersion" (had they expected that the phrases would become policy just because they had coined them?). Nor did they help other people to comprehend the phenomenon that most liberals and radicals were complaining about during those years: the corruption of American institutions under Lyndon Johnson. In their new jobs they might have written articles or given speeches which told potential volunteers about some of the internal battles that had caused them to sour on the Peace Corps, but neither of them did, even though the agency was still using their names and some of their buoyant rhetoric in its recruiting campaigns. But their first allegiance, it seemed, was to the organization that had disappointed them, not to the constituency it would almost certainly continue to fail. They seemed to be so committed to the choice they had made in the 1950s, that the only way to change America was to reform its institutions, that they could not consider the most serious question that had emerged out of the 1960s: whether such reform was satisfactory or even possible.

They were willing to deal with people like Rachel and me who raised that question, but not to respond to us.

Even after I realized that there was still a large part of me which, like the child who drew huge heads on tiny bodies, wanted desperately to reason with Mankiewicz and Wofford, even with Hofmann and Dan Stringer and Caleb Roehrig, wanted to hear them incorporate the things we said into their answers and rebuke our arguments on their merits if that was possible. But a year and a half of trying to talk had persuaded me that the only difference between a long conversation in which I tried to be as careful as possible and a brief, bitter exchange was in the intensity of the headache that followed.

The only other point to conversing with such people in reasonable tones was to impress them. Especially with those I didn't threaten directly, like some of the liberal AID workers in Ecuador, I could temper my radical opinions with manners I had learned at Choate and Harvard, flatter their desire to be regarded as radicals themselves, and linger in their memories as the sort of bright young man who might bring life to their organizations. In other words, I could speak to them in very much the same way as I had imagined myself addressing the members of HUAC, convey through my bearing and my carefully chosen words the somewhat arrogant message that would be at the heart of Eugene McCarthy's Presidential campaign: I am the best of your young, still loyal to your ideals, and you can't afford to waste my talents. That instinct, bred deep, is a hard one to lose. But I was so disgusted with most Peace Corps volunteers and staff, who considered themselves open-minded and boasted of their concern for the poor, that I could no longer imagine myself working inside any organization where I would be expected to cooperate with them once again.

II

IF you can't reason with people who have power, and you don't care about impressing them, you can either ignore them as the hippies urge, or react like the New Left and fight them.

For months after the pot crisis Rachel and I tried to ignore the Peace Corps. The fact that we were instrumental to the success of Jorge's course provided us with a legitimate reason to remain silent, to submit to our persistent fear that the organization would define us as criminals during the next open crisis and expel us.

Then in June 1967, a year after our arrival in Ecuador, we began a new course, quite different in its conception, and Rachel and I lost our justification for our silence. Though more people had enrolled, it met only once a week, in the public library, not the Episcopalian community center, and all the lecturers were Ecuadorian professional people: Javier, Jorge, a city planner, a lawyer. Rachel and I still met with Jorge nearly every day to help him plan future classes, still organized surveys, still spent much of our time with the students. Beyond that, we were trying to organize a trip for thirty of them to visit housing projects, schools, and educational television networks in Bogotá, Colombia, so that they could see what community development meant in a slightly more developed Latin country. But we were expendable enough that if we were sent home we wouldn't betray Jorge.

By that time we were even angrier at the Peace Corps than we had been during the pot crisis. Some episodes that occurred during those months not only made us feel that we would have to fight back soon but also showed us that it was possible to win more than we lost. For the other side of the frightened selfishness that

Hofmann, Stringer, Caleb Roehrig, and their counterparts at AID and the State Department continually revealed to us was their invariably irrational response to the smallest difficulties, grotesque responses which we might be able to manipulate.

Often, when Rachel or I criticized the Peace Corps in Guayaquil, a staff member would remind us of the beach-front camp for slum children, which had been organized by volunteers in the city and funded by the local Rotary Club. The camp was the Peace Corps' Eiffel Tower. Every dignitary who visited us in Guayaquil was chauffeured to Playas, a resort town on the Pacific Ocean, to see it. Even Margot was intensely loyal to the program.

Then one day a child whom the Peace Corps had invited to spend a happy week in the sun drowned.

Though very few of the slum children knew how to swim, the volunteers who were in charge of the camp had never thought to take the most elementary precautions to insure waterfront safety. The staff, which was so proud of the camp, never noticed the lapse. There was no buddy system, no lifeline on the beach, no rowboats for counselors to use to save struggling children. The day the boy drowned storm warnings had been posted, but none of the three volunteers who accompanied the children to the beach was a qualified lifesaver. Two of them barely knew how to swim.

Before the drowning Margot had agreed to help USIS make a film about the camp, and a few days after the incident she went out there with a cameraman from the Consulate. That night she told us about the disintegration that had taken place.

The outdoor area near the cabins was literally filled with piss and shit, she said, although the Rotary Club had installed six new latrines. The counselors were carrying wooden sticks everywhere, using them to hit unruly kids. One of the camp directors, who was about to return to Guayaquil, was telling everybody, "I never want to take responsibility for anything again in my life." Another got furious at Margot because she insisted on talking about the drowning instead of just feeling it. When she told him that everyone involved with the camp should settle down and figure out how they could save the program, he answered her, raging, "Your're full of shit. I wish I could take some and smear it on your face."

One of the people in our course, Wilfrido Pazmiño, was part of the relatively moderate group of students who had taken control of DUC after Hector Montoya's departure.

When Wilfrido asked me to introduce him and his colleagues to someone at the Consulate who might finance his organization, I arranged for them to meet Bob Geis, the USIS attaché in charge of cultural affairs. During the meeting the North American was at least as interested in jotting down the Ecuadorians' names as the Ecuadorians were in raising funds. Names traded for money: I wasn't very happy about my role as broker in the deal. But I had already warned Wilfrido Pazmiño that the CIA is interested in learning as much as possible about student politics, and he hadn't seemed very worried. He probably assumed that he could get more from the Americans than they could get from him.

About a month later Art Nayer, the head of USIS in Guayaquil, called me to his office. DUC wanted to use the facilities of the Ecuadorian-American Cultural Center to offer a course in the co-operative movement, he told me when I arrived there. "You were in Bob Geis's office when they met with him, weren't you? Well, this morning the Ecuadorian who telephoned me read the list of DUC's directors to me, and I didn't recognize a single name on it." He was worried that a group of subversives was trying to disguise itself as DUC.

When I asked the name of the Ecuadorian who had called him, he glanced at his notes and said, "Wilfrido Pazmiño." Then he handed me two pieces of paper, his list of the DUC directorate and Geis's. "The names just aren't the same," he said.

As I read down the two lists, both of them handwritten, I realized that the problem was simply that the two men had scrawled the unfamiliar Spanish names in different orders. Thus, Wilfrido Pazmiño's name was at the top of one list, in the middle of the other. After Wilfrido's telephone call they had compared their lists hastily, decided that the Ecuadorians were trying to outsmart them, and panicked.

I am almost certain that if I had been out of town that morning DUC would never have been able to use the American facilities. Instead, its members' names would have gone into the CIA files as part of a list like the one the State Department used to defend the Marine invasion of the Dominican Republic by asserting that Communists controlled the left-wing movement.

Julio Lucin, the Ecuadorian diver who had broken his neck in the trampoline accident that Bobby Jefferson tried to forget by staying high on marijuana, was still languishing in a clinic in Guayaquil. The doctors said that his chances for survival were less than fifty-fifty. If he lived, he would certainly be paralyzed for life.

It could be argued that the Peace Corps had a special responsibility to take care of Julio. He had fallen in love with a girl in the first physical-education group that came to the city and ever since then had spent much of his time with volunteers. And what was essentially a moral question in Guayaquil might have been a legal one in the States, where the Peace Corps could perhaps have been judged liable for his accident.

Nevertheless, all but one of the volunteers, including Rachel and me, were resigned to letting him die in Guayaquil.

But Jon Warner, a member of Bobby Jefferson's group, was determined to save Julio's life. Jon was the most religious person I met in the Peace Corps. His pious desire to lead a clean, moral life made him the butt of the same sort of scornful jokes that Hank Dawson and his friends directed at Rachel and me. Now, the only person who encouraged him to help Julio was Dave Carrasco, head of the physical-education program. Together, they worked out a plan whereby the Ecuadorian could be evacuated to a hospital in Wilmington, Delaware, where Jon's parents lived, if someone could be found to pay the bills.

Julio was getting weaker every day. It was the rainy season, and the clinic he had been placed in had no air conditioning. The food was poor, the bed was too small, the nurses were incompetent.

The doctors who were treating him now predicted that he would die in a month.

But suddenly Jon's parents cabled that the director of an excellent hospital in Wilmington had offered to treat Julio gratis.

Hofmann was out of the country that week, and Caleb Roehrig, who was Acting Director of the Peace Corps in Ecuador, was extremely nervous about Julio's evacuation. He insisted that Jon keep the Peace Corps out of the entire process, in case Julio should die on the plane and thus tarnish the organization's image. And he refused to let Jon accompany Julio and a doctor from Guayaquil to Wilmington, though it was clear that Jon's presence would have made things a lot easier when they arrived in his home town.

Julio not only survived, he made a remarkable recovery. Within two months of his evacuation he was regaining the use of his limbs. By that time the Peace Corps had decided to cooperate with USIS and the *Reader's Digest* on a short movie and an article which would emphasize its role in the heart-warming saga.

A few weeks later word came through that Caleb Roehrig had been appointed Peace Corps Director in the Dominican Republic.

When I said good-by to him a few days before he left he looked me in the eye, shook my hand firmly, and said, "The job's a big responsibility all right. Our country has a very big stake out there."

Dan Stringer went home shortly after Caleb's transfer. Though it wasn't clear whether he had quit or been fired, my own guess is that he had been made into a scapegoat for failures that should have been attributed to Hofmann, Gshwend, Mankiewicz, or Vaughn. He wasn't very much worse at his job than the rest of them.

Supercop told us about Dan's grand finale in Guayaquil:

A few days before Stringer left, some friends of his, including Supercop, had organized a softball game as his farewell party. There was plenty of beer there, and everyone was quite high by the ninth inning. Dan, who was a shaky driver under the best of circumstances, offered Supercop and two other volunteers a ride back to town in the Peace Corps jeep. He failed to see a traffic light at an intersection and collided with the car in front of him. Supercop advised him to make a quick getaway instead of involving himself in a legal process that might keep him in the country for months. But the car he had hit managed to stay abreast of him. Finally, at another light, Dan dispatched his other two passengers to negotiate with the other driver. Then he and Supercop peeled away, leaving them stranded. He got to the Peace Corps office safely and departed from the country before he received a summons.

The week Dan returned to the States Hofmann came to Guayaquil to supervise our project until Washington could send us a new rep. He was just leaving one of the city's clinics, where he had been visiting a volunteer who was sick with typhoid fever, when a local policeman saw him walking toward the Peace Corps jeep and arrested him for drunken driving and for leaving the scene of an accident. He had to stay at the police station for three hours.

It was a former member of the IWW (Industrial Workers of the World) who told us that Ecuadorian employees of the United States government were forbidden to sleep in an air-conditioned apartment in the American Consulate which had been specially reserved for AID technicians who had to spend time in the muggy city.

John Caldwell had traveled a long political route. As a very young man he had organized miners for the IWW; then he had organized for the CIO; now he had joined other ex-radicals, like Jay Lovestone, in an effort to organize strong anti-Communist unions throughout the world. He was the Ecuador chief of the American Institute of Free Labor Development (AIFLD), an outfit that is widely believed to receive funds from the CIA.

He had come to Guayaquil to visit some community-development projects, and I was supposed to escort him to one of Jorge's centers. As we left the cool Consulate apartment, he remarked to an AID technician who was with us that "Ecuadorians in our organization and AID aren't allowed to sleep here even though the American government has given them security clearance. The directive was circulated a few weeks ago."

Maybe it was my annoyance that my job with Jorge forced me to be friendly to an American who almost certainly had links with the CIA which provoked me to answer that the policy he was describing sounded like segregation. "I've been fighting injustice for thirty years," he told me. "But, man, you have to understand these things. The decision to keep Ecuadorians out of here was made by the experts."

"What experts?"

"The Marines. They have a security expert stationed in Peru, and his responsibility is to see that American facilities in this part of the hemisphere are safe from local people. When you work for the United States Government you can't be too careful about security. And that's something the Marines know more about than any of us civilians."

The genius of American history: the ability of our pluralistic republic to pull a former Wobbly into a coalition with the Marines.

Even if one accepted the State Department's terms, though, it was impossible to distinguish what Caldwell called security from what I called segregation. The Ecuadorians about whom the Marines were so worried had been given extensive security investigations before they were hired by American agencies. The secret documents they might steal were all in areas of the Consulate that were sealed off from visitors every night, in rooms that were always locked. If any left-wing organization wanted to damage the Consulate's physical plant it could infiltrate the Ecuadorian army, which always assigned soldiers to guard the building at night, or find someone with a clean record to work as a night watchman, or send a woman from the *barrios* to apply for a job as cook or nursemaid for one of the many State Department people who lived in the building.

But Americans are accustomed to seeing Ecuadorians in service jobs; it is only when the local people seem to be their equals that the men who plan security become uneasy.

It seemed clear that the State Department had prohibited its Ecuadorian employees from staying in the apartment out of the same vague fear of the unknown that afflicted most Peace Corps volunteers. It was a fear that destroyed reason. The only calculation behind their decision, so far as I could tell, was that the Americans who traveled to Guayaquil might find it convenient to invoke a rule that obliged them to isolate themselves from local people. They felt freer when they were alone with their own kind.

Rachel wrote Wymberley Coerr a strong letter protesting the policy, we both sent letters about it to liberal Congressmen, and I told Erich Hofmann that I might expose it in the *Village Voice*. I'm sure Erich's response was to wonder wearily why we spent so much time worrying about details that seemed so trivial to him and to resent us mightily for continually complicating his relationship with Wymberley Coerr and the rest of the country team. The Ambassador answered Rachel's letter with a platitude ("discrimination is the farthest thing from our intention"), and Erich's tone sounded almost plaintive when he told us that "so far as the 'old man' is concerned, it's a dead issue from now on." He was really asking us to quit making his life so difficult by constantly questioning the wisdom of authority.

It was not an issue that elicited much support from the volunteers. Even Nick wondered why we were so concerned about the right of a few Uncle Tom Ecuadorians to spend the night in the Consulate when they could easily afford to stay at one of the many hotels and *pensiones* in Guayaquil. We usually argued that the State Department's irrational concern for security, its insensitivity about the feelings of its Ecuadorian employees, was a reflection of its attitude toward the entire country. But clearly our feelings about this small episode were produced by our abiding fury at so much of what we had seen during the past year.

We were reluctant to let the issue drop, no matter how ambiguous it might seem to most people. As we discussed it with State Department officials like George High, Deputy Principal Officer of the Consulate in Guayaquil, we kept finding fresh evidence that the Americans who formulated such policies were unable to think about them logically.

High was supposed to be the most promising American diplomat in all of Ecuador. He was the ideal representative of the sterile paradise, so far as we were concerned: the kind of man who is able to befriend a variety of local people and talk to them about their ideas and problems, but not become so involved in defending their interests that he disturbs other, more conservative people in the State Department.

"Oh, I know how you feel about that apartment," he said, "and believe me we've done everything in our power to let Ecuadorians sleep there. Someone in Quito even suggested that we build a huge iron gate in front of the office where all the files are kept. The Embassy thought it would be a good idea, because, you know, the office could be made completely burglar-proof that way. But you understand our relations to those Embassy people up in Quito. Their political experts just don't understand our security problems down here. You see, the apartment you want the Ecuadorians to sleep in is directly above the office where all the files are kept. You never know what lengths a man who wants classified information is likely to go to."

Did he mean that some Ecuadorian agronomist would sneak away from the American AID people who had accompanied him to Guayaquil, drill a hole through the floor of the Consulate apartment while they slept peacefully, and somehow shinny down to the files? Or perform like a human fly and rapelle from window to window? I didn't know how to ask that question directly.

"But that's not our biggest worry," he said. "Someone might plant a time bomb, that's what really concerns us. He might get a good night's sleep at our expense, and then leave the building before the device exploded. Oh, I know what you're thinking, and you're probably right. We do invite Ecuadorians to our parties here and sometimes they stay until midnight or later. I suppose they could plant a bomb then, too."

What I was really thinking was that there was no way of attaining the degree of security George High wanted without segregating the building altogether. As a matter of fact, there was no way of obtaining that degree of security without leaving Ecuador altogether. Then, American property and information would be completely safe from the Ecuadorians.

At a Fourth of July picnic in Guayaquil George High tried to formulate a working credo for Americans living abroad. His theme was a reinterpretation of the Declaration of Independence.

It speaks to all of us here. To the businessman it says, Help your Ecuadorian counterpart, show him the most effective techniques of management, help him to stabilize his economy. To the banker it says, Be good citizens of your community, teach it the most modern methods of financing and cost accounting. To the corporation executive the Declaration of Independence says, Worry about the social development of the country where you are living. Organize your workers. Teach them that you support stable, responsible trade unions.

Our enemies around the world complain about monopoly capitalism. They are wrong. We do believe in the small businessman, but we now realize that we must have large corporations to suit our increasingly complex society. On the Fourth of July we would do well to think of the Declaration of Independence in this light and to realize that it is one of the most flexible documents ever written by the human hand.

III

SUDDENLY, the Peace Corps obliged us to define ourselves through our actions. Jack Hood Vaughn ruled that ninety-two volunteers in Chile could not add their names to one of those moderate "Negotiations Now" petitions that used to occupy full pages in the Sunday *New York Times.* He sent out a cable to Country Directors all over the world insisting that the Peace Corps "must stand clear of all U.S. policies as well as host-country policies. If one volunteer violates this crucial precept, the Peace Corps is by definition in the soup and therefore not quite credible." (The Peace Corps is "in the soup" if one volunteer opposes the war publicly.) "If a trainee or a volunteer cannot accept this obligation as a member of the Peace Corps, he cannot remain in the Peace Corps."

The directive, clearly based on a false premise, provided us a more powerful weapon in our war with the bureaucracy than any we could have invented. If there was any "crucial precept" of Peace Corps policy it was that the volunteers' right to criticize the government was inviolate. Time and again, in training and in Guayaquil, we had been assured that the only restriction on our speech was the regulation that forbade us from discussing the internal affairs of the countries where we were stationed. Staff people were always boasting that the freedom to speak out against United States policy was the thing that made the Peace Corps unique among government agencies. Some of them must have felt as betrayed as we did.

Shortly after Vaughn's ruling my brother Geoff and Harold Ickes and Paul Gorman, all of whom were working in Washington, wrote us that there was constant plotting and counterplotting inside the agency. Small cabals were meeting in hallways, talking in whispers. We got a sense of those tortured discussions from a policy clarification that Vaughn mailed to volunteers and staff members all over the world:

The protection of the Peace Corps can be achieved, without any loss in freedom of expression, by making it clear in your private communications to the President or members of the Congress that publication of the message would be inconsistent with the apolitical role of the Peace Corps if you were identified as a volunteer or a staff member. Letters to the U.S. press for possible publication cannot include your Peace Corps connection, or, if a number of you want to join in a petition, your foreign addresses, since the latter makes identification almost inevitable. Such messages could be sent to your families or friends for forwarding from United States post offices.

Rachel and I should have been eager to defy the ruling. As soon as a few volunteers were expelled for protesting the war, thousands of people in the United States would be forced to confront the fact that the Peace Corps was part of the same constellation of unjust, irrational institutions as the State Department and AID. Geoff and Gorman and Ickes in Washington, Jack Newfield in New York, assured us that our case would be publicized as widely as possible. They had persuaded some Congressmen to protest the Peace Corps policy and had discussed the issue with reporters, Kennedy Democrats, and movement organizers. Margot, who had just returned to the States, was willing to spend all her time co-ordinating the campaign which they had begun.

But those maneuvers, which sound, as I list them now, like a classic case of left-wing overkill, took place in a world that Rachel and I could barely imagine. Our reality was Erich Hofmann's warning that we would be sent home as soon as we made our protest public. The fear of expulsion, which we still shared, made us extremely cautious.

We had very little active support from the other volunteers. Though virtually everyone we talked with agreed that his freedom had been abridged, the only people who were willing to sign any kind of antiwar statement were Nick and his friend Bob Mix, and Janine Zimmerman. "I'd throw in with you guys if I could be sure they'd let me pull a Sammy Bernstein when I got back to Washington and then send me back here," one physical-education volunteer told us. "But I have to worry about the draft." He spoke not only for dozens of volunteers in Ecuador, but also for most of the group in Chile which had planned to sign the "Negotiations Now" petition. Just one of the ninety-two who were originally involved, Bruce Murray, actually protested the war publicly. He gave his statement to a Chilean newspaper. The day it was published his Country Director whisked him out of town and back to Washington, despite the protests of Chilean students. Later that week

Bruce was expelled from the Peace Corps because he had "interfered in the politics of his host country."

Rachel and I channeled our caution into the text of a letter to the *New York Times*. Though Nick and Bob wanted to mail it immediately, and Janine didn't care, we wrote at least a dozen drafts of the short statement, searching for a tone which would seem to prove our assertion that our idealism had fallen victim to the Peace Corps' *Realpolitik*. It was a way of stalling for time. We were not yet as radical as we seemed to the other volunteers and the Peace Corps staff. Somewhere in our minds we were still the children who had been brought up in the 1950s to accept the conformist standards of the Eisenhower years.

Finally, though, we realized that we had to quit hesitating and dive into our mild protest as if it were icy water. We had to accept the fact that fear was a natural ailment, just like a cold. If you sat in a draft you began to sneeze the next day, if you contemplated an action that seemed dangerous your stomach was taut, your hands were clammy for weeks at a time. But the ailment had to be ignored.

One morning Rachel and I were in the Peace Corps office, trying to show Hofmann that when Jack Hood Vaughn, in his maiden speech as Peace Corps Director (called "To Peace with Love"), said that he supported America's intervention in the Dominican Republic because he loved the island's people and didn't want to see their blood shed, he had violated his own "crucial precept." The longer Hofmann argued that Vaughn had been talking about people and not politics, the more frustrated I became. Finally, furious, I told Hofmann to phone Bill Moffett, the head of the Latin-American desk in Washington, and tell him that unless Vaughn lifted the ban on volunteer protests within seventy-two hours we would mail the letter to the *New York Times*. Though I blurted out the ultimatum, I must have sounded authoritative. It was thrilling to watch Hofmann obey me, to hear him relay a message I had dictated all the way from Ecuador to Washington. It was a role I had always coveted when I was in the civil-rights movement. Now that I was able to present my own demands I was so buoyed by the militancy I had found in myself, so impressed by the new power it seemed to provide me, that I hardly realized that, when Moffett and Vaughn refused to respond to our demand, we were obliged to act.

Our letter was published in the *News of the Week in Review*, the only publication, besides the *Volunteer*, that is circulated to all Peace Corps members. The day it came out Harold Ickes cabled us that he had found out we wouldn't be fired.

A wire-service story in Guayaquil's *El Universo* said that the Peace Corps had dismissed our case because our letter had challenged the organization's policy and not protested the war (". . . we feel obliged to express openly our disagreement with the war in Vietnam," we had written); a brief story in the *Times* referred to a Peace Corps staff man who said that Vaughn's ruling had "not been intended to silence volunteers but to keep them from participating in the political affairs of the countries in which they were stationed." The next week Wofford supported us in a letter to the *Times*, in which he seemed to assume that the basic issue had been free speech, after all.

That was all we ever heard. Though the article in *El Universo* said that we had been sent to the Quito office for consultations, the Peace Corp never contacted us after the letter was published, nor did it clarify the ruling we had protested. We could not wrench any comment out of Hofmann or his reps.

Nick, who had been both amused and disturbed by our intercontinental plotting, was certain that we had been allowed to remain in the Peace Corps only because of our connections in Washington and New York. Instead of confronting the organization directly, our careers against its contradictions, we had used the access to power that my background had provided to make our risk as safe as possible. As a result, Nick reminded us, we had allowed the organization to save some of the face it lost when it fired Bruce Murray while we salved our own consciences.

Nick's prodding forced us to realize that if we interpreted the Peace Corps' decision not to fire us as a political victory we would miss the point of the entire experience: that members of the American "new class" who persistently dissented from their government's policies threatened the people who controlled the United States about as much as members of Guayaquil's "new class," like Jorge and Lourdes, threatened the people who controlled Ecuador. The Americans could find jobs more easily than most of their contemporaries in Guayaquil, but to succeed in them they had to let institutions like the Peace Corps transform them from men into human machines. The bureaucracies needed interchangeable parts.

Ecuadorians demonstrated against a system that endangered their physical survival; our protest was against a system that made it virtually impossible for us to survive as decent human beings. The Ecuadorians couldn't advance themselves at all. We could advance ourselves only by hurting other people. The distance between their condition and ours was America's definition of progress.

If we had mailed our letter to the *Times* before we consulted our friends in the States (or if we hadn't had relatively powerful friends to consult), we would almost certainly have been fired from the Peace Corps. But because we had proceeded so cautiously, from silence to high-level manipulation, we had helped the organization to disguise its true nature.

Thus, we learned the lesson that radicals like Tom Hayden had known for years: one or two direct confrontations with people in power are often worth hundreds of memos and meetings, those tedious exercises in due process we had been arranging for so long. For the drama of a well-staged confrontation with an intractable institution reaches people as no verbal argument can. If a government agency, a university administration, a welfare department, or a school board overreacts when a group whose moderate demands have never been heeded finally turns to militant action, then some witnesses to the conflict must become aware of the vast gap between the institution's assertions about itself and its behavior once those assertions are tested. And some bureaucrats, obliged to administer policies which they regard as inhuman and irrational, must realize that their institutional roles have subverted their human personalities.

Of course there are confrontations, staged over irrelevant issues simply for the sake of provoking a violent response, that antagonize many people who could have been persuaded. The art (it is like a poet choosing a metaphor) is to select an issue to which your constituency responds, and then (it is like telling your story well) to reveal the institution's personality by allowing people to contrast it with your own relatively decent behavior. Confrontation is the theater of the deed, more suited to winning converts than to winning battles, a full step short of the revolution that might have to follow someday.

But even though our attempt to maintain free speech in the Peace Corps resulted in a political stand-off, as Nick said, it still represented a personal victory for Rachel and me which enabled us to make increasingly bold use of techniques like confrontation. For we had finally overcome our fear of expulsion. When we took our letter of protest to Guayaquil's post office and mailed it to the *New York Times* we were certain that we'd be fired within a few weeks. We thought that our connections would help us publicize the Peace Corps' reprisal, not avert it.

Afterward, as we walked down Nueve de Octubre, holding hands, we finally felt as if we had declared ourselves independent of the America that George High had invoked in his Fourth of July speech, the selfish, irrational system that forced even good men like Harris Wofford to accept Nixonia's terms if they wanted to remain inside it. We were becoming able to disregard the definitions of successful careers and reasonable behavior that we had learned while we were growing up in America. We were learning to trust our own anger.

We were ready to disrupt the sterile paradise. If it had been a year later we might have done so physically, by using our new-found skill at rifling files to steal classified Peace Corps or AID documents that related to programs in Ecuador and searching for a newspaper or magazine to publish them. But in the summer of

1967, a few months before the demonstration at the Pentagon, such acts were virtually unthinkable. But frank words were frightening enough to the people who staffed America's foreign-policy institutions, men thoroughly unaccustomed to democracy or even debate.

Two American artists living in Quito, Lennie and Esther Weisberger, had discovered that the city's largest supermarket, La Favorita, discriminated against Indians. Its owners had decided to sell leftover meat at fifteen cents a pound to wealthy Ecuadorians and North Americans, for use as food for their watchdogs. Some Indians who lived near the Weisbergers knew about the bargain because they worked as maids and houseboys. They wanted to buy the inexpensive meat to make nourishing stews for their families. But Esther had seen the manager of La Favorita refuse to sell it to one Indian woman and order another to make her purchases at a small window behind the store. Other people in her neighborhood had complained of similar treatment. She knew that Rachel and I had been in the civil-rights movement, and one day when we were visiting Quito she asked us whether we thought it would be possible to organize a protest campaign.

That afternoon we had a long discussion with one of La Favorita's owners, an oligarch who had traveled throughout the United States, and then went across the street to talk with the manager of La Fuente, a modern soda fountain owned by the same family. Both men admitted that their establishments, home to most Americans, were segregated, by class as well as by race. The manager of La Fuente told us that "our customers refuse to eat with Indians [*la gente con ponchos*], so we keep them out unless they are accompanied by North Americans like your Peace Corps volunteers." The owner of La Favorita, who established policy for the soda fountain, too, was even less ambiguous. No poor people were allowed inside the supermarket, he told us, except those who were obviously shopping for their employers: "You haven't lived in this country long enough to know these people. They would rob hundreds of *sucres* of merchandise from us." When I said that I'd heard the same arguments from the owners of segregated stores in the American South he answered that "the two situations are very similar."

Of course there was no way that we could apply the kinds of tactics to La Fuente and La Favorita that SNCC had used in the early sixtys. No North American could serve as a spokesman for the Indians in negotiations with the Ecuadorian storeowners, and the Weisbergers' neighbors were much too intimidated to protest themselves or even to join demonstrations that we might organize on their behalf. Besides, as a practical matter, Rachel and I couldn't spend much time in Quito. We decided to try to interest local student groups in the issue, to find out if they were willing to confront their oligarchs, and then returned to Guayaquil.

But we also decided to use the fact that the Ecuadorian stores were segregated as a way of challenging our own oligarchs. With the Weisbergers, we wrote a leaflet describing the situation and planned to distribute it to employees of the American government through the Embassy mails. Our actual demand, that people who disapproved of La Favorita and La Fuente's policy toward Indians "minimize their purchases" there, was so weak that even the most moderate civil-rights organizations in the United States would have laughed at it. But we surrounded it with rhetoric that must have been particularly galling to the good citizens of the sterile paradise. "To us it seems astonishing that anyone, North American or Ecuadorian, who claims to be working for social progress in Ecuador should patronize establishments that exclude any portion of that society. It is hypocrisy, we think, to say that Indians should be part of the economic and social life of the country during working hours, while at mealtime you eat food purchased from people who [say by their actions] that Indians are essentially dirty and dishonest: unfit to be permitted in civilized society."

Before we released the leaflet we talked with some American officials in Quito who thought that a large portion of their community would participate in our campaign. Several AID workers, including its program director, agreed to circulate a petition inside the mission which suggested that the stores alter their policies.

"This can be a very good thing for the United States," one of them said. "It can win us a lot of support among the Indians, and at almost no political cost." We even heard from the man who was acting as Caleb Roehrig's substitute that Wymberley Coerr might support us, though for unusual reasons: the Ambassador's wife had already tried to organize a boycott of La Fuente after one of its owners had gotten annoyed at her son's rude behavior at the Tennis Club and tried to have him expelled.

But it quickly became clear that, except for the very few liberal AID employees and Peace Corps staff members who had at least learned the language of protest, none of the Americans in Quito was able to understand our campaign, let alone to sympathize with it. If anything, their sympathies were with the oligarchy. They certainly didn't have the same delusion as Erich Hofmann and Caleb Roehrig that they were in Ecuador to help its poor. The salaries of United States Government employees are tax-free, comforts they could never have afforded at home were dirt cheap. They could maintain large houses, employ two or three Indian maids, enjoy excellent brands of liquor at the cut-rate commissary prices, send their children to private schools staffed by Americans and Americanized Ecuadorians, and still save five or ten thousand dollars a year.

They were even more self-righteous about the United States, more scornful of lower-class Latins, than all but the worst of the Peace Corps volunteers. People who had never been able to afford housemaids at home quickly came to perceive all poor Ecuadorians as their servants (while they longed to be invited to the oligarchy's lavish parties) and constantly complained about their dirtiness and their stupidity. You could hear their attitude toward the entire country in the history of personal disillusionment that most of the women shared: "I used to treat my servants democratically, as if they were my friends. I used to invite them to eat lunch with me and stay in the kitchen while they cooked. But then they began to steal food from my refrigerator. Now I'm convinced that the rich Ecuadorians are right. You have to treat them like animals if you want to get any service out of them."

There were even fewer institutional checks on their selfishness than on the volunteers', since they were employed by agencies whose purpose was plainly to protect America's economic interests, as in the State Department, or to make a commercial profit off Ecuador's problems, as in most AID projects. (One reason that the American business community supported foreign aid is that each loan carried with it at that time the precondition that the recipient nation reinvest most of the money in the United States by purchasing American goods, even though tractors, bulldozers, refrigerators, machine parts usually cost less in Europe or Japan.)

If you spend any time with an AID program director you realize that his office is a bazaar to which representatives of all private agencies must come if they want to sell their wares. It is very much like the Big Fiesta: packaging is more important than content. I saw that very clearly one night when AID's program director invited Rachel and me to dine with him and the president of Southern Illinois University, which makes a great deal of money on AID contracts. Though the educator knew nothing at all about Ecuador, he was an accomplished pitchman.

The sales representative he sent to Guayaquil, an internationally known community-development expert named Richard Poston whose tedious writings we had studied in training, was another in the procession of Americans that we had to introduce to Jorge. Though Poston spoke no Spanish, and knew very little about Latin America, he was charging a substantial consultant's fee. As I listened to his interview with Jorge, I was convinced that he had no real context in which he could put the information he was receiving. He kept confusing the simplest facts. The report he finally prepared was so full of clichés, so badly informed, that even some AID people who had been prepared to admire him admitted that the paper was probably a standard form, written years ago in Illinois and used all over the world, in which he included enough topical references to make those who knew nothing about the situation think that he had done some research.

You could see the vicious circle as it rotated. Selfish institutions sent greedy shills overseas to quote Thomas Jefferson or Abraham

Lincoln in their discussions with Ecuadorian bureaucrats, and use some of the noblest words Americans have written to prove their own concern for the poor. Of course, once a university got its contract, nobody there really cared about the quality of the job that was done in the field. In Guayaquil AID was paying the University of Houston one hundred thousand dollars a year to establish a basic-sciences program at the Central University. One of the three people who had been sent down there spoke virtually no Spanish, though he was supposed to teach two classes. That wasn't as much of a problem as it seems, though, since the University was closed down by strikes about one-third of the time the team was down there, often because the students didn't want a basic-sciences program sponsored by the United States. The three Texans seemed to spend most of their time at the Phoenix Club, shooting pool, or at one of the local casinos, testing out mathematical gambling systems they had devised in their considerable leisure time. After they had been in the country for about a year a small scandal developed over the fact that two of them, both married, had been dating Ecuadorian girls. One displayed his new mistress at public places like the Key Club, where Americans and Ecuadorians frequently gathered.

Our mailing about the stores was so threatening that the Embassy mail office was told to destroy it before it was circulated. Only a very few people saw the letter during the next few weeks, while we were preparing to send it out again through the Ecuadorian post office. But rumors spread very rapidly. By the time it arrived, most people must have been convinced that they had already read it and decided it was the work of traitors. The wife of an AID technician spoke for Nixonia when she condemned our campaign because "I pay two hundred dollars a month for the food I buy in that store, and I have a right to expect that meat will be saved for my dogs, not given to some Indians who aren't good customers anyway." Esther, who supported Lennie and herself by giving piano lessons, lost three students the week the letter was supposed to have been circulated, and was told by the Canadian who served as head vestryman of the Anglican church in Quito, where most Americans worshiped, that she was no longer welcome to teach on the premises. (The minister at that church, a Cuban refugee, was also in trouble with his congregation, which claimed that he was spending too much time organizing projects for Ecuadorians.) One of our friends at AID reported that once when our essay was discussed in an Embassy staff meeting someone attributed our behavior to the fact that the Weisbergers and I are Jewish. One man in the room stood up for pluralism, American-style. "I'm Jewish, too," he said, "and I would never do anything like that."

Wymberley Coerr was as angry as the American community he represented, despite the optimistic prophecy we had been given. He must have been involved in the initial decision to suppress our letter. People who went to the Embassy that week told us that he spent several hours each day trying to persuade the State Department in Washington to send him a cable ruling that any American who signed the petition which was being circulated in the AID mission could be expelled from the country. (Our friends at AID voluntarily decided to withdraw the petition when they found that no one at all was willing to sign it.) Once Coerr called in one of the three AID workers who supported our project, a man who administered a two-hundred-thousand-dollar education program about which he had been trying to get an appointment with the Ambassador for more than a year, and spent almost an hour with him talking about us. The conversation didn't begin very auspiciously, our friend said. "What are these Cowans really like?" Coerr had asked him. "Publishing letters against the war in Vietnam, and now this thing. They must be real publicity seekers. Don't you think they're trying to use people like you?"

"Mr. Ambassador, did it ever occur to you that the Cowans really believe in what they're doing?" our friend answered. Apparently it never had.

But Coerr's reaction to our campaign was mild compared to Erich Hofmann's. He seemed even angrier than he'd been after the pot crisis. When he visited Guayaquil shortly after our petition should have been circulated, he appeared to be happy to greet us with the news that the Ecuadorian government was about to declare the Weisbergers *personae non gratae*. (We were still protected by the fact that we were in the Peace Corps.) "Your campaign has been a total failure. You've united all the Americans against you. They think you're all wet, and so do I. There is no segregation in those stores."

We were standing in the Peace Corps office, arguing in front of a dozen volunteers. Poor Erich. I can never write about him without remembering that he was a nervous man trying to protect a job. Something like the sales clerk you yell at after the department store which advertises its fancy furniture and rapid delivery service has shipped the sofa you ordered, a month late, with a leg and a cushion missing. You want to talk to Mr. Bloomingdale or Mr. Sears, but instead you are forced to direct your anger at some poor employee who has to support his wife and three kids on the salary he earns. I wanted to talk to Mr. Johnson or Mr. Rusk or Mr. McNamara about their crazy war in Vietnam and racism at home, but instead I found myself confronting a poor *schlemiel* of a Luftwaffe veteran whose professional future I was probably imperiling by my insistence on causing controversy. I had always had mixed feelings about fighting Erich, and now I wished more than ever that I could reach past the shell of his adult personality to find the brave boy who had circulated petitions against the Nazis.

I might have been smiling as I began to speak to him. I often smiled when I argued with Peace Corps staff members. At first the expression had been a nervous response to the tension I felt when I argued with people in authority, but then I learned that it gave me a tactical advantage. "That Paul Cowan loves to argue with people until their back is against the wall, and then he loves to laugh at them," Caleb Roehrig had once told Ed Fagerlund. I began to use the grin as a mannerism to disconcert my enemies.

But it was also genuine. I was laughing at the man I had become, at the actions which that odd moral sense of mine was always forcing me to take. How crazy that Paul Cowan should be in Guayaquil, Ecuador, using whatever intelligence and courage he possesses to combat a local Peace Corps Director! That action had nothing to do with the reality I cared most about. Real life was driving with Rachel past the ancient, isolated farmhouses in Pennsylvania on our way to become graduate students at the University of Chicago, talking through the autumn afternoon as we began to fall in love; the way Odetta sounded when I listened to her sing "The Battle Hymn of the Republic" while I was sitting in the Last Chance, accepting the congratulations of the other customers for my triumph over Itzhak; the way the smell of the tortillas that Paula Guzmán cooked for Mingo combined with the smell of kerosene; the way I felt when I first heard Pete Seeger at a hootenanny on Houston Street in Greenwich Village, and knew that somehow I would try to accept the invitation he hollered as he sang the wonderful spiritual "Twelve Gates to the City,"

"Step right in, you're welcome in the city."

Rachel and I had tried to make that invitation echo through our lives. We had tried to make as many people as possible welcome in whatever place we happened to be. But it wasn't enough.

"If you're going to have great love, you'd better have great anger": I would hear Pete Seeger sing that line at a concert I went to a few days before the 1968 Democratic Convention in Chicago. It would stick in my mind as we walked down Michigan Avenue to face the troops and the tanks.

I had developed my anger in Ecuador. And as I faced Erich Hofmann in the Peace Corps office in Guayaquil, all my spurned lover's rage toward the greedy United States, all my hatred for the selfish American community in Quito, began to focus on him.

I stood as close to him as I could and cocked my fist. I was virtually bellowing as I told him that he didn't believe that there was segregation at La Favorita and La Fuente, or in the Consulate apartment, or in the Peace Corps' decision-making process, because his career was so tightly bound to a segregated system that it had made him numb to its evil. "The organization you represent is imperialist, Erich. You're a colonialist."

As I talked, I stepped toward him so that he had to retreat to avoid a collision. To snap the spell of fear under which he still held most of the volunteers, I had to make him seem to be frightened of me. "Tell me why you won't show Ecuadorians your five-year plan. Tell me why you won't let them come to meetings where you make decisions."

"Call it colonialism if you want," he said, "but all I know is that if Ecuadorians were involved in the Peace Corps' programing decisions, ninety per cent of our projects would be failures."

Some of the other volunteers began to laugh.

"Besides, it will take two generations until they can make wise decisions for themselves," Hofmann continued. "Until then we have to show them how to do things."

Ed Fagerlund, who had been listening to the discussion very carefully, looked at Erich for a long time. "You know," he said finally, "I used to think that Paul exaggerated when he criticized all of you, but now it seems to me that he might be right. That really is what a colonialist would say."

Hofmann looked as hurt as he did angry. "I keep trying to talk with all of you, but I never understand what we're arguing about. I think it's a waste of time. I'm going into my office to do some Peace Corps work."

Of course, we had to help Lennie and Esther if they were in serious trouble, and we wanted to go to Quito anyway so that we could meet with some Ecuadorian students who had said they were interested in our campaign. But before he left Guayaquil Hofmann refused us permission to travel on Peace Corps time and Jake Bair, who had replaced Dan Stringer as rep, backed him up.

So, after we wrote Hofmann a letter explaining exactly why we planned to make the trip and got Jorge's permission to be away from Guayaquil for a day, I telephoned Erich to tell him that we'd be there the next morning.

"You can't come on official Peace Corps time, Paul. I forbid you to come."

"I appreciate your feelings, Erich. We'll be there at nine."

"You don't understand. The Director forbids you to come."

I could literally hear his secretary gulp when we arrived in his office the next day. No one had ever displayed such a strong response to my physical presence. I felt like Spencer Tracy in *Bad Day at Black Rock*.

Rachel handed Hofmann Jorge's letter of permission, but he refused to read it. "The only relevant opinion about your work is that of the Peace Corps staff," he said.

"Would you say that sort of thing to Jorge's face?" Rachel asked.

Instead of answering, Erich gave us a memorandum and sat silently, fiddling with his pipe, while we read that we were now on probation because we had committed a "serious breach of discipline" by spending time away from our "duty station." "This means that during the next thirty days any infraction of a Peace Corps rule or any conduct unbecoming to a volunteer may well result in your dismissal from the Peace Corps."

That, for a twelve-hour trip to Quito (less time than most volunteers spent on the beach, away from their "duty stations," during most weekends in the rainy season) to see if some friends were in trouble because they had joined us in circulating a muckraking letter within the American community (they weren't expelled) and to talk with Ecuadorian students about ways they might ally themselves with some Indians who wanted to use public facilities which the oligarchy had closed to them.

But we got what we wanted out of Hofmann's clumsy response. Seventeen volunteers mailed him a letter which complained that the penalty was too severe (if Nick hadn't been out of Guayaquil for a month he would have helped elicit much more support), and one man even persuaded a *comité* of slum dwellers to send Hofmann a petition requesting that our probation be lifted. It was the first time that most of the volunteers had ever contested the Director's decision.

I also tried, for the last time, to write Hofmann a letter that would make him see what I had been talking about for the past year and a half—what Bob Moses had taught me at Oxford, Ohio: "The work that we do, as you must understand, proceeds by example, rather than rhetoric. . . . I could spend years trying to persuade Ecuadorian students that they must be bold and willing to sacrifice if they want to change their country. But my words count nothing next to my actions. The example Rachel and I set is the important thing. The students with whom we work are impressed when they see that we are willing actually to mail the letter against the war in Vietnam or continue participating in the campaign against La Favorita and La Fuente." He never answered me.

Part of his response to the volunteers' letter was surprisingly defensive. "One of you spoke of the 'recent series of events in which the Cowans have been seriously harassed.' I'd say the shoe is on the other foot." The rest sounded angry and frightened. For example: "Paul and Rachel decided to go to Quito without asking for leave, in defiance . . . of both the Country Director and the Regional Director, thus in effect saying that they could determine better than the Peace Corps Director what is and what is not legitimate Peace Corps work. In doing so they attempted to put the Peace Corps in Ecuador in a dangerous and untenable position."

So the main standard for judging a volunteer was not his effect on any segment of Ecuadorian society, but whether he conformed to orders he had been given, whether he would damage the Peace Corps' corporate identity. We're here because we're here because we're here because we're here.

When Rachel and I got back to the States we learned that this time there had been some substance to Hofmann's fears. A friend of Rachel's who works in the Latin-American division of the State Department told her that the owners of La Favorita and La Fuente had convinced the Ecuadorian government that we should be expelled. We were saved by Wymberley Coerr, who argued that when we organized our campaign against the two stores we had hoped to provoke that response. He had to protect us, of course, just as he had to use threats and coercion to make certain that no American institutions seemed to be involved in our campaign. The Peace Corps, the State Department, and the Ecuadorian government all would have looked silly if two volunteers and two artists had been sent home because they circulated a letter within their own community asking Americans to "minimize their purchases" at a soda fountain and a supermarket until Indians were allowed to trade there.

I suppose that Coerr and the owners of the two establishments could have told each other that they had won a victory. The bureaucracies had simmered but never burst, the student organization never joined the campaign openly, the stores were still segregated.

But when the Ecuadorian government did finally expel someone from its country it was Wymberley Coerr, not us. He was given just twenty-four hours to get out after he had delivered a speech in English to a primarily American audience in Guayaquil in which he criticized President Otto Arosemena's government for its failure to participate adequately in the Alliance for Progress.

Rachel and I were in Bogotá at the time, but some volunteers told us that Hofmann claimed that our letter about La Fuente and La Favorita was partially responsible for creating the climate in which Coerr felt obliged to insult the Ecuadorians, in which the Ecuadorians felt obliged to send him home.

It seems to me that Hofmann was indulging his anger at us, no more. So far as I could tell, Otto Arosemena had proved to himself that he could gain popularity by attacking the United States during a hemispheric Summit Conference in Punta del Este, where he was the only Latin-American president who refused to sign a document, composed by the State Department, reaffirming the solidarity of all the nations in the OAS. When he returned to Ecuador he was treated like a hero.

Of course Arosemena was a cunning man, as brutally subtle as Juan Marcos or Antonio Parra Velasco. Three centuries of power had made the Ecuadorian oligarchy much more skilled at protecting its interests than any group of American diplomats or foreign-assistance workers could ever be. (I often thought that a meeting between Arosemena and a few populist-imperialists like Bill Gshwend and George High would be like a scene out of Henry James, rewritten by Joseph Heller.) He must have realized that he could exploit the Ecuadorians' dislike of the Americans who staffed the State Department, the Peace Corps, and AID, their craving for the material goods which they saw in American movies and on television (wealth which the United States seemed to be withholding from them) to protect the oligarchy's interests. So the progressive America that Mankiewicz and Wofford had sought to incorporate into the Peace Corps, "the revolutionary force," not only became an outpost of Nixonia when it traveled abroad and did the work assigned to it, or was regarded as a bunch of publicity-seeking troublemakers when it began to do battle with the conservatives who control U.S. foreign policy; it was also part of the American country team that Ecuadorian oligarchs could manipulate almost at will (demand a loan today, expel an ambassador tomorrow) to preserve their control over the country. Because of its blind arrogance, the Peace Corps was twice damned.

But I would like to believe that Hofmann was right and take some credit for Coerr's expulsion. What a triumph if our modest one-page letter had helped to cause a major conflict between two of the most selfish oligarchies in the world!

Our final confrontation with the Peace Corps began in Bogotá.

From the point of view of our course, the trip seemed to be a success. Rachel and Jorge and I had organized it for the same reason as we had agreed that Ecuadorians should lecture in all the classes. We wanted to emphasize the fact that Latins must learn from one another, not from Peace Corps volunteers or AID technicians.

From all we could tell, the students agreed. Most of the social institutions in Bogotá are much more sophisticated than those in Guayaquil, and as the Ecuadorians visited low-cost housing projects, educational-television stations, model towns in the *campo*, they seemed to feel that the programs the Colombians organized were considerably more relevant to their country's problems than the moral exhortations they so frequently heard from the North Americans who had been sent across a continent to spread their method of change. They appeared to be freer, more receptive, when they compared experiences and ideas with students from Bogotá's Xaveriana University, which helped arrange the trip, than when they talked even to good friends from the United States like Rachel and me. Almost every night the Ecuadorians and Colombians got together to talk, to drink, to go dancing. By the end of the week a group of Colombians had decided that they would visit our students in Guayaquil in several months.

A year later, long after Rachel and I had left the Peace Corps, those two small exchanges resulted in the First Multinational Student Congress of Community Development, for which more than ninety students and professional people from Chile, Panama, Colombia, and Ecuador gathered in Guayaquil to discuss their common problems. Whatever its politics, whatever its conceptual limitations, at least its center of gravity is Latin America. Perhaps, in time, it will move from the bogus field of community development into direct, committed conflict with the oligarchy, as so many North American organizations have done over the past decade.

Jorge was very happy with the trip, and Rachel and I might have shared his feelings if we had been able to forget our own nationality. But we had to spend time with Peace Corps people in Bogotá, and we quickly came to resent them as much as those we knew in Guayaquil.

One Sunday morning we went to the house of the volunteer whose work had been praised most highly by the Colombia staff to see if he had any suggestions for the students' visit. We had gone there with Ralph Craft and his Ecuadorian girl friend, a social worker from a middle-class family who was enrolled in our course. After a few minutes they decided to tour Bogotá by themselves. As soon as they walked out the door Rachel and I found ourselves listening to a speech against integration. "I just can't understand a guy like Ralph who goes with a 'camp,'" the volunteer said. ("Camp" = *campesino* = "Ekkie." I later learned that some volunteers in Colombia called them "Japs" because of their high cheekbones.) "Can't you see it. You bring her home to your family in America and she has to go to the bathroom. Your mother shows her where the toilet is, but she pisses in the fireplace. 'Son,' your mother asks, 'what have you brought home?' I know how badly trained these people are. I don't want any part of that."

Later, when I mentioned the conversation to another volunteer in Bogotá, he said, "I hate to admit it, but I know how he feels. The Peace Corps is kidding itself if it thinks that the Americans who come down here are going to be generous citizens of the world when they return home. Most of the ones I know leave the country hating Colombians."

The cheapest place to eat in Bogotá was the cafeteria of the National University, the most radical school in the country, and the next day everyone on our trip went there for lunch. From the start the atmosphere seemed unusually volatile. As we were standing in line I noticed a great deal of whistling and some stamping, though I assumed that it was just some students impatient to eat. Then, in the dining room, I was conscious of people staring at me, but I figured that, like so many Latins, they were amused by my height and by the sweat that so often pours off my face. So I ignored them. I concentrated on a conversation in which Rachel and I were trying to persuade Father Roen, who still supported the war, that the CIA was implicated in the assassination of Ngo Diem Dinh.

But I had a headache, and I went up to the counter to buy an aspirin. As I headed back to our table, I began to hear a great clatter. People were banging on their plates, their cups, their chairs: any hard object. And yelling!—in English and Spanish, "*Yanqui, go home,*" "*Afuera, Cuerpo de Paz,*" "*Abajo imperialismo.*" I saw one of the Ecuadorian students restraining a Colombian who was about to throw a bottle at me.

I suppose that James Meredith, walking through the dining hall at Ole Miss, must have felt the same nervousness as I did at National University. Only Meredith was the good guy.

Well, I thought for a moment, I'll not only be the bad guy, I'll embody evil. I'll give a Peace Corps speech! say what most volunteers would feel in that situation. "You ungrateful sons of camps!

We've come down to train you in how to behave, and now you want to run us out of your dining room. Spic bastards! Too stupid to see what I can do for you. You know, the Marines have invaded entire countries for less than this. Just wait until I get back to America and go into the State Department. Then I'll have power over your miserable lives." A real John Wayne speech, uncensored. Did Richard Nixon have similar thoughts when the students stoned his car in Caracas?

If I'd had the nerve to give that speech I would have provoked the kind of anti-American riot that I believe should sweep the continent.

Instead, I returned to my table, trying to look as calm as possible, and continued to chat with Rachel and Father Roen until the shouting ended. Then we got up to leave and the noise resumed, louder than ever. If I am ever trampled because of my beliefs, I decided, I want it to come after a confrontation with my real enemies, not political allies who don't know me.

At Choate I had learned that if you turn your back on taunts, and seem stubbornly docile, you are relatively safe. For the first time I put that coward's lesson to sensible use. Fortunately, we had been eating near an exit so we didn't have to pass many people on our way out the door. Soon the bus we had rented came to carry us to freedom.

"Don't take it personally," one of the Colombian students said as we were leaving the university. "To them you are not Paul and Rachel Cowan, two special people who are doing a special job. You are symbols of a government that is exploiting this country. If I hadn't known you I would have been yelling, too."

Everyone who was listening to the conversation, Ecuadorians as well as Colombians, said that they agreed.

Take it personally! In a way, my friends, that was the moment I had been waiting for ever since my Peace Corps group first arrived in Guayaquil. Nick had said, " '*Yanqui*, go home' is the most lucid piece of political theory that has ever been devised in this century." I agreed. The angry cries of the Colombian students exhilarated me. They reminded me that there must be tens of millions of people throughout the continent who wanted us to help them put that theory into practice.

Those cries told me that we must go home soon, too, and carry our fight with our own kind from a remote outpost of America to its decaying core.

I included most of it in an article I wrote for the *Voice* that night—the incident in the cafeteria, the segregated American agencies in Guayaquil, Hofmann's attitude toward the Ecuadorians, the remarks of the volunteers in Colombia. It was the first serious piece I had published there in two years, the first since my essay in praise of the Peace Corps. Though the article seems a little moderate now—I was still too timid to include my fantasy about provoking a riot—at the time it felt much closer to the sort of risky, personal style I was trying to develop than had anything I'd written when I was on the *Voice* staff. Maybe Dan Wolf would see that I had begun to change.

The paragraph I cared about most said:

"At this point [Rachel and I] are trying to combat [American arrogance] by programs like the student exchanges, and by trying to fight American imperialism wherever we see it. But it is not easy, for we are part of what we oppose. We are trying to wrench ourselves free of our past, of a youth spent snug inside the United States, and somehow make ourselves into citizens of the world."

Dan wrote a fine headline for the article ("Yanqui Go Home—and Maybe We Should") and ran the piece October 26, 1967, the issue which carried an account of the March on the Pentagon that Rachel and I might well have helped organize if I had been courageous enough to resist my government's authority two years earlier.

"Cowan, Hofmann is going to run your ass right out of here when he finds out about that article." Jake Bair, the new rep, was lecturing me about my disloyalty shortly after the piece came out. (The Director was in Loja, a town near the Peruvian border from which it was difficult to communicate with Peace Corps headquarters.) "The staff in Washington is already pissed off at you. Protect your record and resign before you're fired."

"You sound like you're panicking, Jake. Don't you see how ridiculous they'll look for kicking us out now, after we've opposed the war publicly, just because I wrote an article against the Peace Corps?"

"I don't know, man. Hofmann's coming down here the day after tomorrow. You'd better have your bags packed and be ready to go."

Our bags had been packed since we mailed our letter to the *Times*.

We spent the next two days working with the Dodges and Nick and Ed Fagerlund, and Ralph Craft and Bill Hennemuth on a long critique of the Peace Corps which the eight of us intended to publish in as many newspapers and magazines as possible. "We joined the Peace Corps because we thought it would afford us a means of helping nations without imposing the United States' cultural and political values on them," it began. "We were wrong. We now see that the Peace Corps is as arrogant and colonialist as the government of which it is a part."

I wanted to use the words "declaration of independence" somewhere in the statement, but everyone else felt the term was too pretentious.

But I don't want to suggest that Rachel and I were calm about Hofmann's visit. If anything we were even more nervous than we'd been when we mailed the Vietnam letter.

We walked over to the Peace Corps office to meet him, filled with the kind of fear that literally makes you wonder whether you can take another step. But as soon as we arrived we felt protected, for the other six people who had signed the statement were there, too. We must have seemed calmer than we felt. At least Rachel did. In her pink print dress and deep-purple hat, she looked lovely enough to win a genuine compliment from Hofmann.

He had to receive a phone call from Washington before he could tell us whether we had been expelled. "I have never wanted to say this to you, Paul," he said, "but everyone in the Peace Corps thinks you're crazy."

"Not here they don't," Joyce Dodge answered. "We think that all of you are crazy with your rules, your threats, and your lies." For the next ten minutes I was silent as I listened to Bill and Ralph and Rachel and Nick and Ed and Bill attack Erich far more harshly than I would have dared just a few months earlier.

When the call from Washington came through Erich vanished for a very long time. But he finally re-emerged from Jake Bair's office with the broadest smile I had ever seen on his face. He was staring straight at me when he said, "Well, we're not so rigid after all. The Washington staff has agreed to state that your project was a mistake from the start and to let all of you go home who want to, with honorable discharges on your record. Paul and Rachel, I guess it will be home for Thanksgiving for you, won't it?"

"No, Erich, we can't leave until our course ends. You should realize that. But maybe by Christmas."

The eight of us had lunch at the Pensión Helbig, where we spent part of the meal fantasizing about the vacations we would take before we returned to the United States, the rest planning ways of publicizing our statement as broadly as possible while we were still active volunteers, still entirely credible. (Portions of it appeared several weeks later in the *New York Times*, the *Washington Post*, the *Chicago Sun-Times*, the *Miami Herald*.)

I suppose, though, that I should have felt guilty about one thing. Both Hofmann and Jake Bair claimed that I had misquoted them in the *Voice*. Though I was certain Erich had actually said it would take two generations until the Ecuadorians were ready to program for themselves, I also knew that it was Ronald Peterson's replacement as staff doctor, not Jake, who had made the statement I'd cited as the most accurate summary I had ever heard of the real reason the United States has a Peace Corps:

You have to realize that our country has world-wide responsibilities now. Our President is not only the leader of a country isolated from the rest of the world by two huge oceans. He is President of the world now. And what a wonderful thing the Peace Corps is for a country with America's responsibilities. Soon we will have a hundred thousand citizens who speak all the languages of the earth and know all its cultures. They can advise the President and Congress about how all the people around the world for whom America is responsible should be treated.

The mistake had been made because I corrected my copy in sloppy handwriting, and I told Jake that I'd retract it as soon as possible.

But when we came back to the Peace Corps office after lunch and found Jake in one small room, Erich in another, both busily composing letters to their superiors in Washington which claimed that I'd misrepresented them, I began to feel more contempt than guilt. "I'll bet that neither of you guys has the balls to write a letter to the Voice defending your beliefs or attacking mine. You're so worried about your careers that you can't even say what you think in public."

It was as if we had won the building, at least for the day. While they typed their letters, we pinned up copies of our declaration of independence and told each volunteer who came in that he was free to leave the Peace Corps whenever he wanted.

Months later, back in New York, when I read that the Viet Cong had attacked the American Embassy in Saigon during the Tet offensive, I was almost able to imagine that I was a member of the raiding party. How I would have loved to invade that segregated building and give all the information I could find there to my government's enemy, the people.

I want to help fling the doors of the sterile paradise open to the people of the world. But once that happens many problems will remain. Can the wealth which America and its allies, from Russia to Ecuador, hoard at present be shared by a vast number of people, from the widest ranges of cultures imaginable, with ideas and values which will remain in constant conflict? How can people retain their individuality, cultures their integrity?

Those are the kinds of questions that a sane, democratic America would have faced during this decade of bullshit, and wanton, crazy violence.

INDEX